Uptight & Off Center

About the Author

Sharon Heller, PhD is a developmental psychologist and consultant. She suffers sensory processing disorder, and visual and auditory processing problems. Her "aha" moment that she had the dysfunction didn't come until age 43 and profoundly transformed her life. She lives in Delray Beach, FL where the sun, ocean, and the many yoga studios offer a plethora of sensory activities for her daily sensory diet.

Also by Sharon Heller, PhD

The Vital Touch, How Intimate Contact with Your Baby Leads to Happier, Healthier Development (NY: Owl/Holt, 1997).

The Idiot's Guide to Conquering Fear and Anxiety (NY: Macmillan, 1999).

Too Loud, Too Bright, Too Fast, Too Tight: What to do if you are sensory defensive in an overstimulating world (NY: HarperCollins, December, 2002).

Anxiety: Hidden Causes, Why your anxiety may not be "all in your head" but from something physical (Symmetry, 2010).

Yoga Bliss, How Sensory Input in Yoga Calms & Organizes the Nervous System (Symmetry, 2021)

Uptight &

Off Center

How Sensory Processing Disorder Throws Adults off Balance & How to Create Stability

Sharon Heller, PhD

Symmetry
Delray Beach, Florida

Book cover by Robert Heller
Cover painting by artist Sharon Heller
    "Anya Heller": anya-heller.pixels.com
Printed in the United States of America
2nd printing—October, 2021
www.sharonheller.net

To K, whose transformation from a friendless, depressed, "lazy" 11-year-old child, lost in her own world and barely able to read to, in a few short years a popular scholar and superstar, astounded all who had the supreme delight of working with her.

viii

"The body never lies."

~Martha Graham

Acknowledgements

I wish to express my gratitude to the many sufferers of SPD who shared their stories, and especially Rachel Schneider, whose story opens the book.

I am indebted to the many wonderful OT's who informed my understanding of SPD and taught me a whole new way of looking at human behavior. Special thanks to the extraordinarily insightful Patti Oetter, Moya Kinnealey, who guided me with wisdom and kindness, Teresa May-Benson, who opened more new ideas for me, and Lucy Miller for her generous input and indefatigable energy.

Without these new lenses, I would not have been able to unravel what made me and everyone else tick, often discordantly. To know why we do what we do and think what we think, we must first explore how our senses lead us to perceive or *misperceive* the world.

CONTENTS

Introduction

"Behavior is a reflection of the organization of your nervous system at that moment and under those conditions.

~Patti Oetter, O.T.

A divorced mother of a darling little girl, Rachel is a 40-year-old woman of creativity and compassion, wit, and intelligence. She attracts easily platonic friends and romantic partners with her down-to-earth and vulnerable approach to people, and prides herself in making a deep connection to others.

After successfully completing her BA in psychology and MS in mental health counseling, she quit her job as a technical editor and copywriter and became a learning disabilities specialist and a psychotherapist in private practice.

Rachel has always been noticeably more sensitive than others, hyperaware of bodily sensation and of every situation she encounters. Energetic, vivacious, and bubbly one minute, in the next she will crash—typically in a pool of her own tears. After the crash, she feels burnt-out and exhausted and too lethargic to engage with others and the world outside of her home.

As a child, Rachel remembers feeling the same deep, bone-weary tiredness and nervousness, especially when faced with unfamiliar and unexpected situations and places that disrupted her daily pattern of activities. Often, she would ask to be kept home from school with non-descript illnesses. Nevertheless, because she was a bright and dedicated student who loved to learn, she did well in her studies—aside from math, which she struggled with as far back as third grade.

Starting at age thirteen and escalating at age fourteen, Rachel experienced panic attacks in new or unfamiliar places. De-realization and depersonalization, clammy hands, a racing heartbeat, and an inability to see or hear clearly left her feeling temporarily disabled. These attacks seemed to happen mostly at night and especially when she was somewhere unfamiliar with many people moving about, bright lights, or unexpected sounds. Soon, she feared participating in activities that might trigger an attack and became more and more homebound.

When she was fourteen-and-a-half, a cognitive behavioral psychotherapist diagnosed her with Panic Disorder. The therapist recommended that Rachel engage in exposure therapy and face her fears head-on. These exposures were painful for Rachel, and triggered attacks, especially when she and the therapist moved from the dark outside to inside a fluorescently-lit setting like a store.

During this time, she underwent biofeedback that reduced her heart rate and steadied her breath, relaxing her. The therapy helped Rachel feel calm enough to leave home and attend a private university just outside of Boston, where she completed her BA in only three years.

Ever the homebody, Rachel felt homesick at college and, for the first two weeks of school woke up in tears. The unfamiliarity of the place and people, and the change in routine appeared to be at the root of her distress.

After college, Rachel moved back to New York City and lived with her parents for a few years. During this time, her anxiety increased, and Rachel found herself crying more deeply and more frequently.

She met with a psychiatrist who confirmed her Panic Disorder diagnosis and prescribed Clonazepam for her anxiety. The medicine lowered her anxiety enough for Rachel to switch jobs and grow her social circle. Although she still felt uncomfortable in places that most 20-

somethings visited, like clubs, she felt reasonably comfortable in a few familiar, local bars, and she would join her friends after work once a week for an hour.

While she maintained a mostly typical existence, she lived in fear of her attacks and what others might think should she have one in public.

What Triggers Rachel's Anxiety?

What drove Rachel's anxiety? The trigger did not appear to be primarily psychological, as she lacked the markers for a psychiatric condition: her childhood was normal; her parents were loving and supportive and she was close to them and her sister; there was no history of anxiety in her family or of her unexplainable sensitivities.

Nor did she appear to have problems relating socially. She enjoyed many long-term friendships and relationships with people who, despite her peculiarities and rigidity, enjoyed her warmth, compassion, and quirky sense of humor.

Yet, Rachel always felt different and knew that her emotions and subsequent behaviors were atypical. She was aware that she reacted severely to minor things that didn't seem to bother most others, and she was hard on herself for her perceived differences.

In her early 20s, Rachel's psychiatrist once mentioned "sensory integration disorder" (now called *sensory processing disorder*). Unfortunately, the therapist quickly discounted the diagnosis, as she believed that Rachel's anxieties were entirely psychological in origin.

Rachel had her doubts. She felt something going on in her body might be triggering anxiety. Pondering the true root of her concerns, she felt the need to get educated about mental health issues and she entered a graduate program in mental health counseling.

There, she saw a psychologist with a background in both behavioral neuroscience and psychology. In her second session, her therapist mentioned the possibility that Rachel had *Sensory Processing Disorder. SPD* is a common, but relatively unknown condition in which sensory messages get scrambled in the brain. This causes a traffic jam on the sensory highway, and you cannot make sense of or respond appropriately to your world.

The two found an SPD evaluation online that Rachel completed. It confirmed her hunch that her anxiety was body based, not mind based. Shortly thereafter, an occupational therapist diagnosed her officially with SPD. This realization changed her entire life. What appeared to be causeless anxiety had a logical trigger.

With treatment and a bag full of tools, Rachel has lived a fuller, happier life. A leading adult advocate for the condition, she is the author of *Making Sense, A Guide to Sensory Issues.*

What is Sensory Processing Disorder?

Like Rachel, millions of functioning adults suffer *sensory processing disorder.* Ordinary life feels like watching TV and suddenly the image blurs or becomes double; the color dulls or becomes overly bright; the sound is static or the volume becomes too low or too high; or the screen goes blank altogether. Understanding what you are watching takes effort and feels horrifically frustrating and upsetting.

Developmental psychiatrist Stanley Greenspan describes it well.

"Imagine driving a car that isn't working well. When you step on the gas the car sometimes lurches forward and sometimes doesn't respond. When you blow the horn, it sounds blaring. The brakes sometimes slow the car, but not always. The blinkers work occasionally, the steering is erratic, and the speedometer is inaccurate. You are engaged in a constant struggle to keep the car on the road, and it is difficult to concentrate on anything else."

The concept was first recognized and researched in the 1960's by occupational therapist A. Jean Ayres, whose theories and work with learning disabled children pioneered the theories, research, and therapies for the field known as *sensory integration (SI)*.

SI describes how you make sense of the sensations that constantly bombard you, so you know who you are, where you are, what you are doing, and what is going on around you. Knowing this, you respond with appropriate attention, body position, movement, and emotions. It is happening every millisecond as you attend to something out in the world or inside your own body.

To grasp the meaning of sensory integration, think of it as negotiating your moment-to-moment world by focusing on a stimulus, attending to it, and creating a goal-directed, adaptive action. Consider for instance what happens if you start to start to fall. You spontaneously and skillfully touch something to help you balance, focus your eyes to help you re-orient in space, and respond by correcting your stance.

For the average person, SI happens automatically, effortlessly and is accomplished mostly outside of conscious awareness. For instance, your phone rings. Your brain registers the sound and distinguishes it from the jingle on the radio. You walk skillfully to the table where the phone sits. You pick up the phone and new sensations register like the hard, smooth feel of the phone, slight pressure against your ear and face, and the high-pitched voice of your mother saying, "I fell. I can't get up." Your brain quickly dismisses these irrelevant sensations, as well as others like the dog barking or the smell of newly cut grass, allowing you to focus on your mother's words. You automatically respond, "I'll get there as soon as I can." You press the correct button to turn off the phone, grab your purse and keys and dash out the door.

In this example, your brain mapped out a plan for how to move your body skillfully and efficiently to the table. As you picked up the phone, your sense of muscle and joint position (proprioception) enabled you to know where to place the phone in relation to your body. You ignored the many other objects on the table (sensory modulation) and instantly honed in on your phone (visual discrimination). You picked up your phone using touch awareness, motor planning and fine motor skills.

You screened out other sensations going on around you (sensory modulation) and tuned into the speaker and then responded, all without conscious thought. In short, you weren't distracted by other sensations. Nor did you need to concentrate on moving your body efficiently, or on figuring out what was being said to you.

Such nervous system integrity makes you adaptable and goal directed, curious and motivated. You are engaged and grounded, focused and alert. In sync with others, you tend to take initiative, manage transitions, think on your feet, and go with flow, monitoring, sustaining, and changing attention.

In people with SPD however, a glitch exists in the reception, organization, and response to sensory information; what should be automatic takes conscious effort.

When the phone rings, your brain may not register exactly where the ring of the phone is coming from, and you run around in circles trying to find your cell phone. You see the phone on the table and walk to pick it up but poor body awareness causes you to knock into a chair in your path. Stressed, you pick up the phone which may feel annoying against your ear and face, further overloading you. The unpleasant squeaky, groggily voice of your mother adds to your already irritated state. Overloaded, the words "I can't get up" don't immediately register and you foolishly blurt, "Can you walk?" Your mother screams "No!" and, after telling her that you'll be right there, you press the wrong button to turn off the phone. You then run around in circles looking for your keys.

In this example, messages get scrambled and over- or under filtered and you feel confused by the input. What seems simple and automatic to the normal brain becomes perplexing, irritating, effortful, and at times impossible. Spontaneous behavior takes conscious effort and energy. Despite best efforts, your behavior is inefficient, excessive, or useless and you innocently say and do things at the wrong time, in the wrong place, in the wrong way. This chaos goes on day in and day out, making you feel *uptight and off center.*

SPD SIGNS

OVERSENSITIVE TO SENSATION
- **Touchy** about light touch, textures, clothing, ordinary affection
- **Picky** about food
- **Bothered** easily by noise, odors, bright light
- **Fearful** from movement, like elevators, escalators, roller coasters, going fast, or spinning
- **Avoid** eye contact

UNDERSENSITIVE TO SENSATION
- **Slow** to get moving; tire easily
- **Seem** oblivious to environment
- **Seek** intense sensation, like loud noise, spicy food, strong perfumes
- **Crave** roller coasters and fast movement
- **May** not notice if cut or bruised
- **Hard** to get up in morning
- **Thrill** seeker, ignoring potential danger
- **Seek** stimulants — caffeine, tobacco, cocaine
- **Hyperactive** & fidgety

COORDINATION PROBLEMS
- **Clumsy**, awkward, or accident-prone

- **Poor** balance
- **Rigid** & tense posture or floppy & slouching
- **Jerky** movements
- **Poor** fine motor coordination – sloppy handwriting

UNDERACHIEVER
- **Fail** to work up to capacity
- **Learning** problems but normal intelligence

POOR ATTENTION
- **Distracted**
- **Driven**
- **Perseverate** on small detail
- **Unaware**/spaced out
- **Hyperalert**, not processing
- **Turned** inward

POORLY ORGANIZED BEHAVIOR
- **Disorganized**, distracted, spacey
- **Problem** following directions or adapting to new situation
- **Frustrated**, aggressive or withdrawn when encountering failure
- **Compulsive**, obsessed
- **Impulsive**
- **Rigid,** controlling, short-tempered

POOR SELF-CONCEPT
- **Feel** weird, crazy, different & inept
- **Feel** you disappoint, anger & frustrate
- **Feel** "lazy," bored, unmotivated, depressed

EMOTIONAL INSTABILITY

- **Unable** to unwind & self-calm
- **Emotionally** labile or flat
- **Withdrawn,** shy
- **Explosive**
- **Inappropriately** loud, silly, attention getting

AREAS OF OTHER POTENTIAL PROBLEMS

- **Poor** Posture
- **Faulty** visual processing
- **Faulty** hearing & language processing
- **Allergies** & compromised immune system
- **GI** disorders
- **Psychiatric** Disorders

SPD SUBTYPES

Sensory processing disorder gets played out in different ways and no two people experience it the same way.

Sensory Modulation Disorder-SMD: Those who suffer sensory modulation disorder lack the ability to turn up or turn down volume of sensory input, and to focus in on and respond appropriately to relevant sensation. This varies from *hypo-responsiveness* where you barely register sensation, e.g., not hearing the phone ring to *sensory craving*, e.g., programming your phone ring with a loud hip-hop tune to *hyper-responsiveness* where you feel overwhelmed by slight sensation, e.g., startling when the phone rings. Some flip from craving to avoiding and vice versa.

Sensory Discrimination Disorder-SDD: Those who suffer sensory discrimination disorder have difficulty distinguishing one sensation from another: the taste of lemon from lime; the sound of a cat's meow from a bird chirp; whether your thigh or your knee is being touched. This makes it difficult to accurately assess information and causes you much confusion, frustration, and anxiety.

Sensory-Based Motor Disorder-SBMD: Those who suffer sensory-based motor disorder have difficulty navigating through space and are clumsy, uncoordinated, and often gravitationally insecure (over-responding to position changes) and fearful. You may also have a sloppy handwriting.

Do You Have One or the Other?

SMD may exist independently of the other two while SDD generally co-exists with motor and modulation problems and SBMD generally co-exists with discrimination and modulation problems. Consequently, while some people experience difficulties largely with sensory modulation, others will experience some problems in all three areas. Studies suggest that 27% of children who have sensory modulation disorder will present with multiple subtypes.

How Common Is SPD?

Good chance that some of you reading this book will not have heard of SPD. Yet, it afflicts to some degree anywhere from five to thirty percent of children and adults.

According to occupational therapist and researcher Lucy Jane Miller, founder of the nationwide SPD research program and recipient of an NIH grant to study the disorder, only around 10% of children with SPD will likely be diagnosed and treated by occupational therapy, the profession involved with understanding, researching, evaluating, and treating sensory processing problems.

These 10% are mostly children who have severe over- or under-responsiveness to sensory stimuli that interferes with daily life, including social skills, attention, self-regulation, and skills development, and in whom SPD co-exists along with other diagnoses, such as autism, pervasive development disorder, ADD and other learning disabilities (some estimate that many as 70% learning disabled children have sensory processing disorder).

Many suffer severe abnormal responses to sensation and live constantly traumatized by the condition, especially those on the autistic spectrum. Recall how the autistic savant Raymond in the film *Rainman* (played by Dustin Hoffman) screamed at the sound of the fire alarm or at being touched.

Amazingly, such severe disability exists as well in people who appear to function normally, though they tend to be quirky, exceptionally shy, antisocial, or highly emotionally volatile.

Undiagnosed & Untreated

What happens to the 15% to 20% of "normal" but "out of sync" difficult children with sensory processing problems? Most will remain undiagnosed and untreated. Few parents, teachers, caregivers, physicians, mental health workers or parents are aware of sensory processing disorder. Of those professionals familiar with the condition, many deny its existence as an actual and treatable condition, particularly psychologists and psychiatrists who treat the child entirely from a psychiatric perspective. Consequently, many children grow into adults never having been identified with or treated for SPD.

Moreover, SPD might afflict many more people than the presumed 30% of the population. Consider this. In a fascinating study at UCLA in 2017, students responded to a "healthy brain" student advertisement. But only 32 percent passed the initial telephone screening process.

Of those who qualified for the in-person health history and physical examinations, only 52 percent passed these screening procedures. In other words, only 11 percent of those that believed they were healthy/normal qualified for brain imaging.

Of the original 2000 students, just over 200 ended up meeting the criteria. The actual study concludes by saying, "The majority of individuals who consider themselves normal by self-report are found not to be so." In fact, almost 90 percent of human brains are atypical, damaged, or in some way not healthy.

How many people do you personally know who are uptight and off center? Probably quite a few.

"The majority of us have 'escaped' diagnosis but know our limitations well. We have learned strategies to capitalize on our strengths and cover or avoid those things most difficult."

~Patti Oetter, OT

Out of Sync

Having a brain that makes you feel off center, out of focus, missing a beat and out of sync with the rest of world enacts a huge price on well-being, even for those who suffer it mildly enough to escape diagnosis.

You experience more failure than others. This leads many to feel stupid, clumsy, inept, frustrated, embarrassed, and often self-conscious and humiliated, as well as frustrated and guilty for unintentionally disappointing.

Such feelings make you feel weird, crazy, and deeply flawed. You lambast yourself: "I can't do it;" "I don't have fun like others;" "I'm not normal;" "People don't understand me;" "People don't like me."

Frenetic, inappropriate, withdrawn, aggressive, self-absorbed, disorganized, or crazed behavior is common and reflects a confused, chaotic inner state.

Missed Potential

SPD truncates skills, causes spaciness, distractibility, disorganization and disorientation, restricts work choice and location, and robs you of stamina. Further, it creates extreme stress that ultimately leads to a barrage of stress related illnesses like headaches, GI problems, dizziness, and chronic fatigue, as well as psychiatric disorders ranging from anxiety to disassociation.

As most people will go through life not knowing why this is happening, they don't know how to help themselves and fail to come near their potential. As a result, many flounder through life, and often a lonely one.

Loneliness

As few people understand or know of SPD and the problems it creates, family, friends and coworkers expect you to behave "normally." When you don't, people become frustrated and disappointed in you. They tend to attribute your behavior to character flaws: you are fussy, stubborn, short-tempered, picky, unfriendly, disorganized, impulsive, lazy, depressed, silly, spoiled, manipulative, annoying, obsessive/compulsive, and neurotic. You drive others crazy or *are* crazy.

Assuming your failings must be your fault, you view yourself equally negatively: "Stupid me!" "Weird me!" "Crazy me!"

How do you explain to them *or to yourself* that you are doing your best to adapt to the world as *your brain perceives it*? You can't. How do you make sense of why life is a constant struggle when you don't know *what is wrong with you*? You don't. How do you explain to others that tell you that you "don't try hard enough" that you try *harder* than others just *to stay above-board*. It's hard.

Finding it difficult to belong and not knowing how to be more normal, many people live isolated and lonely lives. This is especially so for the sensory defensive who feel overwhelmed and overstimulated by the ordinary sensation involved in social situations, like noise, lights, and crowds, and social relations, like eye contact, closeness, sounds, smells, and touches.

Mis-treated

As few professionals have heard of SPD, most treat you with tranquilizers, antidepressants, and psychotherapy, as if you have a psychiatric disorder.

Such treatment generally improves quality of life by helping you cope better and feel better about self. But it impacts little the sensory and regulatory issues underlying this dysfunction: sensory processing problems stem not from negative thinking or critical parenting but from miswiring in the primitive brainstem. Consequently, your functioning improves little and, still not knowing what is wrong with you, you feel invalidated and remain anxious. Says one woman with tactile defensiveness,

> *"A psychiatrist once told me the reason why clothes bother me sooo much is that I was probably smothered as a child."*

What are the causes of SPD?

SPD comes from an insult to the nervous system. Trauma is a major cause. Often it happens prenatally from drugs, illness and maternal stress or from birth complications, such as asphyxia, post-birth trauma or prematurity, as well as trauma in the early weeks of life.

In fact, you can identify sensory processing problems at birth. Researchers will present the newborn with an aversive stimulus, like ringing a bell next to the ear, and the newborn typically startles. To see how quickly the newborn habituates to the stimulus and stops responding, the researcher will continue to repeat the stimulus.

In the normal infant, habituation occurs typically after seven or eight trials. But in newborns that may have sensory processing problems two extreme patterns emerge.

In the first, infants don't habituate but keep responding with increased intensity until they cry out of control, and it takes much intervention and effort to quiet them. These are the fussy, colicky infants who react intensely to the slightest sensation, and whose parents often need to hold them tightly and rock them for hours to calm. A study by Davies and Gavin in 2007, that looked at habituation to sensory stimuli in 28 children with SPD, confirmed similar poor habituation to noise.

In the second, newborns hardly startle at all as if they didn't pick up the stimulus. These infants tend to be quiet, easy, and uncomplaining. Though described by their parents as happy and content, they may be motorically delayed and hypo-responsive to sensation.

Other sufferers show normal development but later trauma to the nervous system that creates sensory processing problems. Such trauma includes head or brain trauma, physical, sexual, or psychological abuse, chemical abuse, or post-traumatic stress disorder when people become hypervigilant, hyper-alert, and sensory defensive.

Take Peter. A 22-year-old law student, he suffers severe sensory defensiveness, low libido, depersonalization and TMJ disorder that gives him an ongoing headache.

His mother doesn't recall problems as an infant. Rather, problems started after he fell from a bicycle at age eight and cracked his skull open. He appeared to heal well and did not suffer hard neurological signs like loss of balance.

His problems likely resulted from a misaligned his skull from the fall. This caused the TMJ disorder and headaches, and threw off his neck and spine, preventing the neurotransmitters in his brain from communicating clearly, profoundly impacting the integrity of his nervous system. Defensiveness and depersonalization were the result. The sexual issues came largely from a locked pelvis from spinal contortion.

Other causes of SPD include:

- Viruses
- GI problems like food allergies, food sensitivities, and yeast overgrowth
- Auto-immune disorders
- Drug reactions
- Nutritional deficits
- Poor posture that prevents the nervous system from working efficiently
- Genetics

FOOD FOR THOUGHT: *I hypothesize that the genetic component might be weak liver functioning that interferes with the release of toxins from the body. The toxins build up and impact the nervous system. More and more it is believed this results from poor gut flora.*

Do I Have It?

Many of you might wonder if you or someone you know might be suffering SPD. This is not unusual. Most people will resonate with some of these symptoms.

This does not mean you suffer SPD. Those with SPD fall on the extreme ends and have sensory processing problems that disrupt everyday functioning. This disruption ranges from mild and life is hard but you get by, to severe and life is highly restrictive.

What Can You Do to Help Yourself?

If you suspect you may suffer SPD, what should you do?

Self-Evaluate

To see if you suffer SPD, to what extent, and in what categories of dysfunction take the self-test for sensory processing disorder found in Appendix A.

Get Educated

Pour carefully through this book to learn about the dysfunction. In this way, you no longer need to be left in the dark about what drives your perplexing and disturbing difficulty to make sense of and respond appropriately to the world.

And you will learn if your anxiety, panic attack, depression, OCD, substance abuse, eating disorders and other psychiatric diagnoses might be the result of or associated with sensory processing problems.

Get Treated

Begin your journey with a complete medical evaluation to rule out medical problems for symptoms. For instance, dizziness and loss of balance can come from various medical conditions.

Ideally you should get a proper evaluation and diagnosis from an occupational therapist who will give you a battery of tests to evaluate your specific sensory processing problems.

The OTs trained in sensory integration therapy are generally pediatric occupational therapists who, though they work primarily with children can generally accommodate adult clients.

Seeing a pediatric OT does present challenges, explains Teresa May-Benson, research director of the Spiral Foundation points out in her article

"Occupational Therapy for Adults with Sensory Processing Disorder," (*OT Practice*, June 15, 2009).

For instance, adults often need after hour appointments, may feel discomfort in getting therapy along with children, and lack insurance to cover therapy. But it is well worth getting as treatment is most effective, writes May-Benson "if it can be started with an intensive period ... during which the individual can observe significant changes in sensory processing over a several-week period." In finding an OT, look for one with the most training in sensory integration and present them with this article as it clearly outlines the approach occupational therapists should take in treating adults.

If you are an adult and unable to see a pediatric OT, you can use this book and others to learn how to employ your own sensori-motor activities to help modulate your nervous system. These will help you calm down when you are anxious and jumpy, rev up you up when you are bored, lethargic or depressed, and wind down to sleep.

Problems with sensory discrimination and sensory-based motor problems, however, are not easily self-treated and require occupational therapy intervention. You may also need other therapies such as visual, auditory, cranial/sacral, and neuropsychological like neurofeedback.

IMPORTANT INFO: *According to an article by OT Tina Champagne, "Sensory Processing Evaluation and Evaluation in Mental Health" (AOTA Continuing Education Article) more and more mental health practitioners within and outside the field of occupational therapy have begun to understand the relevance of sensory integration interventions in mental health. If you are receiving mental health services and your practitioner is not so informed, educate him or her on the need for incorporating sensory processing evaluation and treatment into your wellness plan.*

Get Positive

Should you also see a psychologist or other mental health worker to deal with mental health issues? For many people this is useful to cope with the sequela of SPD. This includes low self-esteem and low motivation from having experienced so much failure in your life. Chapter 14 includes many mind-body techniques to give you the motivation needed for change and to change your mind chatter to a more positive tone.

Get Natural

As for medication, many of you are likely on or have been on meds to cope with the stress, anxiety and depression associated with SPD. My bias is to substitute drugs for natural substances like amino acids that don't have side effects, and those with SPD experience more side effects than the average person. There's much information on this in the last chapter of the book.

Tell Others

Spread the word. It's time for sensory processing disorder, or SPD to become a household word and especially since the American Psychiatric Association (APA) still does not recognize SPD as a cause of mental illness.

After careful examination of research presented by Lucy Miller and her team from the SPD foundation, the APA chose to *not* include SPD in the newly released DSM V, the holy bible of the mental health system because there's no biological marker. This has now been debunked. A groundbreaking study from San Francisco's Benioff Children's Hospital, conducted by Elysa Marco and her team shows that kids with SPD have differences in brain structure compared with other kids. This finding reveals for the first time a biological basis for SPD that sets it apart from other neurodevelopmental disorders.

In the study, the researchers used an advanced form of MRI called "diffusion tensor imaging" on the brains of 16 boys, ages 8 to 11, with SPD but without a diagnosis of autism or prematurity. They compared their results with 24 typically developing boys who were matched for age, gender, right- or left-handedness and IQ.

The results showed that the boys with SPD had abnormal tracts of white matter in their brains, particularly in the back part of the brain in areas known to play roles in tactile, visual and auditory systems. The strongest correlation was for auditory processing.

"These are tracts that are emblematic of someone with problems with sensory processing," study researcher Dr. Pratik Mukherjee, M.D., Ph.D., a professor of radiology and biomedical imaging and bioengineering at UCSF, said in a statement. "More frontal anterior white matter tracts are typically involved in children with only ADHD or autistic spectrum disorders. The abnormalities we found are focused in a different region of the brain, indicating SPD may be neuroanatomically distinct."

The researchers concluded that the abnormal microstructure of sensory white matter tracts likely alters the timing of sensory transmission and results in the processing of sensory stimuli and integrating information across multiple senses as difficult and even impossible.

Unfortunately, as this study was conducted after inclusion was possible for DSM V, psychologists, psychiatrists and other mental health workers will continue to misdiagnose symptoms of SPD as a psychiatric disorder. Giving them this book will be a huge wake up call. In fact, we should have a bumper sticker of OT Patti Oetter's insightful words.

> *"Behavior is a reflection of the organization of your nervous system at that moment and under those conditions."*

Can I Rid Myself of SPD?

SPD is a complicated neurological dysfunction that does not have a cure per se. Nevertheless, by following the sensorimotor interventions and mind-body techniques presented in this book, symptoms can be greatly reduced, and in some cases eliminated so that your life no longer seems one of never-ending left curves. This will happen from neuroplasticity, meaning the brain's ability to rewire itself. And though neuroplasticity happens in leaps and bounds in the young, developing brain, it amazingly continues throughout life.

I suffered visual spatial processing problems my whole life, as well as slow auditory processing. As I was bright, I compensated well enough, and problems were never picked up. Nevertheless, I felt dumb, and my family thought I was dumb.

In my youth, I took years of dancing, mostly jazz. In class, you learn a dance routine taught in sequential small sequences. By the end of the class, the students are joyfully dancing away, the steps learned and automatic. My brain did not translate what the teacher's feet were doing into my feet and I had great difficulty learning even a small sequence. By the end of the class, I was still struggling to figure it out and each step took effort. Needless to say, I never made it to Broadway.

At age 60, I became an avid painter and painted virtually daily for hours. I painted mostly from my imagination and without formal training and it would often take me months to finally get a face to look like a face, as I continually reworked the shape, mouth, nose and eyes. Six years after I started painting, I began Zumba classes. Amazingly, I picked up the steps immediately as the teacher demonstrated and danced away! No lag. No effort. All the hours spent figuring out space on a small canvas had grown loads of brain highways that rewired the visual cortex in my brain and greatly improved my visual spatial processing.

The idea that you can't teach an old dog new tricks proves false. Granted, neuroplasticity doesn't happen overnight. You must persist, persist, and persist. And you must make the interventions in this book your lifestyle for the rest of your life. And... you can't stop there.

Is There More I Need to Know?

Though sensorimotor and mind-body interventions can change your life substantially, healing sensory processing problems means healing all nervous system imbalance: sensory, psychological, neurological, nutritional, digestive, body toxicity, environmental toxicity, musculo-skeletal problems, and cranial/sacral misalignment.

In this book, I focus on sensory and mind-body interventions. To learn more about healing digestive issues, hormone imbalances, immune system compromise, drug reactions, toxicity, and cranial/sacral misalignment refer to my books *Too Loud, too Bright, too Fast, too Tight* and *Anxiety: Hidden Causes*. The latter book especially has long chapters on diet, digestive issues like food sensitivities, and detoxifying both body and environment. Doing so is crucial as you need proper nutrition to feed your brain and balance your biochemistry. If not, all the sensory interventions in the world will not give you stability and equanimity.

Part one consists of four chapters that provide a basic overview of sensory processing disorder and its subtypes and how it creates psychopathology and other associated problems.

Part two consists of eight chapters on how to create a sensory diet unique to your specific needs so you don't have to stumble and fall through life.

Part three consists of three chapters on how to change your thinking, free your mind with meditation and visualization, and use natural substances in place of drugs.

Appendix A is a self-test of symptoms of SPD. At the end, you will find references for your referral. I have included essential websites throughout the book.

Part One

Sensory Havoc

1

*

Senses off Balance

"All we have to believe is our senses: the tools we use to perceive the world, our sight, our touch, our memory. If they lie to us, then nothing can be trusted."

~ Neil Gaiman, *American Gods*

The mantra of the new century is *being present*. When we are living *in the moment*, we are engaged, focused, and optimally alert, calm and balanced.

What is the key to hanging out in the present? *Fix your nervous system so it works as it was designed.* In any given moment in time, what we see, hear, feel, taste, smell and how our body is moving against gravity determines how alert, focused, stable, and connected we feel.

To achieve this, you must first be aware of your senses. And that means correcting a misconception: we don't have "5" senses—touch, vision, hearing, smell and taste; we have at least "7" and probably more.

Let's now explore our "seven" senses.

OUR SEVEN SENSES

What sensations are impacting your brain at this moment? Visual of course as you read this page and tactile from any surface of your body touching a chair, the floor, or a book. What about other sensations? Do you hear any sounds? Do you smell any smells? Are you chewing gum and tasting the flavor?

Now bend down to pet your cat. Perhaps he will lick you as you do. In this act, you engage three other senses. The first is the sense of being touched (tactile) so you are aware of sensations impacting your skin, activated as your cat licks your hand.

The other two few people are aware exist:

Sense of balance (vestibular) so you don't fall, activated when you bend forward.

Sense of joint and muscle input (proprioceptive) so you know where you are in space, activated by the input into your hip, knee and ankle joints as you bend forward.

These three "near" or internal senses inform us of what is happening inside our bodies and are the main players in our sensory repertoire. Our "far" senses, seeing, hearing, smelling, tasting and touching inform us of what is happening outside our bodies and are only supporting players.

Ponder this. We could live without sight, hearing, smell and taste. But if we did not feel our skin burning, our tactile sense, or know we are about to fall, our balance sense, or where our bodies are in the dark, our body awareness sense we could not survive long. In fact, the far senses evolved from and are dependent upon the near senses to make sense of our world.

When you have sensory processing disorder, these three near senses don't function properly, and especially your balance sense. To understand why and what's happening inside your body, let's explore what makes these three senses the key threads in the neurological web of your brain and what happens to the organized symmetry of that web when your brain distorts sensory messages.

NEAR SENSES

VESTIBULAR/SENSE OF BALANCE

Did you ever get car or seasick or have a middle ear infection? If so, you know the awful feeling of dizziness and, worse, vertigo. It's impossible to focus on anything than stopping your head from spinning. This mayhem is coming from your inner ear, where the vestibular apparatus resides.

Our most important sense, the vestibular sense governs balance (gyroscope), orientation (compass), and movement to orient us in space as we move against gravity. It does this every second of our lives automatically and without thought. In this way, we know where our bodies are in space, experience gravitational security so we feel in control of our movement, and have a tripod for a stable visual field.

It accomplishes all this by gathering information from the position of the neck, head, and eyes relative to the ground. It kicks in when our eyes move or the head goes offline in different positions: up or down as we get up or sit down; side to side as we tilt our head or sway a baby; back and forth as we nod or swing on a swing; backward and forward as we look down or back, bend down or bend back; or in a circle as we turn our head around or spin. In this way, we know, at all times which side is up so to speak so we can move stably against gravity and accurately perceive the world around us.

FASCINATING INFO: *The organizing effect of vestibular sensation is why babies calm when you rock or sway them and perk up with delight when you toss them in the air. Likewise, **you** calm when rocking or swaying a baby and get a huge rush* *when flying through the air on a roller coaster.*

Muscle Tone

What is your body like? Are your muscles firm or are they floppy or stiff? It makes a difference: your muscle tone directly relates to pull of gravity—to how much your vestibular system is up to par.

To control muscle tone, the vestibular apparatus tells muscles how much they need to contract to stay upright and maintain your body against gravity. If you have poor vestibular functioning, you can have too little or too much muscle tone.

Too Little: You will have floppy posture that makes it difficult to counteract and move against gravity, to transition from one position to another like getting up to walk, and to start and stop movement. This makes you afraid of falling and, trying to keep your head steady you don't move it much and lack vestibular input. Good chance that you sit slumped in a chair or lie sprawled across a desk—a red flag for "Balance system in need of repair!"

Too Much: You will have stiff posture and stilted movement. Rigidly upright, you lack free movement of your head that gives you vestibular input.

As the vestibular sense influences muscle tone and body posture, blame having two left feet or being unable to catch a baseball on faulty vestibular processing.

Attention

The vestibular apparatus influences attention because it feeds sensory impulses into the reticular activating system (RAS) in the brainstem. The

RAS sets arousal to an optimum level to calm us when we are hyped and rev us up when we are bored. When the vestibular system is under-active, it doesn't feed the RAS enough stimulation to modulate alertness. The result is hyperactivity and distractibility. We will talk more about this in chapter three.

Orchestrator of Other Senses

In addition to controlling balance, muscle tone and influencing attention, the vestibular system fine tunes other sensory systems except for smell. Along with body awareness that I'll talk about shortly, the vestibular system picks up information from skin receptors through touch, temperature, pressure and movement of our feet, hands, and the rest of our body, as well as information from our eyes and ears, and sends all this information to our brain. If you have poor vestibular integration, you will have weak or inconsistent connections between the vestibular system and the visual, auditory, and even the tactile systems; being touchy and balance and coordination problems often go hand in hand.

Vision

We use our eyes to guide our hands and feet for walking down stairs, walking in the dark or any new skill—imagine learning to type at the computer without looking at your hands.

If the vestibular system is impaired, you will over-rely on vision. When you walk downstairs, you will look carefully at where you are stepping. If you are on a raised surface like a rooftop, you will try and fix your eyes on an object on the roof. If adequate visual cues are lacking, you may panic in an elevator, a tunnel, a windowless room, or going up and over a bridge, and you fear darkness. Wide open space as when peering out at the ocean can equally discombobulate.

Here is one person's experience of moving from where she had mountains all around her, which gave her visual cues of where she was in space, to living in wide open space.

> When I joined the Air Force and was sent to Texas for Basic Training, I actually felt as if I was going to fall off the earth. I didn't feel grounded. My balance was off, and I fell over more easily. I have always lived where there were mountains in every direction so that mountains and trees punctuated the sky: I felt as if the mountains hugged me. Here all I saw was sky as if it touched the ground.

Hearing

Hearing is impacted as well as vision, as hearing and balance both happen in the inner ear: hearing activates the gravity receptors; moving activates the auditory receptors. For instance, you boogey when you hear rock music; moving in turn enhances the pleasure of the music. Therefore, auditory issues typically involve faulty vestibular integration.

Language

The vestibular sense also has a part in language skills as the balance function is located in the ear. In the movie *Akeelah and the Bee*, a young and smart disadvantaged girl living in an impoverished area of Los Angeles is determined to win a national spelling competition. To do so Akeelah must be able to overcome her problem with spelling the large words. Together with her coach, Akeelah discovers the key to her success: jumping rope as she practices spelling the words enables her to spell the words effortlessly. In the national competition, Akeelah pretends to jump rope as she spells the final word. In the end, she wins.

Seeing & Hearing

When both hearing and seeing get scrambled in a sensory overloaded environment like a mall, you get a double whammy as bright lights, talking, shouting, loud music, much movement, signs and other visual pollution bombard you at once. Unable to tease out visual and auditory information to compensate for inner-ear static, you feel light-headed, dizzy, disoriented, and anxious.

Signs of Vestibular Dysfunction

Given the importance of the vestibular system to create stability, life can become hell if it functions poorly. You might experience dizziness, lightheadedness, loss of balance when changing head position; abnormal eye positions when you stand or lie in certain positions; dizziness and nausea when you close your eyes; car or seasickness.

Ordinary things make you light-headed or dizzy, like walking on an uneven terrain like grass, bending over to pick up your baby, tilting your head up to kiss your husband, or standing over the sink to brush your teeth.

Falling asleep can feel frightening and you suffer insomnia. When you do fall asleep, closing your eyes may evoke terrors and nightmares related to falling, floating, and spinning. As vestibular problems also cause problems with alertness, you might easily zone out, finding it hard to get moving or engage with the world.

Imagine living off balance daily! Yet millions who suffer SPD do.

Coping Comes at a Price

How do you cope? You compensate. For instance, you might unknowingly hold your head to the side, tighten certain muscles around your joints, not breathe deeply, and limit the directions your eyes look. Or you might hold onto something to help maintain balance.

While this will help keep you from falling you pay a heavy price for feeling at odds with gravity. Physically, you may suffer nausea, dizziness, adrenal overload, low muscle tone, tension, pain, or many other symptoms.

Emotionally, you may suffer low self-esteem, loss, sadness, depression, frustration, desperation, anger, fear, and even hostility. Mentally, you might feel confused, disorganized, spacey, and unable to remember, and have phobias and even disassociation.

As you can see, determining the course and direction of your life requires a vestibular system on course and following the correct direction. If not, the best of intentions and positive thoughts will do nothing to lessen the feeling of being off center and filled with anxiety, fear, and phobias.

Hypersensitivity to Movement & Fears

If you experience any of the following, think twice before you run to a psychiatrist to get Zoloft or Xanax.

- *Claustrophobia*
- *Fear of flying*
- *Fear heights, enclosed spaces or wide open vistas*
- *Fear falling, especially on uneven surfaces*
- *Dislike bending upside down or having your head backward*
- *Dislike rapid, sudden or rotating movements*

These space related fears are less likely to come from fearful thoughts running through your head than they are from hypersensitivity to movement, or from *gravitational insecurity*.

Gravitational insecurity results from an overloaded vestibular system trying to process too many sensations at once. It leaves you feeling as if you are walking a tightrope.

Basically, a severe reaction to change in head position, especially sudden, creates dizziness, vertigo, light-headedness, or nausea, as well as fear and anxiety as the slightest movement registers in the brain as "Falling!" Everyday activities like bending forward to change a sheet, bending backward to get your hair washed, or turning your head while driving feel traumatic. Unsteady on your feet, you are also accident prone, further increasing spatial insecurity and fear.

Such fears can start with or escalate to panic attack as vestibular dysfunction involves the same symptoms as panic attack:

- *Disorientation*
- *Dizziness*
- *Lightheadedness*
- *Vertigo*
- *Depersonalization*
- *Floating sensations*
- *Imbalance*
- *Falling*
- *Nausea*

It happens something like this.

You experience *balance and coordination problems (broken gyroscope)*. This triggers a fear of heights, bridges, stairs, escalators, and wide-open spaces and provokes anxiety, dizziness, lightheadedness, feeling off balance, floating sensations, spinning, falling fainting, tipping or swaying.

You experience *disorientation in space (broken compass)*. This triggers fear of tunnels, shopping malls, or other disorienting situations and provokes anxiety, disorientation, confusion, floating sensations, spaciness, light-headedness, depersonalization, dizziness.

You experience *motion sensitivity to change in direction, speed of movement or sudden movement*. This triggers fear of riding in a car, elevator, plane, escalator, roller coasters, boats, rocking chair and provokes anxiety, dizziness, light-headedness, nausea, and vomiting.

You now have a space-related phobia, a primal persistent fear of physical harm coming not from your thoughts but from a problem residing in your inner ear. This phobia in turn can trigger panic attack, or the fear may initially set off a panic attack that quickly escalates into a phobia.

Not knowing why this is happening, you don't know how to control it and panic attacks might start to hit in many different places. Phobias multiply and become pervasive, and you anticipate having a panic attack when you venture out the door. Feeling no place is safe, you become agoraphobic, the most crippling phobia, where you become housebound.

FOOD FOR THOUGHT: Double-Jointedness: *Those with "hypermobility syndrome" or double-jointedness, an inherited trait, commonly experience panic attacks. Apparently, they appear to inherit a fear gene. At the same time, people with hyper-mobility syndrome have wobbly ankles and feet and therefore poor balance. Their panic may be set off by this instability, in other words by vestibular dysfunction, as well as a faulty gene sequence.*

In his practice, psychoanalyst Harold Levinson, author of Phobia Free, found that some *90 percent of specific space related phobias and panic attacks resulted from an underlying malfunction within the inner-ear balance system.*

Levinson happened upon this startling discovery in the 1960's when treating dyslexic children. Dyslexia was believed to be caused by a disturbance in the cerebral cortex, or thinking brain. But after examining 1,000 patients, Levinson found only 1% showed evidence of cerebral dysfunction but 750 of the children exhibited problems with balance and coordination. He concluded that dyslexia correlated with problems related to inner-ear, or vestibular dysfunction.

This would not have surprised A. Jean Ayres, the founder of sensory integration theory. While Levinson was doing his research, she found the same relationship between vestibular processing and learning disabilities. Nor would this surprise astronauts. In space and without gravity present, astronauts routinely reverse numbers and letters to produce "mirror writing."

Hyposensitivity to Movement

As movement can be frightening so can it be thrilling for those with a sluggish vestibular system who, hyposensitive to movement crave it. A thrill seeker, you love the adrenaline rush of fast cars, motor boats, roller coasters, flying, and so forth and never seem to get dizzy. You groove to the sensation of getting your body pummeled, as when white water rafting, and defying gravity, as when diving from the high board is great fun. Unable to sit still, you burst with energy and constantly move some body part, like shaking a leg.

Hyposensitivity results from the brain only receiving a limited amount of vestibular stimulation as it is either not receiving or not processing correctly movement experienced against gravity. Those on the autistic spectrum routinely rock and even spin for hours as the only way to feed a sluggish vestibular system and quell jumpiness.

PROPRIOCEPTIVE SENSE

Close your eyes and bring your index fingers together to touch in front of your nose. You can do this by sensing the position of your muscles and joints in space. This ability is called *proprioception*.

Our second power sense, proprioception gives us our "place in space." It does so through receptors located in our joints, muscles, tendons, and ligaments that give us our sense of body position and body awareness. This enables us to coordinate movements without having to use vision, as in the above example. Movement and gravity stimulate proprioception.

We tap into the proprioceptive receptors when we contract and stretch muscles, bend and straighten, pull and compress joints between bones, and create resistance into joints and muscles—"heavy work"—like when you lift heavy furniture, bike uphill, or work out with weights. When you are feeling out of whack, heavy work is your magic bullet to get your system quickly balanced. In chapter six, we'll talk much about heavy work.

Grand Modulator

Proprioception is the *grand modulator*. When we are hyped, it calms us; when we are lethargic, it jazzes us up. In technical terms, it has a neuro-modulatory effect on the central nervous system, meaning it can either facilitate or inhibit neural signals.

It does all this by grounding us so we can feel our edges and know where our body ends, and the world begins. Such body awareness allows us to move in the world and be part of it, yet to have boundaries so we don't lose self—to feel connected to the earth and to have roots, but also to have wings and be able to take flight. Feeling this control of our bodies in space makes us feel a solid, strong presence on this planet that we inhabit and translates into emotional security and confidence. This physical sense of self lays the foundation for psychological self-awareness.

Feel Good Serotonin

Balance and stability from proprioceptive input comes in large part because input into your joints and muscles increases the neurotransmitter serotonin, the feel-good hormone: the bigger the joint (hips, for instance), the greater the release of serotonin. Serotonin influences mood, passivity, anger, and aggressiveness. It sets the firing level for all other neurotransmitters.

IMPORTANT INFO: How much deep, restorative sleep you get, whether or not you eat nutrient dense food and remain hydrated all affect serotonin level.

Often called the policeman of the brain, serotonin helps keep brain activity under control. For instance, serotonin breaks up dopamine, our pleasure-seeking neurotransmitter to enable us to experience passion and pleasure.

When the brain has too little dopamine, we crave food, sex, or stimulation, feel unsatisfied, become depressed, and can't focus. When the brain has too much dopamine, we're driven toward non-stop pleasure seeking, the basis of obsessions and addictions. Researchers suspect that high dopamine leads to mania in those who are bipolar.

Serotonin keeps this extreme behavior in check.

An increase in serotonin also causes natural melatonin to be released in the brain creating even more tranquility. Writes John Ratey in *Spark, The Revolutionary New Science of Exercise and the Brain.*

> *"I tell people that going for a run is a little bit like taking Prozac and a little bit like taking Ritalin because, like the drugs, exercise elevates these neurotransmitters.... A deeper explanation is that exercise **balances** these neurotransmitters."*

IMPORTANT INFO: *To keep the brain primed with fuel and alert and ready to learn the body must move. When we don't, we pay a price. And not just those of us who suffer SPD. Think of all the people you know who must go to an extreme to counter-balance imbalance and overeat, smoke, shop till they drop or abuse drugs, and who suffer anxiety, depression, hyperactivity, and spaciness.*

Orientation Association Area

Orientation in space and time happens in the posterior superior parietal lobe, an area just behind the top of the head. Also called the "orientation association area," it is where our brain sorts "me" from the vast "not me" of the infinite universe. Inactivity in this area from lack of sufficient proprioceptive input may play a part in depression, eating disorders, body dysmorphia, and depersonalization, while damage to this area by trauma or stroke results in difficulty maneuvering in physical space. Little wonder that numerous studies have found exercise to be more effective than antidepressants in controlling runaway depression, anxiety, and obsessive-compulsive disorder, and with longer lasting effects.

Poor Proprioception

Given the supreme importance of proprioceptive input, what happens if you have poor proprioception?

To start, you lose key information about how much tension the muscles need for good muscle tone. This makes you unaware of what muscles you are using, and you are clumsy, disconnected, uncoordinated, disjointed, and unsure of your footing. You may be unable to identify objects by feel and need to look at what you are doing, like typing. In the dark or other times when you can't rely on vision, you feel afraid.

You cannot figure out where your weight is when you stand and don't feel grounded. Nor do you know where your body ends and the other's body begins. To find your edges, you seek intense pressure into your skin. In the extreme, you may feel shut off from your body and slightly numb. Emotionally, you merge with the other to feel whole and dependency characterizes your relationships. In short, you have a tough time in figuring things out.

Poor Proprioception in Everyday Life

How does poor proprioception play out in everyday life? Here are some ways that might strike a chord.

- **Unable** to identify objects by feel, you need visual cues to zip, button and unbutton clothes and so forth; dress messily and look disheveled with shirt sticking out; shoes untied, pants not pulled up.
- **Unsure** which finger is which or where each one is located, you have difficulty with fine motor skills, such as buttoning, zipping, writing, or

using silverware.

- **Over-relying** on vision, you need to see your keys to believe that they are in your hand; you don't put them in your pocket until the door is locked.
- **Misjudging** spatial relationships of objects, you bump into furniture, mis-step on stairs and curbs, drive over a curb or hit another car.
- **Misjudging** the weight of an object, you push too hard on your pencil, e.g. and easily break them.
- **Unable** to tell if touch is friendly or threatening, you lash out aggressively if someone taps you on the shoulder, which you perceive as an attack.
- **Feeling** an "unbearable lightness of being," you compensate by seeking weight into your body to feel terra firma. You may do so by choosing a spouse larger than yourself, by owning a big dog and, with women even by getting pregnant often.

Proprioceptive Modulation Problems

If you are over-responsive to proprioceptive input, you will be clumsy, bump into things, move stiffly and lack coordination. If you are under-responsive to proprioceptive input, you will overly seek affection, crave bear hugs, and like to be up close and personal, often invading the other's space. You may prefer tight clothing, grind your teeth throughout the day and night for jaw input, crack your knuckles, and behave aggressively, especially as a child.

Interoception

Interoception (internal proprioception) is the sense that puts us in tune with the inner workings or our body.

Connected to our internal organs are nerve endings that send signals to the brain. This allows us to interpret inner, physical states and to know if we're hungry or satiated, hot or cold, alert or fatigued, need to urinate or defecate, in pain or not, and so forth. In this way, we recognize and are in tune with the internal workings of the body—interoception—so that we maintain *homeostasis*, or a balanced state.

Poor Interoception in Everyday Life

Here are some ways that poor interoception plays out in everyday life.

- **Unable** to gauge when you need to urinate or defecate, you may let your bladder get too full and you may suffer constipation.
- **Unable** to recognize if you are hungry or full, you over-or under-eat.
- **Feeling** reduced pain sensation, you may be unaware you have a broken toe.
- **Unable** to realize you are sleepy, you may push on until you are too wired to go to sleep.

TACTILE SENSE

Our third power sense is our sense of touch. When it's right, *is it right!* Little in life gets us into that just right place quicker than a bear hug from a loved one.

This emotional security starts with the sensations of warmth, deep pressure, and proprioceptive feedback from our muscles and joints that create a chemical buzz of hormones and neurotransmitters. This happens in the limbic area of the brain (the seat of emotions) and creates pleasure (see chapter three).

These neurotransmitters include:

- **Serotonin,** our mood regulating hormone that keeps us calm and steady;
- **Dopamine,** our pleasure-seeking hormone that taps into the brain's

reward "opiate" system;

- **Oxytocin**, the "cuddle" hormone that makes us feel attached to someone; it gets released by dopamine during touching, and in women, during labor and breast feeding.

Touch Receptors

Tactile sensation happens via touch receptors in multiple skin layers that convey information about pressure (light, deep), pain, temperature (hot, cold), and vibration. These allow us to discriminate the feeling of touching, our far sense, and being touched, our primal sense.

Protective Response

The tactile sense keeps us informed about safety in the world.

Light touch triggers "danger!" arousing fear and triggering the sympathetic nervous system. Stress chemicals course through the bloodstream and alert us to pay attention as a bug might be crawling up our leg, a speck of dirt may have alighted on our eyelash, or a stranger in the crowd might be picking our pocket.

Deep touch helps us define our edges. It gets deep into the proprioceptors and tells us we are safe. Triggering the parasympathetic nervous system, it gets us into a relaxed, neutral balanced state, over-riding sympathetic firing and washing away cortisol and adrenaline involved in the fight/ flight response. It calms also by enhancing pleasure chemistry in the limbic areas of the brain that are associated with dopamine.

This sense of security from deep pressure touch happens as well because it involves proprioception to make us feel at once connected to the earth and to others. The more pressure—the bear hug versus the handshake—the more intense the *somatosensory input* (tactile and proprioceptive) and the more powerful the effect. "*Hold* me!" we beg when held lightly.

If you do not get sufficient loving touch, you experience skin hunger and hunt ways to get intense pressure into your body. You might sleep around to get hugs and engage in abusive sex. Some people join a *BDSM* community who use a variety of erotic practices involving dominance and submission, role-playing, restraint, and other interpersonal dynamics.

You might play sports that pummel you like water and downhill skiing, horseback riding, deep sea diving, wrestling, or football. You may even slash yourself as cutting provides extreme skin pressure to confirm your existence. We'll talk about this in chapter four.

Hypersensitivity

If you are hypersensitive, or tactile defensive, ordinary touch feels aversive. Depending on degree of sensitivity, you respond with annoyance to panic. Some will cringe when cuddled, kissed, and lightly touched, especially from a stranger, and get the heebie jeebies when wearing rough clothes, bras, nylons, waist/wrist bands, socks with seams, tight clothes, and jewelry.

They will bristle from hair on their faces, from getting hair or nails cut, from taking baths and showers or from getting hit by waves at the beach. Shocks go through their system when walking on sand, grass, stones, and concrete. They feel too much pain and feel miserable in heat or cold.

Hyposensitivity

Having "crazy monkey sex" all night with the aristocratic women of the Russian court who threw themselves at him, eating with his hands and then licking his fingers and stroking his beard, sprinkling it with greasy food morsels, Rasputin, the Russian mystic peasant who famously stared at and healed people with mesmerizing eyes was classically tactile *hyposensitive.*

If you are hyposensitive, you under-register sensation and miss out on tactile information. This affects your ability to read signals accurately and respond appropriately. For instance, you may hold your baby awkwardly or, when nursing her, you might not know when her body signals that she's satiated. You may be unaware of danger signs and not realize that your hands are dirty, as Rasputin didn't, or that an ant is crawling up your arm.

To get more sensation into the skin so you can better tune into the world, you wear tight clothes with rough, fuzzy, or uneven texture, much jewelry, and may fidget constantly. Needing to feel another's body against yours, you like to get up close and personal even with non-intimates and invade the other's space. You seem to never get cold and don't easily feel pain. In fact, you might even enjoy pain for its intensity and adorn your body with tattoos and piercings, both because you have a low pain threshold and because both are visually highly stimulating. In the extreme, you may be self-abusive, banging your head, pulling out your hair, cutting your skin, and seeking and enjoying rough or abusive sex.

Poor Tactile Discrimination

Tactile discrimination is the ability to feel differences among size, shape, texture, and weight of objects. If you have poor tactile discrimination, you may be unaware of the differences in objects and mis-categorize them. Renee has two dishes at her sink, one for hand soap and one for a brillo pad. As the brillo pad loses its roughness from use and takes on a softer texture, she routinely places it in the soap dish next to the soap as her mind fails to distinguish the two textures. Fortunately, she has an understanding husband who places the brillo pad back in the correct dish, without calling her a lunatic for doing something bizarre.

Poor tactile discrimination makes it hard to be sure where your body parts are or how they interrelate. You may have difficulty orienting arms and hands, legs and feet to get dressed, which feels a chore, and bump into things to figure out where you end and the world begins. In the extreme you feel separate from your body and experience depersonalization (we will talk about this in chapter four).

Low Touch Society

Problems with receiving tactile input may be influenced by our low touch society in which babies spend 90% of the day in containers rather than in human arms. On the mother's body, babies get on-going deep pressure touch, along with vestibular and proprioceptive input. In a container, they lack all three and this affects their developing nervous system. (For more information, see my book *The Vital Touch*.)

Oral/Motor Dysfunction

Tactile receptors in the mouth can also be under or over-responsive to sensation.

Hypersensitivity

If you are hypersensitive to oral/motor input, you are a picky eater with extreme food preferences and limited food repertoire; as an adolescent you may have appeared anorexic. You may gag on textured food, have difficulty with sucking, chewing, and swallowing, be extremely fearful of the dentist, and dislike toothpaste and brushing your teeth. Kissing tickles and you may withdraw from your partner and he or she feels rejected.

Hyposensitivity

If you are hyposensitive to oral/motor input, you crave excessively spicy, sweet, sour, or salty foods, crunchy textures and like excessively hot or cold water or drinks. You likely overeat. Constantly driven by the need for oral/motor input, you may lick, taste or chew on inedible objects, like a pencil or your hair.

FAR SENSES

SEEING

Vision is our dominant sense for learning about the world and to help us navigate through it, with 80% of the information we take in coming through our eyes. What's more, 93% of human communication is nonverbal through picking up facial and body expression.

Vision & Other Senses

Vision depends on the vestibular, proprioceptive, and tactile systems.

Seeing tells you where you are in space. If your head turns to the right, your eyes will typically follow and settle on a target, giving your brain a reference point for the balance system. Conditions that restrict visual acuity, such as the dark, improper eyeglass prescription, glare, or eye disease impair this reference; if you close your eyes and try standing on one leg, you might wobble.

Through movement, the vestibular system works together with the visual system to develop a visual map of the environment, so you can place yourself in space. In fact, ninety percent of the cells in the visual cortex respond to vestibular stimulation. Picture how the vestibular system guides the movement of your eyes, enabling you to track moving cars.

If you have vestibular dysfunction, your brain may scramble visual messages and you have a problem coordinating vision because both eyes fail to work together as a team (binocularity).

Poor binocular vision causes difficulty in perceiving what you see. For instance, you may have difficulty connecting sights with sounds and not know where to look when someone calls your name. You may have difficulty connecting sights with touch sensations and not know by looking that sandpaper is rough. Likewise, you may have a problem connecting sights with movement sensation and swerve around the chair to avoid bumping into it. Lacking good eye-hand coordination, visual perception, and spatial awareness, you may frequently swat past the tennis ball and in school had trouble recognizing letters and learning to read—dyslexia.

Such problems cause you to mistrust your sense of vision. Sarah is an example. When she turns off her car, she holds her keys in her hand until she gets to the elevator. If she puts them in her pocket, she will keep taking them out to check that she has them. She's not obsessive/compulsive. She must feel *and* see her keys for her brain to accurately register "keys."

Visual Processing Problems

Visual processing can go awry in different ways:

- *Light Sensitivity (photosensitivity)*
- *Scototopic Sensitivity Syndrome (Irlen Syndrome)*
- *Poor Visual-Spatial Discrimination*
- *Poor Ocular Motor Skills*

Photosensitivity

Photosensitivity means that you find it difficult to tolerate bright light and visual patterns, a common affliction of the sensory defensive.

The following visual signals are implicated:

- **Sunlight**
- **Bright** incandescent lights & fluorescent, especially older ones that buzz & flicker

- **Color** distortions
- **Various** hypnotic patterns
- **Tiled** floors
- **Moving** cars
- **Oncoming** headlights
- **Wallpaper** patterns
- **Flickering** lights
- **Blurred** images
- **Darkness**
- **Various** visual and color patterns created by stationary or moving crowds

Causes of Photosensitivity

Photosensitivity happens primarily when the vestibular system does not properly filter incoming visual signals. This provokes dizziness and severe anxiety.

Under stress, the pupils of the eye dilate to admit more light and to increase peripheral vision to scan for danger, and sensitivity to bright light and visual disturbance commonly occur. When the stress passes, vision returns to normal.

If vestibular processing is off, the alarm system doesn't completely turn off. Your eyes easily dilate in response to light, and you become photosensitive: a 100-watt bulb looks like a 1000-watt beacon and feels glaring and irritating. If inner-ear dysfunction is severe, the sun or bright lights sets off an alarm system in the brain that creates anxiety and, under extreme stress, you panic and become *photophobic*.

Anxiety Trigger

Light might be a common hidden and undiagnosed anxiety trigger.

Anxiety: Fluorescent lights contain certain colors or color distortions, as well as pulsing vibrations that make older lights start to buzz and flicker. This stresses the body's nerve endings, confusing and overwhelming the nervous system. As a result, fluorescent lights in the workplace, gym, classrooms and supermarkets may unknowingly cause you to feel quickly drained, spacey, agitated and often acutely anxious.

Social Phobia: In social settings, bright lighting will render you unable to make eye contact and you seem social phobic.

Agoraphobia: In public places bright lights may also be the fear finger that pushes the panic button for many agoraphobics, who are commonly photophobic.

Fear of Driving in the Dark: Driving at night for the photophobic is a nightmare as the bright street headlights of oncoming cars scream at you, and the sensation of the flickering, blurring, or hypnotic effects created by objects that pass in front of or next to you overload your visual circuits. The faster you are driving, the worse is the effect. Highway driving is worse than driving on slower, local roads and under stress fear may escalate to panic while you are cruising I95.

Hyperactivity: Bright lighting and fluorescent lighting in classrooms causes or contributes to hyperactivity, something that has been documented for over thirty years with time-lapse cinematography studies.

In 1973, light therapy pioneer and photobiologist John Ott, and the Environmental Health Research Institute compared the performance of four first-grade, windowless classrooms in Sarasota, Florida, under full spectrum, radiation-shielded fluorescent light fixtures, which emit the full range of the sun's colors, or the standard cool-white fluorescents.

Under the cool-white fluorescent lighting, some students demonstrated hyperactivity, fatigue, irritability, and attention deficits. Under exposure to full-spectrum lighting for one month, their behavior, classroom performance and overall academic achievement improved markedly. Several learning-disabled children with extreme hyperactivity calmed down and seemed to overcome some of their learning and reading problems. Since then, other studies of the same nature have found similar results.

Scototopic Syndrome

Some people on the autistic spectrum, the learning disabled and developmentally delayed commonly suffer scototopic syndrome or Irlen syndrome, although it's commonly seen in a neurotypical population as well. In addition to light sensitivity, these folks experience a number of problems that makes reading difficult.

- **Contrast sensitivity** makes it difficult to discern figure from background.
- **Impaired print resolution** makes the letters appear unstable and seem to move, shift, shimmer or break apart.
- **Tunnel vision** renders you unable to move from line to line or from one group of words to another
- **Visual distortions** make objects appear blurry, moving or changing, or as if disappearing and re-appearing.

If you suspect that you might have Irlen syndrome, check out the Irlen Method. It uses colored overlays and filters to filter out offensive light rays and improve the brain's ability to process visual information.

Poor Visual-Spatial Discrimination

Contrary to popular belief, vision involves more than just seeing the world up close or far away. Your eyes must make sense of what you see by perceiving, discriminating, processing, and responding to visual images.

If you have poor visual-spatial discrimination, you will have difficulty discerning similarities and differences among like objects—an orange from a tangerine—and have problems that make you feel anxious and unstable.

- **Uncomfortable** or overwhelmed by moving objects or people, you fatigue easily when using your eyes for close work.
- **Finding** it difficult to quickly comprehend reading, you lose interest quickly and find it hard to visualize what you read.
- **Poor** at distinguishing foreground from background, you find it hard to locate items among other items like papers on a desk, socks in a drawer, items on a grocery shelf.
- **Experiencing** difficulty perceiving depth, distance, boundaries, you misjudge spatial relationships and bump into objects or people, misstep on curbs and stairs and, not surprisingly, fear driving.
- **Experiencing** a problem scanning visual sequences and following rapid movement with your eyes, you find it hard to follow a tennis match or video game.
- **Poor** at recognizing symbols or gestures, you might misinterpret facial cues.

Some obvious signs of visual discrimination problems are seeing double, writing at a slant (up or down hill) on a page, and confusing left and right.

Poor Ocular-Motor Skills

Visual problems are often related to poor ocular-motor skills and eye teaming, when your eyes don't work together, and scrambled vision creates problems learning.

Everyday tasks become difficult. Reading is a challenge because you are unable to scan across the line to read and you may reverse letters. Climbing stairs is difficult as is navigating around furniture, people and other objects. Socially, it may be hard to look into someone's eyes or play sports.

HEARING

Are you bothered by the jolting, screeching, screaming, piercing sounds in our modern world? If so, join the crowd.

Many people in our noisy modern society feel irritated and easily bothered by loud or jarring noise. This does not mean you are auditory defensive. Those who are behave in an extreme.

They will:

- **Pick up sounds** others don't hear, like the whirring of the fluorescent light, and become unnerved by noise at a volume most people tune out and tolerate.
- **Feel acutely bothered** by sudden noise, and ambient noise like people chattering or chewing, sniffling, or coughing which has caused more than one divorce.
- **Get unnerved** by high frequencies like voices, certain speech sounds, or a ringing telephone, or low frequencies like a lawn mower, air conditioning, or vacuum cleaner, or both high and low.

"Certain sounds will cause me to be hysterical. Off-key singers is one of them. I start saying all sorts of awful things about the singer and how I

will kill them. I can't stop myself."

Conversely, if you are hyposensitive, you will underreact to sound and seek loud, sounding music, blast the TV and love arythmic rhythms, like jazz for example.

Auditory Discrimination Problems

Do you have a problem immediately make sense of what you hear? Or find it difficult to follow what people are saying in a film or TV program? Or respond slowly to a question or command? Or hate talking on the phone because you have to concentrate to figure out what someone is saying?

If so, your hearing may be fine. The problem is likely with listening, perceiving, and processing language or sound.

The ear is both the organ of sound and of balance. If the vestibular system is malfunctioning, auditory input drifts or scrambles. Your brain interprets the auditory input slowly or misinterprets it, though your hearing may be normal. As a result you:

- **Become** confused and misunderstand what is said or hear things that weren't said.
- **Blend** foreground and background noises.
- **Demonstrate** oversensitivity or undersensitivity to sounds.
- **Have** trouble articulating thoughts verbally or in writing.
- **Find** it hard to filter out other sounds while conversing and attend to what someone is saying.
- **Respond** slowly to questions: "What?" you say, or "Could you repeat that?" and look at the other person for reassurance before answering: *Love is finding that person who fills in the words for you!*
- **Fail** to respond when called and people think you're ignoring them or, as a child, "playing deaf." In school, your mind would go blank when

called upon even if you knew the answer.

When Tommy's wife asks where he put the cereal box, often he will momentarily stare, not to annoy her but because it takes time to figure out what she said.

- **Fail** to understand or follow two sequential directions at a time and freeze when someone asks you to pass the salt and pepper.
- **Often** talk out of turn or "off topic" and people accuse you of not paying attention and you get misdiagnosed with attention deficit disorder (ADD) rather than a problem with auditory discrimination.
- **Find** it hard to identify people's voices or instruments in the orchestra as you are unable to discern if a sound is near or far.
- **Not** remember that your spouse told you to stop and pick up a dozen oranges and get accused of not paying attention, or of being self-involved and not caring.

SMELLING

"Nothing revives the past so completely as a smell that was once associated with it."

~ Vladimir Nabokov

Smell is our primordial sense, protecting us from imminent danger like smoke or rotten food and sharpens our awareness of nature, people, places, and things. As such, smell powerfully influences how we feel about someone, how close we can get to them, how long we stay at someone's house, and whether we will ever return.

As we inhale a scent, the smell travels across the olfactory nerves located inside the nose and up into the limbic system, our emotional brain and memory center. Here endorphins get released, the brain's natural opiates that give us feelings of attachment and comfort, as well as neurotransmitters and other 'feel-good' chemicals.

Of the five physical senses only smell links directly to the limbic system. This is why the scent of a special fragrance can evoke emotional memories. For instance, upon taking a whiff of apple pie, you recall sitting content in your grandmother's kitchen as a child watching her bake. Overcome with sudden sadness, you miss her warm and chipper ways.

Though everyone has smells they love and smells they hate, those with sensory processing disorder react intensely to smells others will easily ignore. You might be bothered or nauseated by cooking, bathroom and/or perfume smells, refuse to go places or be with people because of smells, and choose foods based on smell.

> "Gardeners and landscapers are at my apartment complex weekly for four hours or more. The noise makes me want to punch the wall and throw things. I pace constantly, angrily muttering, "Get the fuck outta here already." Adding to the noise is the noxious chemical odor from the equipment which wafts into my apartment and makes my head spin. It's torture. Once they stop, I have to lie down in my quiet, dark closet and regroup. If not, I will scream at my husband when he walks in the door if he even says hello to me."

In her book *Sensational Kids*, Lucy Miller reports how in her laboratory she found that smells that are generally not offensive, such as wintergreen, citrus and mint can set off an alarm response in children with olfactory hyper-responsivity that she measures physiologically. Something as benign as milk can trigger sweating, an increase in heart rate, shallow breathing, and other physiological reactions that are normally seen in the presence of a real danger, such as a snarling dog.

Such hyper-responsivity creates enormous stress, and many sensory defensive people suffer adrenal exhaustion as a result. Not surprisingly, studies show a relationship between adrenal exhaustion and heightened sense of smell. Typically, people will be repulsed by noxious odors such as petroleum fumes but also be intolerant of perfumes and even pheromones, those mysterious sex odors that repel or attract.

If you are hypo-responsive to smells, you have the opposite problem: you may not notice unpleasant or noxious odors and eat the rotten egg even if you sniff it first.

If you have smell discrimination problems, you will have difficulty identifying what food you are eating without looking at it, or distinguishing particular tastes or smells, like an orange from a tangerine.

Let's now explore how the senses play out in the different kinds of subtypes that comprise sensory processing disorder.

Summing Up

7 Senses: We have 7 senses: touch, vision, hearing, smell, taste, vestibular and proprioceptive.

Near Senses: Tactile, vestibular, and proprioceptive are "near" senses. They tell us what is happening inside our bodies and are primary.

Far Senses: Visions, hearing, smell and taste are "far" senses and tell us what is happening out there in the world. They are secondary to the near senses.

Vestibular sense: Our sense of balance is the orchestrator of the nervous system. When that is off, other sensory systems tend to also be out of balance.

Proprioception: Our sense of body awareness helps us feel grounded and in touch with our bodies. It is the grand modulator. When we are hyped, it calms us; when we are lethargic, it jazzes us up.

Interoception: It is our internal body awareness and puts us in touch with the inner workings of our organs.

Modulation Problems: A person with SPD may be under-or over-responsive to each sense.

Other Issues: Those with SPD commonly suffer visual and auditory processing problems, as well as learning disabilities such as ADD, ADHD and dyslexia.

Light: It is often a common hidden and undiagnosed anxiety trigger.

2

Different Strokes for Different Folks

"What we think and feel and are is to a great extent determined by the state of our ductless glands and viscera."

~Aldous Huxley

Jenny seeks sensation. Tommy avoids it. Sarah is clumsy and doesn't know her right from her left. Jonathan knows right from left but he can't tell you if you are touching his back or his shoulder. Tamika is clumsy, doesn't know her right from left, doesn't smell rotten food, or feel dirt on her skin.

All five have sensory processing disorder but manifest it differently. Jenny is a *sensation seeker*. She also has a problem with *sensory modulation* and is *hypo-responsive* to stimuli. Tommy has a problem with *sensory modulation* and is *hyper-responsive* to stimuli—*sensory defensive*. Sarah has problems with posture and *bilateral integration*. Jonathan has problems with *sensory discrimination*. Tamika has *dyspraxia*, and problems with *sensory discrimination* and *sensory modulation*.

What do all these terms mean?

SENSORY MODULATION

Every moment of our lives our magnificently designed brain works to keep us safe by evaluating sensations for danger that come from outside and inside our bodies.

Most of this processing takes place outside of conscious awareness. We become aware of a sensation when something is potentially dangerous and a threat, for instance a sudden loud noise in the dark signaling us to prepare to fight or take flight, or when something is safe and interesting, like a baby's giggle and we want to engage. If something is safe and *we don't care*, like a car driving by, our brain registers the sensation unconsciously and ignores it. In this way, the brain doesn't get overloaded with sensory input irrelevant to basic survival. This process is called *sensory modulation*.

Sounds straight forward. It's not. Each of our brains turns up or turns down the volume of sensory input at a different rate and with a different intensity based on individual sensory threshold or arousability. Arousability is defined as how quickly our brain notices and responds to sensation, as well as how quickly we return to baseline or homeostasis.

Seekers (resilients) possess a high sensory threshold. You experience sensation slowly and mildly and require much sensory input to alert to and tune into the world. Once aroused, you quickly return to baseline. Quickly bored and disinterested, you need more and more to feel "just right." Unless you are faced with a charging tiger, you evaluate the world as safe—precisely how our brain is designed to function—and ignore the noxious sound of the smoke alarm, calmly turn off the boiling water, and continue preparing dinner.

Avoiders (sensitives) possess a low sensory threshold. You experience sensation quickly and intensely, requiring little sensation to become alert and tuned in and take long to return to baseline. Quickly over-stimulated, you need less and less to feel just right. You evaluate noxious but safe sensation as a threat and feel disturbed by the smoke alarm, though not enough to discontinue preparing dinner. Nevertheless, you feel distress and distracted to some extent until the sound ceases.

You likely have a good idea where you hang out most of the time. This is because differences in how you respond to a threat underlie basic inborn temperament patterns. They are based on sensory threshold, emotional regulation, and the speed with which you can change from one state to another. This basic modus operandi remains stable throughout life.

Infant Temperament Patterns & Sensory Processing

Seekers–the Resilient:

Languid: happy, easy, undemanding, inactive; unbothered by sensation or changes in routine; adapt easily, cry little, play contentedly alone.

Bold: happy, social, curious and active; quest constant new and different sensation; get fidgety if restricted or not given enough new stimulation, like if forced to be in the house too long or play alone.

Avoiders – the Sensitives:

Shy: quiet, inactive, and quickly alert to sensation; adapt slowly to change and cling to mommy but don't overly fret.

Feisty: fussy, difficult crybabies; easily overstimulated; quickly thrown from change in place or routine; hard to soothe.

These patterns are normal and typical, and most people cash in on their strengths and adapt to their weaknesses.

SENSORY MODULATION DISORDER

Some people strongly under- or over-react to sensation to where it guides behavior and interferes with normal functioning, and they are unable to easily alert to and focus on a task or wind down. They have a sensory modulation disorder, or SMD.

Let's break this down further.

- **Sensation Seekers (often called "cravers"):** Some people strongly *crave* and *seek* input from one or more of the senses.
- **Avoiders:** Some people strongly *avoid* input from one or more of the senses and are called "over-responsive" or "sensory defensive."
- **Under-responsive:** Some people strongly *ignore* input from one or more of the senses and are termed "under-responsive."

High Sensory Threshold/Cravers quest extreme sensory input. They evaluate dangerous sensation as exciting and compromise personal safety. You may dismiss the smoke alarm going off in the middle of the night as a false alarm and go back sleep until you begin to feel hot and inhale smoke. As a young man, my brother skied off the side of a mountain on a skiing trip in Aspen thinking it looked like a fun jump, not a cliff. Luckily for him and his family, he landed in a tree and eventually made his way out of it.

High Sensory Threshold/Under-responsive fail to tune into a danger signal as the brain ignores it. As a result, you might fail to hear the smoke alarm going off in the middle of the night and not awaken. You might ignore the burn from the scalding hot boiling water as you may not register the full extent of pain without more burning, throbbing, stabbing, sharpness, radiating throughout your body and you put yourself in potential danger for extensive injury.

Low Sensory Threshold/Avoiders over-react to what should be evaluated as "don't care" as dangerous. Upon hearing the smoke alarm, you smack your hands over your ears and run out the room. The water boils out and the pasta and pot are ruined.

Such constant misinterpretation of sensation gives rise to extreme behavior to get you to the comfort zone, where you feel neither anxious/threatened nor bored/oblivious. The result is a slew of psychopathological conditions, from anxiety and depression to mania and substance abuse that SMD mimics, exaggerates, or results in. We will go into this in detail in chapter four.

SENSATION SEEKERS

Sensory Seekers require intense sensation to register "pay attention!" They fall into two categories based on: energy level (high/low); muscle tone (firm/floppy); and self-regulation (active/passive control of understimulation):

Languid: low energy/low muscle tone/passive sensation seeking

Bold: high energy/firm muscle tone/active sensation seeking

Low-Passive/Languid

Hyposensitive to sensation, the languid doesn't process enough stimuli and, ignoring it, easily tunes out the world, unbothered by sensations that most find disturbing, like a passing siren, the smell of rancid milk, or the pain of a cut or bruise. This makes you easy going and you go with the flow. At the same time, tuning out much sensation makes you unaware of what's going on and you may appear dull and out of it.

Possessing low energy, you passively seek the intense sensation you need to become alert. You love thumping music, chilé peppers, sequins and bangles, bright lights, strong perfumes, and bold colors; tattoos and piercings commonly cover your body. You crave passive movement like rocking or riding the roller coaster. The quintessential couch/mouse potato, you may watch much TV and often play video games. You are likely to over-eat, gamble, and be addicted to sex. You depend on stimulants like coffee, coke, or nicotine to pump you up enough so you can tune into the world. As you easily ignore sensation, you have poor interoception and you don't know if you are hungry or full, need to go to sleep, or if you need to go to the bathroom, calm a pumping heart, or are in pain.

Low Muscle Tone

In most languids, low responsivity goes hand in hand with low muscle tone, weak muscles, and lack of coordination (dyspraxia). As a result, it takes enormous effort and concentration to resist gravity and to get your body moving (see motor problems in the next section). In fact, it takes *nine times the effort* of those with normal muscle tone for you to get enough punch to use the information being taken in by muscles and joint receptors. Consequently, you slump and shlep as you lack the muscles needed to hold up your body against gravity. You fatigue easily and get little done, making you appear lethargic, "lazy," disorganized, and depressed.

Learned Helplessness

Frustrated and feeling a failure as a result, you fear that you won't succeed and easily give up trying, seeming unmotivated to help yourself. This resignation is called *learned helplessness* and underlies depression. Even when not feeling depressed, you may be perceived as such because your smile might look pasted. Like everything else smiling takes effort as the muscles in your cheeks and jaw may be too weak to sustain a broad, real smile and your smile seems to be forced even when you're genuinely happy.

Response Varies by IQ

How languids cope with hypo-responsivity relies on intelligence. The less intelligent are withdrawn, dull and disengaged. Those with higher intelligence are artistic dreamers who turn inward for self-stimulation and to get out of their wretched bodies. Within their own inner world, they weave fantasies from which they derive intense pleasure. *How many novelists are languids?* Kind, knowing, spiritual and psychic, some fit the profile of the "indigo child," while others that of the computer geek.

The need for unusually intense sensation to tune into the world, along with low muscle tone that makes action effortful can create a range of mental health issues that we will discuss in chapter four.

Low/Active Bold

The bold, often termed "cravers," are easily bored and need constant newness, intensity, uncertainty, challenge, and risk. A pounding heart, sweating hands and fast breathing gives you an adrenaline rush that you interpret as "fun" and makes life sizzle: you thrill to speeding along the narrow mountain path, while the passively seeking languid is your delighted passenger. In the movie *Rush*, daredevil racecar driver James Hunt described his need to chance death by driving in circles at 150 miles an hour as necessary for him to feel "normal." Those who swallow fire or lie on nails are not brave so to speak; they are the quintessential sensation seeker!

Risk taking makes you the leaders of the world and, a divergent thinker you come up with innovative ideas. Always on the go, you stay up late at night and multi-task as you punch your way through life.

Charming, upbeat, and exciting to be around, you are likely to be a people magnet, speaking expressively with your hands and frequently touch others, comfortable to be up close and personal— think politicians!

At times though sensation seeking makes you overly affectionate and you intrude on the other's personal space.

Low Dopamine

If strong sensation is unavailable, dopamine, the pleasure-seeking neurotransmitter drops too low and you zone out or run around frantically seeking something to perk interest. If you are unable to get sufficient sensation, you will create it and might doodle, jiggle your foot, crack gum, giggle loudly, or act silly and other attention getting behavior—think Robin Williams and Jim Carrey. With your high energy level, you may dance around and nudge others and appear hyperactive. As a child, you may have crashed into walls, people, beds and the like to get weight, pressure and traction into your body.

Insensitivity

This constant need for new, different, and interesting sensation interferes with focusing on relevant information needed for everyday functioning. You may forget your wife's birthday, look away and fidget when people talk to you, interrupt them, or change the subject, and finish late the dull report your boss has requested. As such, many seekers are irresponsible, undependable, and self-serving people who miss social cues and are insensitive in social interactions.

Sacrifice Personal Safety

If your time is insufficiently filled with challenge, you engage in sensation seeking behaviors that compromise personal safety regardless of the consequences to yourself or your family: addictive behavior, such as gambling and risky sex; aggression and you may harm others or yourself; extreme sports; substance abuse. You lack motivation to change these patterns as self-help strategies, like therapy, meditation, journaling, yoga—anything that requires quiet focus—offer too little sensation to engage you and satisfy your need for instant feedback to avert boredom. Fortunately, risk taking diminishes as you grow older and by middle age you calm down and are more capable of healthy relationships and greater productivity.

Salvador Dali

The artist Salvador Dali is an example of a supreme seeker/craver. High strung and manic, Dali would throw temper tantrums that his mother found hard to quell. In school, he would throw himself down a flight of stairs to get attention, indicating an extremely powerful need for tactile-proprioceptive input.

On the day he was to meet his future wife Gala at the beach, he wanted to make a suitable impression. But bathing attire was too dull. So Dali shaved his arms and mixed some laundry bluing with powder and died his armpits. He immediately started to sweat, causing the makeup to run. So he shaved again to make himself bleed, indicating low tactile/proprioceptive input and a high pain tolerance. His armpits were now all bloody. He stuck a fiery-red geranium behind his ear, indicating a need for strong visual input. He then smeared goat excrement all over his body, indicating a need for extreme odors to perceive smells. Voila! He was ready to meet Gala.

At the same time, Dali exhibited a terror of touch, indicating possible tactile defensiveness. His famous long oiled mustache is telling. Curved out to either side like bird wings, the hairs pulled his skin and provided comforting pressure touch, but without touching his face and creating aversive tickling touch.

Though Dali may stand out as an extreme, such frantic, non-stop seeking is not uncommon. Many school children suffer it and are often aggressive, "hyperactive," impulsive and lack self-control. They get diagnosed as having oppositional defiant disorder (ODD), a recognized childhood mental disorder characterized by negativity, hostility, and disobedience, and are often put on medication. To some extent, this is a problem with our sensory deprived school environments that seek to keep children for the most part in their seats, quiet and still. In the culture in which we were designed to function, children and adults would have been provided sufficient on-going physical sensation to modulate their nervous systems so they could feel naturally alert and calm.

Writes Miller in *Sensational Kids* about "Ben," a typical sensory seeking child,

> *"... when children pulled their weight on the family farm or in the family business instead of going to school .... Ben would have been a superstar! In that context, his physical stamina, agility, and coordination would have been prized and he would have functioned better because his sensory needs would have been met naturally by the routine of his daily life." (p. 178)*

Driven to sensation seeking, regardless of the task-at-hand or the consequences, sensation seekers may experience many mental health issues that I will discuss in chapter four.

SENSORY AVOIDERS – SENSORY DEFENSIVENESS

> *"And have I not told you that what you mistake for madness is but over-acuteness of the senses?"*
>
> ~Edgar Allen Poe, *The Tell-Tale Heart* (1843)

Imagine a day inside Jenny's skin. The morning alarm goes off and she startles, her heart races, her body tightens, her breathing quickens. Her husband turns to get out of bed, grazing her foot, and she cringes, her bodily rhythms speed up another notch and her body tightens further. He sees that she seems annoyed about something and affectionately strokes her cheek. She bristles and, when he turns around, rubs where he touched her.

She slowly arises to get out of bed, as she feels a bit dizzy, and quickly puts on her soft cotton house slippers, as the feel of the carpet makes her recoil, and walks into the bathroom. The bright lights her husband has left turned on assault her. Her eyes squint painfully. She quickly turns off the lights and turns on a small lamp on the sink counter. Her already overloaded system gets further destabilized. She starts to brush her teeth, but the toothbrush is new, and the bristles tickle her uncomfortably. She leans over to spit out the toothpaste and feels a sudden loss of balance and a surge of panic engulfs her.

She steadies herself and turns on the shower. The soft spray of water from the showerhead feels like pelts of hail hitting her body. Her already stressed system is accelerating fast into overload. And her morning has only just begun! She still has to figure out what clothes to put on, as most textures annoy her and feel uncomfortable on her body. She has to figure out what to eat for breakfast, as anything soft, mushy, or creamy repulses her. Worst of all, she has to figure out how to face the world outside that, for her, is like maneuvering through a sensory minefield.

Jenny is an avoider or what is commonly known as *sensory defensive* (SD), a common mimicker of anxiety and panic. The sensory defensive feel *too* much, *too* soon and for *too* long, and experience the world as *too loud, too bright, too fast and too tight*, becoming easily distressed by everyday sensation. For instance, you may interpret a light stroke on the shoulder as an attack and become anxious, hostile, or aggressive and spontaneously flinch, withdraw or lash out.

After the irritation has passed, you fail to return to baseline quickly and remain in red alert. Feeling constantly hyped, stressed, and agitated, life feels a constant emergency; anxiety is omnipresent.

Anxiety, Panic....

Over time, chronic, unrelenting, and uncontrollable stress keeps your body flooded with stress chemistry and you are locked into a hyper-vigilant, self-protective stance. This is typified by a worried look, rigid posture and inevitable illness as the nervous system and the immune system are intimately connected. This trajectory is especially likely if you live in an urban setting where our fast-paced, noisy, flashy, cramped, sound-bite environment forces you to experience more sensory junk food than your nervous system can digest; ordinary life is a recipe for disaster.

Constant stress and anxiety lead to extreme and often uncontrollable behavior that manifests as a broad range of psychopathology. By adolescence, you were likely referred to as anxious, phobic, depressed, compulsive, hostile, aggressive or controlling. By adulthood you will probably have been in therapy for anxiety, fears or depression as Rachel Schneider relates:

> "It's been a banner week in the world of this SPDer! ... It's only been a week and a day since I had a disabling sensory overload event (call it what you will: panic attack triggered by sensory stimuli, dissociation triggered by sensory stimuli - when it comes down to it, my senses were taxed and I had a physiological reaction), a hugely upsetting occurrence as the sensory world flows in and out of me as if there are no barricades."

No doubt, you've taken tranquilizers, antidepressants, and perhaps betablockers for panic. Good chance you also engaged in alcohol and recreational drugs to self-calm.

Mild to Severe

The depth and scope of the psychopathology is determined by the degree of hypersensitivity, ranging from mild to severe.

The mildly sensory defensive feel irritated by many clothing textures and toss and turn at night to the sound of a dripping sink but life seems manageable. You know that you are more edgy, fastidious and restless than most but you see yourself as neurotic, not someone with a "disorder" and you suffer only mild psychiatric symptoms like generalized anxiety.

The moderately sensory defensive feel bombarded by discomforting sensations and feel constantly hyperalert. This makes you constantly frazzled and anxious and undue stress severely diminishes your ability to interact with the world. You suffer many mental health issues and are likely to be on or to have been on psychotropic medication.

The severely sensory defensive suffer hair-raising sensitivity to barely noticeable stimuli like a gentle touch or sudden noise; minor sensation, like the phone ringing can quickly derail you. Functioning is greatly compromised, and psychopathology is obvious, pronounced, and acute. You are extremely likely to be or to have been on psychotropic meds.

Temple Grandin, who you may know from the popular HBO film, **Temple Grandin** is an autistic woman who writes and lectures all over the world on her experience with autism. Here she gives us some insight into what it's like to be severely touchy.

> *"As far back as I can remember, I always hated to be hugged. I wanted to experience the good feeling of being hugged, but it was just too overwhelming. It was like a great, all-engulfing tidal wave of stimulation, and I reacted like a wild animal."*

Feisty/Shy

Avoiders fall into two categories depending on energy level (high/low) and self-regulation, which is control of over-stimulation (active/passive):

- **Shy:** low energy/passive sensation avoiding
- **Feisty:** high energy/active sensation avoiding

High/Passive Shy

Some avoiders are shy/introverted and fearful. Wishing to not make waves and draw attention, you passively avoid sensation by fleeing or withdrawing. You make an excuse to not go to a noisy restaurant and opt to stay home. You avoid eye contact, need much personal space, cry easily, and have difficulty making friends. At the same time, needing to carefully monitor your world, you read faces well, making you highly tuned into others, and you are sensitive, empathic, and kind.

Your energy is often low, evident by a body that often seems caved in, though inside you are jumping. Nervousness, along with sensation avoiding and a natural cautiousness that enables you to delay gratification gives you the patience to engage in self-development and you may learn more active ways of coping and overcome shyness and inhibition. For instance, you may become a teacher, public speaker, or actor/actress.

This change in strategies was first noted by developmental psychologist Jerome Kagan, who was the first to identify the two temperamental extremes—shy children that cling to mommy, and bold ones that easily explore. Kagan found that when parents actively encourage shy children to explore and play with other children many will switch to a more active pattern of controlling overstimulation and overcome their shyness—assertiveness training!

High/Active Feisty

Feisty avoiders are temperamental, edgy and possess high energy, looking and acting hyper and wired. You actively avoid sensation by fighting more than fleeing. For instance, you will complain in a restaurant that the music is too loud and the lights too bright and demand to sit somewhere quieter and dimmer. Things have to be just so; fussy, stubborn, negative, intense and uncooperative you are difficult and hard to be around. If not over-stimulated, however, you can be upbeat and engaged.

The need to design a world highly specific to your needs makes some feisty avoiders artsy and creative, while high energy and the need for order and predictability makes you productive and you get much done. As you are highly aware of your world, you perceive more than others and often have great insight into human nature.

Like your shy counterpart, constant jumpiness, and an ability to delay gratification motivates you to relieve inner tension and you engage in self-development, enabling you to grow and evolve throughout life.

SENSORY MODULATION DISORDER & BEHAVIORAL CHARACTERISTICS

ENERGY LEVEL	SENSORY THRESHOLD	
	LOW	HIGH
	AVOIDER High Sensitivity, Over-Responsive	**SEEKER** Low Sensitivity, Under-Responsive
LOW	*Shy* (flight) **Passive Self-Regulation** • Fearful/anxious • Quiet/introverted • Cautious/wary • Compliant • Socially phobic • Dependent • Rigid • Overly serious	*Languid* (cautious) **Passive Self-Regulation** • Disinterested, bored, oblivious • Easily fatigued, sedentary (low muscle tone) • Lethargic, "lazy" • Shy, withdrawn, depressed • Unstructured, undisciplined • Unaware • Dreamer, "Indigo" child • Couch/mouse potato
HIGH	*Feisty* (fight) **Active Self-Regulation** • Difficult • Willful • Angry, explosive • Defiant/rude • Edgy • Impulsive • Fussy • Hyped • Rigid • Intense/serious • Aware	*Bold* (reckless) **Active Self-Regulation** • Extroverted • Risk taker/thrill seeker • Impulsive • Hyperactive/manic • Uninhibited • Insensitive • Bored/distracted • Undisciplined • "In your face"

(Sharon Heller, PhD, 2010)

See-Sawing

Some of you will think that you fit into more than one category, for instance you may be touchy but love roller coasters; you may be shy with some people but feisty with others; you may be laid back and placid but freak out by a roaring truck or the odor of bleach.

This is not unusual. Some people commonly seesaw between seeking and avoiding and constantly need to rev up or calm down. Though the quadrant of sensory modulation types helps us to categorize our behavior, it's "too simplistic," says Lucy Miller. As she writes in *Sensational Kids* (p. 65), "Things are along a continuum, not divided into dichotomous boxes."

At any moment behavior is colored by many variables, including context, trauma, parenting and culture.

Context

The basic fabric of our temperament creates a baseline of response that defines our modus operandi. From baseline, arousability moves up or down according to sensory input, which can be external (like bright/dim lights) or internal (like heartbeat or thoughts) and that interacts with conditions such as time of day, health, emotional state, activity, fatigue, hunger, previous pain/ pleasure, expectations, motivation, task-at-hand, and environment. All this varies according to our body rhythms that orchestrate behavior, such as cranial-sacral rhythm, brain waves and circadian rhythm.

If you are in a good place, you can more easily tune out noxious stimulation and even the shy avoider may welcome the boom boom of the bass and the closeness of the crowd. If you are in a bad place, everyone is capable of becoming annoyed by loud noise and touchy.

Trauma

Any trauma to the nervous system can create sensory defensiveness. Birth trauma may alter basic temperamental patterns, modifying inborn tendencies. I hypothesize that some feisty avoiders may be temperamentally bold and seek sensation but early trauma impacted their nervous system and created hypersensitivity, leading to both seeking and avoiding.

And not just birth trauma. Any trauma in your life can create hypersensitivity. In my case, I was always mildly hypersensitive but it did not interfere with my life. After head trauma, I became severely defensive and could barely leave the house. One languid I know passively sought extreme sensation. She dyed her hair red, smoked, drank coffee all day, munched away on comfort food, talked loudly, invaded your space, and blasted the radio all day. After head trauma from a car accident, she remained the same sensation seeker but would startle from the slightest noise or if lightly touched.

Hyperarousal and a low sensory threshold are common with post-traumatic stress disorder regardless of whether you are a bold sensation seeker or a shy avoider. Stated D. Jeffrey Newport and Charles B. Nemeroff in an APA article entitled *Neurobiology of Posttraumatic Stress Disorder*, "disturbances in sensory processing are believed to play a prominent role in the hyperarousal symptoms of PTSD such as the exaggerated startle response." (p. 315)

Teresa, whom I describe in my book *Anxiety: Hidden Causes*, was a classic languid, hypo-responsive, fleshy and overweight. Growing up, Teresa was molested by both her grandfather and her stepfather. Just short of graduating high school, her stepfather turned violent, wielding an ax, and beat up her mother and her. After this incident, she began having uncontrollable crying spells, depression, appetite loss, anxiety, and helplessness, along with frequent headaches, light-headedness and cold sweats that forced her to wear sweaters in the summer heat. She was also light sensitive and wore sunglasses outside even on rainy days.

A month after going away to college, she was studying in her brightly lit dorm room when suddenly she felt claustrophobic, dizzy, short of breath, trembly and disoriented. Filled with terror, she feared she was going crazy or dying and ran to the student mental health building. The psychologist diagnosed her with panic attack triggered by post-traumatic stress disorder (PTSD) and started her on the antianxiety drug BuSpar. But that made her dizzy and caused her moods to fluctuate wildly and she stopped taking it. Unable to concentrate in her classes, she quit school and returned home.

Once home, she was too terrified to leave the house or her mother and they clung to each other. A psychologist diagnosed her as depressed and put her on 20 mg of Prozac. Within three weeks, Teresa felt normal and registered for two night classes at a local junior college.

The first night of classes was a lecture held in a dimly lit classroom and she made it through the hour and a half class with little trepidation. The second night was in a lab, brightly lit with overhead fluorescent lights. She had her second panic attack. "I felt my blood pressure drop and all of a sudden I felt dizzy. I felt my anxiety rushing back. I tried to control myself and my tears. But I freaked out and stormed out of the classroom." The bright lighting, which was likely the result of extreme photophobia from PTSD, set off panic attack, the first time in her overly lit dorm room and again in the college lab.

Early Experiences

Parenting profoundly influences behavior. Warm, sensitive parents calm their babies when they are overstimulated and rev them up when they need sensation. This helps the infant develop strategies for self-organization that help tone down sensory modulation problems.

Conversely, insensitive parents amplify sensory modulation problems; an active child may become hyperactive, a languid child depressed, a feisty child highly anxious and insecure, and a shy child more inhibited and fearful.

At the same time, parents who offer firm guidance and limits, along with gentling pushing the child into new territory create a safe haven for exploring and socializing. As previously noted, Jerome Kagan's found that shy children can become more social when parents encourage them to develop more active social skills.

Culture

Behavior is modified by cultural expectations. For instance, American culture is more likely to encourage bold, competitive behavior than many Asian cultures that encourage modesty and cooperation.

SENSORY DISCRIMINATION

Sensory discrimination refers to the ability to distinguish one sensation from another. It enables you to pluck out the salient characteristics of a sensation and correctly interpret its meaning – gritty, smooth, silky, gooey – and to place sensations correctly in time and space.

Characteristics: You recognize that something you just put in your mouth tastes bitter rather than sour. Fine tuning further, you can distinguish the taste of a tangerine from an orange, the sound of the violin in the orchestra from the flute.

Time: You know that you just cut your finger tip, and that the pain is on the inside tip of your index finger not on the side.

Space: You perceive that a car is coming toward you rather than away from you; you can tie your shoes in the dark and zip up your pants without looking at them as you know where you are touching things without having to see them.

With the ability to quickly distinguish one sensation from another, you immediately evaluate if something is safe, dangerous, or if you care and respond appropriately, ignoring:

- The sound of a child screaming on the TV but alert to the sound of your child screaming in pain.
- Smoke from the barbecue peeling into the house but alert to smoke from your toast burning in the oven.
- The tag in your blouse but immediately flick off an ant crawling up your arm.
- Indifference in a face but quickly discern anger and back off.

But if you cannot easily discriminate sensations, you do not respond to signals from the environment accurately and you:

- Can't find your glasses that are on your face and you run around looking for them (touch);
- Make an incorrect turn while driving and you get lost (vestibular);
- Can't figure out that the announcement of a blue Honda Civic blocking the driveway is yours and fail to move it (auditory);
- Can't easily distinguish the smell of milk turning sour and drink it (smell);
- Don't recognize that a tick just bit you and may have put yourself at risk for Lime's disease and you don't seek medical help (touch);
- Don't perceive that the dead animal in your driveway is a possum, not your cat and you panic (vision);
- Don't discern anger in your boss's face from a remark you just made

and continue to expound on the subject, increasing his anger (vision).
- Misinterpret the lump on your breast as soft, not hard and rocky and fail to get it checked out and it continues to grow until you are ultimately diagnosed with breast cancer (touch).

Such lack of sensory discrimination makes the world confusing, frustrating, taxing, and dangerous and these feeling interfere with how easily you can meet the ordinary challenges of everyday life. Consequently, you worry constantly about doing what you need to do to get your needs met and feel constantly anxious.

To OT Teresa May-Benson of the Spiral Foundation, it is primarily problems with sensory discrimination that underlie languids, who are unable to get enough information to feel a sensation: bumpy feels smooth; stuffed to the gills feels satiated; a broken toe—well, it's barely felt at all.

Greatly compounding lack of discrimination are motor issues that commonly accompany discrimination problems, and languids shlep and trip through a life that, without something bright and loud to tune them in, can seem dull and confusing.

MOTOR PROBLEMS (DYSPRAXIA & POSTURAL ISSUES)

"Praxis is to the physical world what language is to the social, it permits interaction."

~ A. Jean Ayres, 1985

Do you feel like a klutz, unable to move your body without bumping into something or someone? Do you easily trip or fall and hurt yourself? Was gym class your worst nightmare? If so, your brain isn't translating sensory input into organized, purposeful motor output. Most likely you also have low muscle tone and weak muscles that hinder you from voluntarily moving your body easily and gracefully.

If this sounds like you, life has probably often seemed one of never ending *stumbling blocks*. As you don't maneuver space well, doing everyday automatic tasks requires exertion and you feel incompetent, dependent, and lacking control. Such effort, along with the passive hypo-responsivity to sensation that generally accompanies motor problems, interferes with the alertness needed to tune into the world and you may appear and be depressed.

Dyspraxia

If you have motor problems you may be *dyspraxic*, meaning you are unable to plan or execute movement well, or you might have developmental co-ordination disorder (DCD).

Molly, a sixty-three-year-old special ed teacher never felt comfortable moving. Her life reflects the impact of dyspraxia on every day functioning in an adult.

- **Disorganized:** For Molly, sorting, planning, organizing, and physically putting away objects present great difficulty, and she feels constantly disorganized; her house is a constant mess.
- **Clumsy:** Uncoordinated and with poor equilibrium, she is clumsy and accident prone and has fallen and broken bones several times since childhood.
- **Poor Athlete:** She always did poorly in gym, and never could learn how to dance, roller skate, bounce a ball, or ride a bicycle.
- **Poor Fine Motor Skills:** She has poor fine motor skills; her handwriting is sloppy and she has great difficulty typing, sewing a button and other hand skills.
- **Falling Out of Bed:** She has always fallen out of bed, even as an adult because her sense of her body in space is poor and her brain does not recognize when she is lying on the edge of her bed when she's asleep.

Sometimes in the middle of the night she awakens in horror to find herself flopped on the floor and for this reason fears going to sleep.

Bilateral Coordination Problems

Another aspect of problems with motor planning comes from problems with bilateral coordination, the ability to coordinate the two sides of the body and sequence motor actions. Molly's poor bilateral coordination plays out in the following ways:

- **Catching a Ball:** Molly has difficulty catching a ball because this requires extending the hands to the exact location where the ball will be in time to catch it.
- **Dancing:** She had a tough time learning to dance as it was hard to get both feet to work together, and she seemed to have two left feet.
- **Hand Dominance:** She established a dominant right hand late and will still use both hands awkwardly. Her hunch is that she was left-handed and her mother forced her to use her non-dominant right hand.

Postural Control

Postural control enables you to stabilize your body during movement and at rest to meet environmental demands. Such stability is dependent on muscle tone which is determined by the degree of tension generally present when you rest.

Muscle Tone

- **Firm:** Movement feels good and desired.
- **Stiff:** Movement lacks fluidity and grace and moving may not feel enjoyable.
- **Floppy:** Movement is uncoordinated and moving feels effortful, as

does keeping your body upright to resist gravity. Floppy muscle tone made Molly seem lazy, unmotivated, and often depressed.

Cause

Molly's muscles are probably structurally normal. Her floppy muscle tone relates to problems in her vestibular system. It isn't regulating neurological information from the brain to the muscles, telling them how much to contract so she can resist gravity and move with ease and perform tasks skillfully. Unable to do easily what she sets out to do, she has a poor body scheme.

Worst of all she doesn't know why she's clumsy, lazy, and uncoordinated. Little wonder people like Molly feel anxious! The next time you accuse someone of being a couch potato, look at his muscle tone. If he's flopped on the couch, it's probably low— sprawled out takes little effort. He's not lazy. Holding his body up against gravity is hard and moving, which takes effort is hard work and not pleasurable.

Fears & Phobias

Gravitational insecurity, which as you may recall is a strong reaction to slight movement and triggers fear of falling is strongly linked with low muscle tone.

Let's now look at how the brain processes sensory information.

Summing Up

SPD plays out in 3 ways: SMD, SDD, SMPD

SMD: Problems with sensory modulation involve seeking or avoiding.

- The languid are passive seekers and the bold active seekers.
- The shy are passive avoiders and the feisty active avoiders.

SDD: Many who suffer SPD have a problem with discriminating one sensation from another and this causes much confusion.

SMPD: Postural disorders and dyspraxia are a common affliction of those with SPD and result in clumsiness, poor coordination, and poor planning and sequencing of movement through space.

Clearly, these problems are an aberration of how the brain was designed to perceive and respond to the surrounding world.

3

*

Scrambled Brain

"All our knowledge begins with the senses, proceeds then to the understanding, and ends with reason. There is nothing higher than reason."

~ Immanuel Kant, *Critique of Pure Reason*

"Sit still." "Stop fussing." "Stop complaining." Don't be so fussy. "Don't be so lazy." "Can't you be like other people?" "Chill out." "Stop acting crazy." "You're too emotional."

If you suffer SPD, such comments are uncomfortably familiar. Why are you like this? Why can't you be more like other people?

To answer these questions, we need to take a foray inside the brain, from its most primitive part to the most advanced. Doing so will reveal what happens when a traffic jam occurs in our neuronal highway, distorting sensory processing and twisting how we perceive and respond to the world.

TRIUNE BRAIN

Sensations tap directly into the brainstem, the primitive survival part of the brain. Its job it is to evaluate sensory input and keep us alert and tuned into the world so we can immediately detect danger. Though some evaluations occur consciously, most are unconscious, gut survival reactions.

Sensory information enters from the bottom up, from the primitive brainstem to the cerebral cortex, the order in which our brain has grown over the last five million years. From the brainstem, sensory information travels to the higher brain where it enables the whole nervous system to organize behavior and make meaningful sense of our surroundings. This allows us to respond adaptively to the situation. Each layer of the brain functions as an integrated whole and reciprocally influences each other. In layman's terms, your senses tell your brain what's going on, and based on this information, your brain tells your body what to do and your mind what to think.

Organized Brain

In the normal "neurotypical" brain, this process happens smoothly, and you function optimally. For the most part, you are adaptable and goal directed, curious and motivated, engaged and focused, alert and spontaneous; you go with flow as you monitor, sustain, and change attention. Generally in sync with others, you take initiative, manage transitions, and think on your feet.

SPD Brain

In a brain that misconstrues sensory information, both from the world and from inside your own body, what you think and what you do is out of sync with actual reality. The world seems too loud when no one else seems bothered. It feels as if someone is touching your arm when they're touching your elbow. The milk tastes fine when it's sour. You see a splatter of ketchup on the kitchen sink and worry that your child cut her finger. You bend forward to listen more closely to what someone is telling you and fall off the chair. You feel you are leaning to the right when your body is straight.

What is going on inside *your* brain!?

To answer that question, let's explore the path of sensory input into the brainstem to thought and action in the cerebral cortex.

PRIMITIVE BRAIN: BRAINSTEM

At the top of our spinal cord sits the brainstem, our primitive or reptilian brain and our first sensory registrar. In charge of survival, it drives the "Four Fs" necessary for self-preservation: feeding, fleeing, fighting and ... reproduction.

Reticular Formation (RF)

Comprising the central core of the brain stem is the reticular formation (RF), the seat of the "Four As": awake, asleep, arousal and attention, and thus consciousness. The RF acts as a sensory antenna, filtering incoming sensations, except smell, and decides what enters—at this moment the words on this page—and what gets excluded—the traffic outside. Depending on the decision, the RF will perk up if we need to pay attention, tone down if we can ignore the sensation, or wind down into sleep.

The RF continues to monitor stimuli outside of consciousness, which is why, though we can tune out the humming of the air conditioner we still feel stressed by it. Often, we don't become conscious of this stress until the air conditioner turns off: "Aahh," you say as the burden lifts.

Sensory Thresholds and Arousability

Set in the RF is our individual threshold to stimuli. It is determined by our unique biochemistry—by our baseline of arousability, or excitability of our autonomic nervous system. This threshold makes some of us hot headed at the drop of a hat and others cool as a cucumber even in the face of disaster.

From baseline, arousability moves up or down according to sensory input. This can be external (like bright or dim lights) or internal (like our heartbeat or thoughts). These inputs interact with conditions such as: time of day and health; state of mind (avoiding, seeking, "just right,") and activity; fatigue and hunger; previous pain or pleasure experience; as well as expectations, and interest.

Modulated

If you have an organized nervous system, your threshold is set in the RF to keep you modulated, meaning you get neither quickly over-aroused and anxious nor under-aroused and lethargic.

SPD

If you have SPD, research shows that you will demonstrate abnormal arousal patterns. For instance, many operate often at the brainstem level as primitive instincts for survival and protection, demonstrated in fight or flight, take precedence over function and learning.

Avoiders

In avoiders, the "gate" opens too quickly to mild, brief, or infrequent stimulation; you take in too much stimuli, and feel quickly overstimulated and anxious. This response is an immediate, from the gut, survival response. It happens too quickly for the thinking brain to jump in and stop

the reaction and happens even when you are not consciously aware of the stimulus. Take noise. Using MRI brain scans of people who had been stressed by an unpleasant noise, combined with visual images, University College London researchers observed that activity took place in the attention center of the cerebral cortex even when a fearful noise was present only at the unconscious level.

From the attention center, activity gets channeled to other parts of the brain to prepare the body for flight or fight, whether you notice the stimulus or not. The conscious, under-our-control part of the brain only steps into play as an after-thought.

Seekers

In seekers, the "gate" needs more than the usual kind and amount of sensation to open, and you take in too little sensation to keep you alert and tuned in. To compensate, you seek strong sensation to elicit dopamine that the brain needs to perk up and engage in the world, and that is low in sensation seekers.

Rhythmicity

Orchestrating all behavior are the body's rhythms, such as heart rate, respiratory rate, and brain waves. They exist within a circadian or 24-hour sleep/wake cycle, an inner clock that synchronizes body rhythms by the ebb and flow of light and dark. Our body temperature, for instance, is higher by day and lower by night, while the right side of the body is warmer by day and the left side is warmer by night.

Organized System

In an organized nervous system, rhythmicity is regular for the most part and behavior is modulated.

SPD

In those with under- or over-arousability, rhythmicity flows in extremes. Your behavior is unmodulated, and things tend to be off key.

Take sleep. If your system is under-reactive to sensation, you fall asleep in a wink: without light, sound and movement there's nothing to charge your system. This is good. But you may also oversleep as a result and find it hard to get going in the morning, and especially if you have low muscle tone. Not surprisingly, most on the low end of arousal are owls and don't get going until late in the day. Such a late start probably affected how well you did in school and work performance as most jobs require morning alertness.

If you are sensory defensive, you are too wired to fall asleep. Once asleep, you awake easily by noise, movement in the bed, odors, light pouring into the room, or the sensation of your bedding or night clothes.

And not just sleep rhythms are off. Everything is.

Autonomic: You breathe too rapidly and your heart beats too quickly, or you seem a zombie and show little autonomic arousal in the face of stimulating sensation like a fire alarm.

Eating: You have little appetite or can't stop eating.

Eliminating: You urinate frequently, and eliminate irregularly, or get the runs.

Moving: You jitter and pace or can't get your body going.

Sex: You can't get enough sex or run from your partner.

AROUSABILITY

	Organized System	SPD
Alertness	Modulated	Difficulty or inconsistent calming or alerting
Attention	Visual & auditory focus	Inattentive
Filtering	Filter & prioritize incoming stimuli	Filter out too much relevant or too little irrelevant stimuli
Vigilance	Vigilant in real danger	Hypervigilant or not perceiving danger
Sleep	Easily fall asleep, stay asleep	Difficulty falling asleep, staying asleep or waking up; oversleep

RHYTHMICITY

	Organized System	SPD
Heart rate	Normal rate	Fast, irregular, vacillating
Respiration	Normal rate	Fast, shallow
Cranial sacral rhythm (CSR)	Flows normally	Stuck in specific areas
Temperature Control	Generally comfortable	Often too hot, too cold, vacillating
Appetite	Normal	Under or overeat
Digestion	Normal	Problems ingesting, digesting & eliminating
Sex	Normal sex drive & sexual activity	Avoid or overly seek

Cerebellum

Wrapped around the back of the brain stem sits the cerebellum. The puppeteer of the nervous system, it is responsible for coordinating muscle tone, balance, and all our body movements so we can move easily, smoothly, precisely, and with good timing. By controlling movement, it also influences speech movements by coordinating and modifying both planned and ongoing speech. If words gush or a sentence takes forever, blame it on the cerebellum.

Cerebellum & Vestibular & Proprioceptive Input

To plan and execute movement well, the cerebellum relies on clear messages from the vestibular and proprioceptive systems. A circus performer walking the tightrope shows the cerebellum at peak performance. If the cerebellum receives faulty vestibular and proprioceptive messages, you will have poor coordination and stiff or flaccid rag doll muscle tone—red flags for SPD.

Cerebellum & Volume Control

The cerebellum appears also in charge of volume control for all sensory input, inhibiting or dampening sensory information so the cortex can better respond. In those on the autistic spectrum, research shows the cerebellum to be smaller, and they lack the filter needed to dampen or turn down sensory information: touch, vision and taste all feel "too loud."

Cerebellum & Learning

The cerebellum appears also to be connected to learning. Research by Peter Strick and colleagues of the University of Pittsburgh reveals a path from the cerebellum to parts of the brain involved with memory, attention, and spatial perception. Damage to the cerebellum results in lack of muscle coordination during voluntary movements, such as walking or picking up objects, as well as a problem with speech, eye movements and ability to swallow.

CEREBELLUM

	Organized System	SPD
Movement	Normal	Over/underactive
Muscle tone	Normal	Floppy/stiff
Balance	Normal	Off
Movement patterns	Graceful	Clumsy, uncoordinated
Automaticity	Ordinary movement automatic	Movement often takes conscious effort
Speech	Normal; smooth flowing	Too fast, too slow, forced, choppy, out of sync

As you see, from the getgo the SPD brain processes sensations within a disorganized framework that can distort the body's rhythms, arousability, movement, and speech. These distorted sensations skew your reality of what is safe, what is dangerous and what is irrelevant, making it hard to tease out and respond adaptively to the world around you.

EMOTIONAL/LIMBIC BRAIN

After the brainstem has coded sensation for danger, safety or irrelevant/ignore, the information travels to the limbic system, our old mammalian brain and the seat of our feelings. Here neurotransmitters like serotonin, opiates, and hormones like oxytocin, the bonding hormone make us *feel* what has made our heart go pitter patter and our palms sweat: fear or excitement; sadness or joy. And it is here, as touch makes us melt or squirm that our mood changes, as a chemical cascade streams through the hippocampus, amygdala, and hypothalamus.

Hippocampus, Amygdala, Hypothalamus

The *hippocampus* in the limbic system stores long-term memories, coloring every sensation our body picks up with a feeling based on our past experience. If that memory is aversive, the *amygdala*, the seat of emotions will evoke fear biochemistry (norepenephrine and adrenaline).

This drives the flight/fight response from the *hypothalamus* in the limbic system. The "master gland," the hypothalamus controls body temperature, hunger, thirst, fatigue, sleep and circadian rhythms to keep our internal state in sync so we stay calm enough to meet demand. Input uses dopamine and output uses GABA, a neurochemical that dampens excitement (See more on GABA in chapter sixteen).

How comfortable are your emotions? Do you allow yourself to experience sadness and disappointment, fear and excitement or do you limit what emotions you allow into consciousness? Do you feel anxious and easily overwhelmed or do you barely feel at all? Are you even keeled or are you moody? Do people know what's on your mind or are you a poker face? Are you socially in sync or are you on a different wavelength from most people? The answer to these questions lies in both natural born temperament and how the limbic system colors the sensory messages coming from the brainstem.

Emotional Regulation

If rhythms are steady and arousal modulated, you are likely comfortable with emotions, which are mostly content, and you express the full range of emotions, neither getting carried away nor lacking them. You can modify your emotions to meet the appropriateness of the situation and your mood is stable.

If rhythms are out of sync with your needs and basic arousal is too high or too low, emotions will reflect the same, and you are unstable and moody, inhibited or overflowing.

Hyper-responsiveness

If you are hyper-responsive and arousal is too high, constant amygdala hijacks are on-going. This happens because so many experiences connect in memory in the hippocampus with irritation, annoyance, distress, and even pain. For instance, if in the NICU Bach was played in your isolette, that music will be associated with negativity and fear because it will be associated with pain, loud beeping, discomforting bright lighting and so on; unknowingly the sound makes you squirm. The result is extreme and intense emotions that evoke acute discomfort as everything feels *too much*.

Hypo-responsiveness

If you are hypo-responsive and your arousal is too low, you may feel little or nothing at all, as is common in bold sensation seekers and cravers, or you may feel consumed by discomforting emotions like fear, sadness and get easily depressed, as is common with languids. Languids will also get easily frazzled and scattered in response to frustration and under-stimulation and, when frustration becomes too much, go over the edge and have a meltdown. The hypo-responsive may seem moody or even bipolar as you fluctuate from boredom or lethargy to sensation seeking that leads to manic-like activity.

Social Regulation

If your emotions are steady and stable, you likely feel comfortable with people and do well in the social arena.

If your emotions get easily out of hand or if you feel little emotion, you will find social engagement hard to manage. You may be a loner because you feel too overwhelmed by people to make eye contact or initiate conversation or engage, or you may be disinterested in human relationships. You may also be socially awkward because auditory problems, visual problems, and problems with sensory discrimination cause you to respond slowly to social cues and misread the other's intent.

SOCIAL REGULATION

	Organized System	SPD
Emotional regulation	Stable; predictable Moods	Unstable, labile (moody), inhibited, excessive, overbright
Emotional State	Mostly content	Overly fearful; inappropriately fearless
Emotional Range	Experience full range of emotions	May lack depth & range; Deadness
Emotional comfort	Comfortable with emotions	Overwhelmed by emotions; out of touch with emotions
Social Regulation	Eye contact; in sync	Poor eye contact; slow responding; out of sync
Emotional expression	Easy to read facial Expression	Facial expression & body language hard to read; may not match communicative intent
Social aptitude	Engaged; appropriately Interactive	Isolated; lonely
Behavior	Appropriate; in sync	Inappropriate; out of sync

As you can see, we now have a biochemistry that creates unstable arousability and irregular rhythms colored by extreme, disorganizing, and uncomfortable emotions, or lack of emotions. What happens when this translates into thinking in the frontal lobes of the cerebral cortex? Let's explore.

THINKING BRAIN: CEREBRAL CORTEX

In the third level, the frontal cortex and specifically the prefrontal cortex, lies consciousness where thinking allows us to interpret what the senses perceive. Here is where self-talk can say, "Okay, calm down. I didn't gauge where to turn and hit a curve but I didn't puncture my tire. Everything is fine!" In other words, the cortex gives us some control or will power over the primal lower messages. But as we've seen, the thinking brain must rely on the maturation of the feeling and primitive brain to respond adaptively to the world.

Organized

When all works as it should, you perceive the world accurately and behavior is efficient, goal-directed and purposeful, while good vestibular, tactile and proprioceptive processing produce a feeling of being centered, grounded and having it together.

SPD

If the neuronal connections between the three parts of the brain are not properly established, your brain cannot easily organize sensory messages from the skin, muscles and joints, inner ear, eyes, and the environment. As a result, the brain fails to get the information necessary to develop properly, and especially the experience of support against gravity.

The reptilian, protective brain, and the limbic, emotional brain take over and the brain attends to real or imagined survival needs, trumping thinking. Forced into flight/flight, the brain releases the stress hormone cortisol, inhibiting dopamine that the higher brain needs for paying attention and learning.

If dopamine is low, you cannot give something your full attention and easily process the information, and you will have learning problems. What's more, if you are operating on auto pilot from the primitive survival mode, you will be unable to exert control over runaway feelings and bring them under your reign because "free will" or control happens in the frontal lobe of the cerebral cortex.

The result of faulty sensorimotor processing in the brainstem, colored by uncomfortable emotions in the limbic system is disorganized, negative thoughts, poor memory and focus, and lack of sufficient communication and cognitive skills, all of which affect well-being, basic skills, learning, coping, self-esteem, identity, and everyday functioning.

Let's look closely at how SPD distorts thinking processes and their effect on functioning.

Cognitive Impact

You may be spacey, easily distracted, disorganized and have poor focus, making everyday living a challenge despite normal intelligence and you fail to work up to capacity.

You may suffer short-term memory problems that make you seem dumb, and you joke about senior moments, while poor communication skills and slow auditory processing makes it seem as if you're not listening and paying attention and people call you a space cadet.

You may lack good problem-solving skills and strategies to modify your behavior, that at times seems inappropriate, and seem as if you lack inner drive and motivation to change your behavior. As a result, you constantly get accused of "just not trying," as if you are intentionally sabotaging your life. Does anyone consciously do that?

Repeated failure from these cognitive glitches makes doing something about them risky because you worry that whatever you do won't work anyway, and you fail to take action. "Why try and fail?"

Negative Self-Talk

All these challenges make you feel inept, clumsy, stupid, crazy, "weird" and easily self-conscious as you fear doing or saying something wrong in social or learning situations.

Not surprisingly, your head fills with self-talk, like: *"I can't," "I don't have fun like others," "I'm not normal," "People don't like me," "I'll never succeed."*

Self-Esteem/Identity

As most people feel that you should be able to control your behavior, you fail to get validation from others that your problems are real and should be taken seriously. Consequently, you assume that your problems are self-willed and your fault, that you are just an annoying, negative person.

You lose touch with other aspects of your authentic self by internal design and experience identity confusion. For instance, Amanda, whom I describe in the next chapter, was a hypo-responsive, low tone teenager with visual and auditory processing problems that interfered with her learning. A loner, she refused to be with other children because she felt they would perceive her as "dumb" and reject her. Once her sensory issues were resolved, so were her learning problems and social inhibition. She became a national merit scholar and a social butterfly—she became *Amanda* who by nature was bright, social, and engaging. If her sensorimotor problems were not fixed, her true essence would have remained buried beneath sensory chaos.

Coping Strategies

To cope with the confusion, humiliation, stress, anxiety and physical upheaval that you experience as a result of living with SPD, you erect defenses to better manage your behavior.

Hyper-Responsive

If you are *hyper-responsive*, you control overwhelming sensory input by:

Avoidance: To reduce sensory overload, you keep people at arm's length by averting gaze and withdrawing, appearing aloof, preoccupied or unfriendly; or you push people away by lashing out.

Control: To constantly sidestep sensory overstimulation, you take extreme measures to control your world and interactions and you appear stubborn, difficult, willful, and bossy.

Predictability: To create a predictable sensory world, you compulsively adhere to strict schedules, rigid routines for eating, waking, and going to sleep, carefully choreographing your sensory environment to avoid anything new or unexpected. This makes you seem picky, inflexible, selfish, and self-involved.

Hypervigilance: As sensory overload forces you into fight or flight, you are in a constant state of hypervigilance and continually monitor even safe environments. This makes you appear fidgety, agitated, short-tempered, impulsive, impatient, and volatile when extreme.

Aggression: When you go over the edge, you have a meltdown and lash out or even become violent.

Hypo-Responsive

If you are Hypo-responsive, you may:

Seek Attention: You clown, act silly, talk loudly and so forth to force more sensation into a starved system.

Self-medicate: You rev-up by self-medicating with controlled and illicit substances.

Withdraw: You may turn inward into your own highly imaginative world that you find immensely stimulating and satisfying putting you at risk for depression.

Poor Relationship Regulation

Such negative self-regard affects how well you can relate to others and the nature of your relationships, and many with SPD feel isolated and live lonely lives.

Here are the many ways it might play out. You might:

- **Show** overdependence on others from lack of acquiring sufficient life skills and from emotional neediness.
- **Exhibit** false independence to hide deep dependency and to compensate for lack of relating.
- **Experience** social anxiety from feeling different from others, and from being easily rejected.
- **Be self-absorbed** from feeling constant distress, making reciprocity difficult.
- **Demonstrate flat emotions** as you find it hard to tune in and engage and people feel rejected.
- **Lack intimacy** from being unable to tolerate affection, the other's odors, noises they make (especially while eating), and so forth.

COGNITION

	Organized System	SPD
Organization	Organize space, tasks, environment, time (prioritize)	Disorganized, messy
Memory	Good working memory	Memory deficits
Communication	Communicative competence	Poor communication
Focus	On task	Distracted by overload or can't tune in
Attention	Sustained, self-directed	Intermittent, other-directed
Language	Articulate	At a loss for words
Sequencing	Able to sequence Information	Difficulty sequencing information & easily confused
Persistence	Keep trying	Give up easily
Problem Solving	Good	Poor problem solving skills
Motivation	Largely intrinsic	Largely extrinsic
Perspective taking	Can infer mental states of others	Poor perspective taking
Adaptability to change	Flexibility to new plans	Inflexible; difficulty with transitions

SOCIAL/EMOTIONAL

	Organized System	SPD
Emotional regulation	Stable - can modify emotions	Unable to modify emotions
Self-talk	Generally positive	Generally negative, destructive, self-blaming
Coping strategies	Normal	Lack strategies to modify behavior
Self-monitoring	Aware of & able to modify behavior	Poor self-awareness
Self-esteem	Healthy	Low, feeling "crazy," "weird;" self-demeaning
Self-image	Steady, coherent sense of self	Feel at odds with body, brain, social self
Social Regulation	Responding, initiating, joint focus, turn taking	Social ineptitude, inappropriate or lack of initiating; out of sync
Social impact	Engaged; appropriately interactive	Isolated; lonely
Relationship Regulation	Autonomy, interdependence, independence, reciprocity, capacity for intimacy	Dependency, false independence, self-absorbed, incapacity for intimacy

ADD & SPD

You may have noticed the similarity between SPD and attention deficit disorder. In fact, ADD and sensory processing problems have much in common, including short attention spans and hyperactivity, and they can be mistaken for each other or co-exist. For instance, ADD children commonly demonstrate aggression, sensation seeking, and tactile sensitivity, suggesting sensory modulation difficulties, as well as clumsiness, dyspraxia and sensitivity to movement (poor vestibular processing) and become easily dizzy.

If sensory processing problems cause you to be inattentive and hyperactive, how do they differ from attention deficit disorder? This is a hotly debated question. Some believe that many diagnosed with ADD actually have sensory processing problems. In his practice, psychoanalyst Harold Levinson found that 90 percent of children diagnosed with ADD and with dyslexia had problems with vestibular functioning. In other words, their inattentiveness, hyperactivity, and reading problems emanated from sensory processing disorder.

Here's one person with SPD's experience with ADD.

"I have found that the more I get proper stim, the less problems my ADD causes me. The less stim I get, the more the tweaks bother me, the more the ADD causes problems. When I am tweaked, I have a horrible time being able to ask for what I need, and that is proper stim. It also makes it hard for me to 'concentrate/be aware' long enough to know which stim I need. All I know is that I need 'something.'

Here are some of the ways that sensory processing problems appear similar to ADD.

Noise: If noise distracts you, it is hard to concentrate and focus on what you are reading.

Seeing: If your brain scrambles what you see, you may ignore, or have difficulty following written instructions and seem distracted.

Hearing: If your brain scrambles what you hear, you may ignore, or have difficulty following verbal instructions and seem distracted.

Touch: If you are bothered by the tags in your shirt or, when you were a child by other children sitting too close to you, you will squirm, wiggle, or jump about and appear hyperactive.

Overstimulation: If your work environment overwhelms you with people too close, constant chatter, buzzing fluorescent lights, intense colors, and cold air conditioning, your mind will be in a fog. Finding it hard to make sense of what you see, hear, or feel, you appear spacey.

Sensory defensiveness: If you are auditory defensive, noise makes it hard to concentrate and focus. If you are visually defensive, hypersensitivity to lights, patterns, and movement make it hard to focus.

Sensation seeking: If you are a sensation seeker, you get too easily bored to focus on anything but the next buzz and might appear hyperactive.

Hypo-responsiveness: If you are hypo-responsive to sensation, you tune out to your world easily and may not pay attention.

Discerning whether you have SPD, only ADD, or both conditions is crucial as the treatments differ. For instance, if distractibility and hyperactivity result from SPD, taking the psycho-stimulant Ritalin, the standard treatment for ADD, will delay your progress as the sensory issues that underlie the behavior will persist.

Now that we have a clear picture how sensory processing disorder impacts emotions, thoughts and behavior, let's now look at the mental health issues that result from or are associated with SPD.

Summing Up

The Triune brain is divided into the brainstem (primitive brain), limbic system (emotional brain), cortex (thinking brain).

BRAINSTEM:

Reticular formation: Controls awake, asleep, arousal and attention and acts as a sensory antenna, filtering incoming sensations, alertness; In SPD, arousability is unstable and rhythmicity irregular.

Cerebellum: Responsible for coordinating muscle tone, balance, and all our body movements. In SPD this process is often off and movement tends to be clumsy and uncoordinated.

LIMBIC SYSTEM:

Hippocampus: stores long-term memories and colors every sensation our body picks up with a feeling based on past experience.

Amygdala: the seat of emotions and evokes fear biochemistry (norepenephrine and adrenaline). In SPD, gets easily set off in those with modulation problems.

Hypothalamus: "master gland" that controls body temperature, hunger, thirst, fatigue, sleep and circadian rhythms to keep our internal state in sync so we stay calm enough to meet demand. Off in those with SPD.

All in all, those with SPD show extreme, disorganizing, and uncomfortable emotions, or lack of emotions.

CEREBRAL CORTEX:

In the frontal lobe in the cortex lies consciousness where thinking allows us to interpret what the senses perceive. In those with SPD, messages get misinterpreted.

Cognitive Impact: You may be spacey, easily distracted, disorganized have poor focus, problems with memory and problem solving.

Poor Self-Esteem: You feel inept, clumsy, stupid, crazy, "weird" and easily self-conscious as you fear doing or saying something wrong in social or learning situations and your head fills with negative self-talk. The result is low self-esteem.

Coping Strategies: To cope with the confusion, humiliation, stress, anxiety and physical upheaval that you experience as a result of living with SPD, you erect defenses to better manage your behavior.

Poor Relationship Regulation: Such negative self-regard affects how well you can relate to others and the nature of your relationships, and many with SPD feel isolated and live lonely lives.

4

*

Being Off Center Makes You Uptight

"Your perspective on life comes from the cage you were held captive in."

~ Shannon L. Alder

Tammy is terrified of heights. While walking up or downstairs, taking an escalator or walking along a catwalk, she feels vertigo, loss of balance and terror. She has been diagnosed as phobic and has been put on Paxil to control her panic. The medication has helped reduce symptoms, but she still becomes unstable when facing heights. This is because the true cause of her fear is not a learned phobia but faulty vestibular processing. The phobia was a result of this dysfunction.

Nadia has panic attacks when in a crowd. Suddenly, a wave of panic overcomes her—her heart races, her pulse throbs, the world spins, and she can hardly catch her breath. She feels as if she's dying and losing her mind. She has been diagnosed with panic disorder and put on Zoloft. This has helped reduce the intensity of the attacks, but they still occur. This is because her panic attack is not based in her head but in her body. Darlene is severely sensory defensive and panics in sensory overloaded environments like crowds.

Jackson finds it hard to talk to people. Often, he can't follow what they are saying and will awkwardly say the wrong thing. This makes him so anxious that he avoids socializing and has been diagnosed with social phobia. He is in cognitive behavioral therapy to help him overcome his fears and he tries to think positively. CBT helps to boost his confidence but he still he finds it hard to focus on what the other is saying. This is because social phobia is not the cause of his shyness. Jackson has auditory discrimination problems that create a disconnect between what people are saying and what his brain processes.

As is clear from the above examples, SPD and psychiatric illness go hand in hand: almost all who have sensory processing issues report psychiatric symptoms. These symptoms range from anxiety to bipolar disorder to substance abuse to depersonalization.

Writes one woman:

"Since my teens, I've seen psychiatrists for depression, anxiety, panic attack, phobia, alcohol abuse – you name it. I've been on a slew of psychiatric drugs, from Prozac, Zoloft, Paxil, Valium…. And still am. They have helped me greatly and I am grateful. But they haven't stopped me from lashing out when you touch my shoulder, or storming out of a restaurant that's blasting rock music. The doctors told me I was born sensitive and get easily anxious. OK… but I always knew it was something more… At age 43, I discovered what. I was sensory defensive. Light bulbs went off like… All those years in therapy and seeing doctors. Maybe I wouldn't be on medication if I was treated when I was a child."

Relevant Research

Though the relationship between SPD and mental health issues is not well studied at this point, and especially adult disorders, several studies have confirmed the association. I mention them throughout this chapter.

Among the most significant studies is one by Lucy Miller and colleagues at the SPD Foundation. The study investigated parasympathetic nervous system (PNS) functioning in children with SPD. Researchers found significantly lower vagal tone in SPD children than in a typically developing sample.

This is telling. Vagal tone is directly related to the state of the vagus nerve, our largest cranial nerve. This nerve fiber is central to the "rest and digest" functions of the parasympathetic nervous system and gives us inner peace. People with high vagal tone have bodies and brains that are more resilient under stress. This makes them able to slide from an excited state to a relaxed one. For instance, someone with high vagal tone would recover faster from a slight from a co-worker than someone with low vagal tone, who is more sensitive to stress.

Not surprisingly, those with low vagal tone have more difficulty handling emotions and are more likely to suffer depression and anxiety, as well as chronic pain, weak digestion, increased heart rate, and epilepsy. In other words, those with SPD have a biological constitution that makes it more difficult for them to manage the slings and arrows that life presents, whether sensory, physical, or emotional.

Does SPD cause this vulnerability or does a more fragile nervous system make someone more vulnerable to sensory processing issues? Likely both interact in those born with SPD. Those who develop SPD later from trauma likely show low vagal tone as a result of a damaged nervous system, and this contributes to the emotional and physical vulnerability of the post-traumatic nervous system.

Let's now explore how SPD creates emotional and mental turmoil that causes, contributes to, or mimics the psychopathology that people with SPD commonly report suffering.

SENSORY MODULATION DISORDER

LANGUID PSYCHOPATHOLOGY

As you recall, languids are hypo-responsive to sensation and experience low energy and high but passive sensation seeking. They generally have low muscle tone and tend to fatigue easily, appearing lethargic, and "lazy."

How might these characteristics create psychiatric problems? Let's take a look.

Anxiety

Generalized Anxiety

Low responsiveness to sensation results in much missed information and the world often doesn't make sense. For instance, you might not see that your eye make-up is smudged and feel embarrassed when your date takes a tissue and wipes your eyes. You might wonder why everyone is running to the kitchen as you have misinterpreted the resounding smoke alarm as a passing police car. You might feel the stew needs more salt, making it too salty for many of your guests. Such constant confusion makes it hard to get things done efficiently. Easily confused and scattered, you get quickly frustrated and anxious.

As you likely have low muscle tone, clumsiness, and poor fine motor coordination, it's hard to get routine things done and you fatigue easily. As a result, you worry excessively about completing the day's tasks like shopping, cooking, getting dressed in the morning, and getting your kids dressed, washed, fed and out the door and so forth. Such worry and difficulty in making it through the day efficiently makes you stressed and irritable. At the same time, poor body awareness and interoception leaves you unaware of body signals indicating irritability, like rapid breathing and tense muscles. Consequently, tension escalates until you explode or collapse.

Phobias

Because of low muscle tone and vestibular dysfunction, you feel uneasy in space and may experience space related phobias like fear of heights or claustrophobia, as described in chapter one.

Post-Traumatic Stress Disorder

The whole constellation of needing much sensation to tune into the world, of finding it hard to get your body moving, of feeling out of touch with your body, and of being unable to easily makes sense of the world can be so traumatizing some people experience post-traumatic stress disorder. Amanda is an example.

A quintessential languid, Amanda was hypo-responsive to sensation, had low muscle tone and poor posture, balance issues and great difficulty in getting herself engaged and going. When I met her at age 13, she was reading at a first-grade level and being home schooled because the children had bullied her for being a "retard." She refused to be with any other children because when they discovered "the real me" they would reject her. She spent her time at home flopped on the couch watching TV or listening to audio tapes of her favorite books, mostly about sorcery.

Her mother was clueless. "I don't think she's autistic. But I don't know what's wrong with her. She's not normal." Spacey, dependent, irresponsible, noncompliant, inept at the simplest things, and unmotivated, Amanda tried her mother's patience and taking care of her was a full-time job.

Feeling frustrated and desperate, her mother fervently wanted to help her daughter and she was willing to do everything I suggested. She put her on a whole food diet that excluded gluten and other allergens, as well as processed sugar, all of which helped Amanda control her weight and improve her energy and alertness. She made sure Amanda took the amino acid tyrosine to up dopamine receptors to increase alertness and focus. She took her for biocranial therapy which improved her posture.

She had Amanda evaluated for visual processing issues. As it turned out, she had conversion problems that explained why, though bright she couldn't read. After a year of vision therapy, she was reading at a normal grade level and an avid reader.

I worked with Amanda on self-esteem issues and, with much persuasion she finally agreed to attend a small private school. Her first year, she could read well enough to do her work, but she had problems following what the teacher was saying and her work was often late and disorganized. After an intense program of the Tomatis method of auditory integration therapy, these problems abated, and she became an honor student.

As Amanda was getting so much other therapy, her mother did not wish to take her for occupational therapy. Instead, I outlined a home sensory diet to give her intense proprioceptive and vestibular input. This included jumping on a trampoline, swimming deep under the water, walking up and down the stairs wearing a weighted vest, sitting on a therapy ball at the computer and while watching TV, and sleeping with a weighted blanket. As Amanda loved being held, I encouraged her family to cuddle with her as much as possible.

To increase alertness, Amanda sipped iced water with lemon through a straw throughout the day, and especially when feeling lethargic. To spice up taste, she threw hot peppery spices into her food, and inhaled peppermint essential oil throughout the day.

Almost from the start, Amanda thrived in school and neither peers nor staff saw Amanda as anything but a warm, friendly, funny, kind and engaging young lady who everyone liked. The director could not relate to the Amanda her mother described before she started school! Today, she is an honor student, the star in her school musicals, and the most popular student in her small school. She has maintained her weight, takes yoga, meditation, and Zumba, and works with a private trainer at the gym.

When I ask Amanda to tell me how she feels about the changes in her life, she looks miffed. She doesn't remember her life before she started school and of being different. She knows that she was a "couch potato" but doesn't recall specifics except remembering how she used to tell me that she was "allergic to reading."

Freud proposed the idea of repression, that traumatic memories become buried in the unconscious. This theory was denied for many years. Recently science has confirmed that traumatic events can create damage in the hippocampus in the limbic system, where memory is stored, and literally destroy the connections containing these memories. Amanda had been so crippled by SPD as a child that these memories were literally erased from her mind, and she could not remember her life before the mantle of SPD was removed and she became who she is in essence.

Mood Disorders

Depression

When you are hypo-responsive to sensation, getting engaged takes a huge pow. If you don't get it, you are risk for depression. This risk is compounded by low muscle tone that, by making moving effortful and not pleasurable results in exercising little if at all. As movement is the primary means for releasing stress chemistry and for releasing the feel-good hormones needed to modulate the nervous system (see chapter 5), not moving destabilizes biochemistry and creates lethargy and depression. Says one languid,

"I am depressed which equals laziness."

As you don't associate feeling depressed with lack of activity, you don't know what's wrong with you or how to fix it. Frustrated and feeling a failure because you lack control to change your state of being, you fear that you will *never* succeed. You give up trying or don't even attempt to try and seem unmotivated to help yourself. "Why bother to exercise. I'll never like it." "Why go out on a date, he'll find me too quirky and soon break up with me anyways." "Why give up the junk food I love. I'll never stick to healthy food anyways." This despondent state of mind is called *learned helplessness* and is the precursor for depression.

Here's how one languid woman sums it up.

The way things have been going, I'll never afford getting any help for my sensory issues. So if that's life, I'm dealing with it more or less. When you've been abused and disempowered, you gratefully accept that a peaceful isolation is as good as it can get."

A study by Beth Pfeiffer and Moya Kinnealey that looked at children with Aspergers (mild autism) confirmed a relationship between hypo-responsiveness and depression.

Bipolar II

Bipolar II is characterized by hypomania (less severe than mania) and depression without psychosis. Many people who suffer Bipolar II reportedly have sensory issues. Some may suffer both conditions; others may get their sensory issues misdiagnosed as depression and mania and benefit little if at all from psychiatric drugs or therapy.

Here is one woman's experience.

"I wonder whether or not SPD is often diagnosed with bipolar and people feel that they benefit from treatment for it or if people with SPD are misdiagnosed with bipolar. I was diagnosed with "cyclical" bipolar and

found out later that under unbearable pressure I dissociate and go into multiple personalities. I did not benefit from treatment for bipolar disorder or any brain based psychiatry and acquired post-traumatic stress disorder from the mental health intervention because it was that bad."

Sensation Seeking as Hypomania

When depressed, the senses are dulled. To snap out of it, languids need extreme sensation and may flip into sensation seeking that appears as hypomania. In fact, psychologist Marvin Zuckerman found that virtually all with bipolar disorder are sensation seekers.

But sensation seeking can also co-exist with sensory over-stimulation, a curious but common conundrum in those with SPD that constantly befuddles the OTs who work with this dysfunction. Here's what might happen. Overstimulation makes you highly agitated and you become manic. To reduce overstimulation, you tone down sensation but at the same time feel antsy and want more, not less sensation. This person describes the utter confusion.

"Over stimulation seems to lead to hypomania for me and ... my solution was to shut myself in a completely quiet, dark room as I recognized that further stimulation would only cause me to become more manic. But sensory deprivation was difficult because I had very strong urges and almost physical sensations in my body that I needed to be doing more.."

Winston Churchill

Winston Churchill stands as an example of depression, mania, and low muscle tone. Fleshy Churchill felt hounded by depression— his "black dog." He hated sports but loved horseback riding, a powerful means of vestibular and tactile-proprioceptive input, and swimming, which permitted easier mobility and provided water pressure to hug the body. Quick tempered and easily bored in school, he was an abominable student and a discipline problem, indicating a problem with emotional modulation. And he showed signs of reckless sensation seeking—mania—indicating a problem with sensory modulation. In a well told anecdote, he flew off a bridge and landed in a tree when he was eighteen, to prevent his two cousins—hunters flanked on either side of the bridge—to catch him, the deer. He woke up with a concussion and ruptured kidney.

Dyspraxia & Mania

In a study done in the UK that followed a group of dyspraxic children into adolescence and adulthood, the researchers confirmed that they were likely to have emotional and other behavioral difficulties, especially depression. If they were taking certain drugs, like steroids, MAO inhibitors, tricyclic antidepressants, or L-dopa, or if they had infections, metabolic disturbances, or tumors, all of which can create mania, they appeared bipolar and could get misdiagnosed and mistreated as such.

SAD

"His body, he said, was like an aneroid barometer-thermometer reacting violently to every oscillation of atmospheric pressure, temperature, or altitude. Gray skies depressed him, leaden clouds or rain enervated him, drought invigorated him, winter represented a form of mental "lockjaw," the sun opened him up again... His nervous system cried out for sun and dry, still air."

-*When Nietzsche Wept*, by Irvin Yalom

If you are under-responsive to sensation, you will need much light for it to register in your brain so you can wake up. This makes you vulnerable to *Seasonal Affective Disorder* (SAD) when you get grumpy, lethargic, and down in the dumps in October as the days start to get short and the sky gray.

Brought on by the decrease in sunlight, SAD is believed to result from an increase at night of the sedating hormone melatonin, which gets turned on as lights gets turned off, as well as from a lack of sufficient light to regulate emotions. Light produces the neurotransmitter serotonin, which governs mood. As light decreases, serotonin levels in the brain drop and people get depressed. In the winter, SAD sufferers crave carbs to get serotonin. Consequently, they overeat, a problem for those with low muscle tone.

Low serotonin levels also make you anxious and though SAD is called "winter blues," anxiety may be the primary symptom, according to some experts. One study in 2006 and published in *Psychiatry and Clinical Neurosciences* found that 9 of 22 panic attack patients had panic attacks more frequently in winter.

SAD & Female Hormones

The hormones involved in SAD are closely related to the female hormones, making women four times more likely to suffer it than men and particularly during childbearing years. Half or more of women with SAD also suffer PMS, a common problem in those with SPD as estrogen plays a large role in how the brain collects and interprets sensory information. For instance, low levels create sound sensitivity while high levels, and especially during pregnancy create smell sensitivity. Says one woman,

> *"For me, sensitivity varies dramatically with the female cycle. I'm in premenopause. When my estrogen is correct, sensory problems mostly go away. When it's low, I have a terrible time with auditory processing and other sensory problems."*

Addictions

Substance Abuse

As your biochemistry is so off, you may rely on stimulants to rev up enough to tune into the world. This leads easily to substance abuse, for instance with cocaine or amphetamines as both release dopamine in the brain that is low in sensation seekers. At the very least many languids drink strong coffee throughout the day, smoke cigarettes, and crave chocolate as it also provides a caffeine buzz. Says one sensation seeking person with SPD.

> *"When I really hit rock bottom, I go back on my Wellbutron. It's my drug of choice for the time being in addition to of course alcohol, nicotine, caffeine, and pot."*

Compulsive Over-Eating

Another common way of trying to balance biochemistry is compulsive over-eating. Low muscle tone makes it hard to get moving and, as you don't exercise much, you passively seek sensation by overeating food with intense taste, especially rich food, and you gain weight easily. Further, if you have low muscle tone and are relatively inactive, you will overeat because chewing offers needed proprioceptive input into the jaws to balance you.

Over-eating & Proprioception

You also like to feel full as proprioception is strong along the GI tract. What's more, having this extra weight is oddly comforting. The heavier you are, the more gravity has to work on, and the more firm is your grip to the earth, giving you better body awareness and ability to feel your edges. Unknowingly you overeat to feel more grounded and secure. This may be one of the reasons why most heavy people regain the weight back. Some women will become frequently pregnant as pregnancy adds weight, enhancing bodily sensation and body awareness, as does holding and carrying a baby, while swaying and rocking offers intense vestibular input.

Gravitational Insecurity

Inability to lose weight may also relate to gravitational insecurity, suggests Kathryn Smith, an occupational therapist in England. If we feel grounded, we feel secure moving through space and having our body leave the ground, as when jumping, diving, trampolining, riding elevators. "But without gravitational security about our body's relationship to gravity, we are unable to free ourselves from being stuck down to earth," says Smith, and to feel grounded, you need to keep your feet firmly planted to the earth. If you do lose weight, you may feel an unbearable lightness of being as if you will float off into the air. Hypothesizes Smith, "those who fit the profile may have fearful dreams of flying off in space."

Comfort Food & Overeating

It's also hard to control over-eating because the food you are likely to eat creates addictive eating. Contained in many of the comfort foods we gobble down are endorphins, our brain's natural morphine and, like a drug, we desire more and more. Gluten found in wheat, oats, rye, corn, lentils, buckwheat, and peanuts contains endorphin mimics called exorphins, as does casein, a cow's milk protein. Since most processed foods, and especially junk food, contain either gluten or casein and often both, as does pizza, cheeseburgers, and cheesecake for instance, the body craves these foods. Eating meat also ends up creating addictions. This happens because it takes long to digest and makes you sluggish and you turn to stimulating substances to rev you up. How many of you order coffee or a chocolate desert in a restaurant following a heavy, meat- based meal?

Nor is it easy to wean from these comfort foods as abstaining from eating them creates withdrawal symptoms and you crave the food even more. Unknowingly, such cravings affect your moods, thinking, and behavior and, in some, lead to extreme behavior like eating disorders and learning disabilities. Gluten for instance is a major source of brain inflammation that might underly depression. Not eating gluten may be one way of alleviating depressive symptoms.

As a result of all these factors, many languids are overweight and fail at dieting as did this woman.

"I seek sensation with food. I have been in a 12- step program for overeaters for many years. They encourage eating plain food but I can't do it. I like food to be very chewy or crisp or to have a combination of textures. I like to gnaw on tough food and I lick my fingers... when on one's looking of course! They also insist on portion control but I have to feel very full so I eat lots and lots of vegetables.

*The worst was when I was a teenager. I was very fat because my whole life I had always needed to stuff myself nonstop. A psychiatrist told my mother that I had to fill myself because I felt empty and unloved. This confused my mother because I was very loved. An OT told her that the stuffing was due to lack of sensation in my mouth. Aha!...**that** made sense."*

Eating Disorders

Bulimia

In some cases, over-eating leads to bulimia as you gorge and purge to control your weight. Providing strong odors, loud noise and violent movement of the body, purging also provides intense sensory input. Writes one SPD woman.

"All I want to do is eat. Especially when I'm anxious. I have to have something in my mouth all the time. I am obese... I hate it... But I can't stop myself... I've tried taking a walk... going swimming... but it's exhausting. I WANT TO EAT AND EAT AND EAT. Lately I've been throwing it up to lose weight. I feel better after... I'm starting to lose some weight."

Sexual Disorders

Sexual Acting Out

You may engage in frequent sex as intense odors, sounds, movement, heavy pressure into the skin that increases body awareness, and sexual arousal provides intense sensory stimulation. As your body is loose, you can move your hips easily and, if you are female readily achieve orgasm while men can have more intense orgasms. Says one woman,

"Who needs exercise... Sex gives me the most amazing workout... I love... love... sex... I'm a complete slut..."

Personality Disorders

Dependent Personality

Lack of motivation and poor fine and gross motor skills leads you to rely on others to force you out of lethargy and to get you going and organize you, creating dependency.

Disassociative Disorders

Depersonalization

Hypo-responsiveness to touch and poor body awareness makes it hard to figure out your edges. Under severe stress you may lose physical and personal boundaries and feel unreal and the world distant. V.S. Ramachandran, M.D., Ph.D., director of the Center for the Brain and Cognition at the University of California, San Diego, proposes that a shift occurs in boundaries of self-perception when incoming sensual input defies what one perceives and requires as the norm. Here's how one sufferer of depersonalization describes her reasoning for depersonalization.

"I view derealization and depersonalization, intense perceptual alterations, as the mind's self-protective reaction to the ultimate perceived state of overload. It just seems to me that when the mind believes it's mega-overwhelmed it flips the switch on a perceptual filter, believing even the slightest additional bit of stimuli may lead to various degrees of psychic meltdown ... the mind is trying to give itself a fighting chance to sort and process that with which it's already wrestling, so it chooses to inhibit the sensory messages streaming in from one's immediate internal and external experience."

Implicated as well in depersonalization is poor vestibular functioning because you experience a mismatch in your sensory experience of the world and reality. That makes you feel spacey and, when severe, detached from your surroundings.

A study published in 2006 and conducted by F. Yen Pik Sang and colleagues found a prevalence of depersonalisation/derealisation symptoms in patients with peripheral vestibular disease, evoked by presenting them with disorienting vestibular stimulation. The researchers concluded that in vestibular disease, frequent experiences of derealisation may occur because distorted vestibular signals mismatch with the other sensory input to create an incoherent frame of spatial reference. This experience makes the patient feel detached or separated from the world.

Impulse Control Disorder

Cutting/Hair Pulling/Skin Picking

If you have low muscle tone, you have poor body awareness and feel out of touch with your body. Under severe emotional turmoil, you may feel emotionally frozen and cut off from your body. Cutting your skin or pulling out your hair (trichotillomania) provides intense skin sensation and pressure that helps you re-connect with your body and know you are alive and okay. And cutting or pulling distracts you from intense emotional pain as it is proposed to release endorphins, the body's natural painkillers, explaining why cutting and pulling rapidly reduces tension rapidly. Some have described the feeling afterwards as a "calm, bad feeling."

> *"I have problems accidently hurting myself... When I was younger it was worse. I used to pull out my hair, cut myself and crash into everything so that I could feel my body... this sensory seeking behavior is sometimes embarrassing."*

Cutting may also give you an increased sense of mastery and control for those who feel out of control and powerless to change their circumstances or experiences—a common mindset of those with SPD, and especially for those who have suffered the dysfunction their whole lives.

University of Washington psychologists have discovered that adolescent girls who engage in behaviors such as cutting themselves had lower levels of serotonin, along with reduced levels in the parasympathetic nervous system of respiratory sinus arrhythmia (RSA), a measure of the ebb and flow of heart rate along with breathing. RSA is related to vagal tone. As you may recall, Lucy Miller and colleagues at the SPD Foundation found significantly lower vagal tone in SPD children than in a typically developing sample. This is another example of how biological vulnerability associated with SPD lends itself to mental illness.

Skin Picking

Skin picking, which falls under trichotillomania is also a common issue in those with SPD.

> *"I am a 'picker.' I will spend up to an hour a day in front of the bathroom mirror picking at my skin. I also scratch my head constantly (not from itchiness) and pick at my fingernails. It is referred to as "compulsive skin picking" and is essentially the same disorder as hair-pulling (trichotillomania). When I pick at my skin, I get intense sensation, I fall into a trance state that shuts out the outside world, and I focus inward. It's a great way to balance sensory input."*

In some cases, skin picking may relate to the need to have smooth textured skin. Says one tactile defensive woman,

> *"I do not self-injure but I do the skin picking. I pick at my scalp, scabs, dead skin, etc. not to the point of bleeding or anything. I just cannot stand blemished skin. I like it smooth."*

Learning Disorders

ADD

As you need much sensation to tune in, you appear unfocused and out of it and have poor memory. Working memory relies on serotonin. As low serotonin causes depression, which many languids suffer, problems remembering five to seven thoughts at the same time could reflect low serotonin in the cortex.

BOLD/ACTIVE SENSATION SEEKING

Extroverted, social, and uninhibited, bold people get easily bored. For life to sizzle, you crave constant newness, intensity, uncertainty, challenge, and thrills. In the quest for constant sensation, you seem impulsive, hyperactive, and undisciplined. As you ignore the other's needs in the nonstop quest for sensation, you are insensitive to the other's feelings.

Here are the many ways sensation seeking can play out as mental illness:

Mood Disorder

Mania

Constant sensation seeking makes you appear manic, and you may be misdiagnosed as bipolar. As you may recall, psychologist Martin Zuckerman found that virtually all with bipolar disorder are sensation seekers.

Addictions

Substance Abuse

You use stimulants to rev up and tune in, and to escape. Here is one man's experience.

"I hate this life that was given to me. I became a drug addict because of SPD. Thank God I have been sober for almost 4 years. My life was totally on hold for about 7 years starting at 14 yrs old. As soon as I started heroin which got me kicked out my house and put in jail. My first drug was my savior: LSD. It was the great escape. I didn't care about the sounds because I wasn't paying attention to them. But with drugs came problems with the parents and problems+ LSD= paranoia=bad trips. Tripping wasn't fun anymore. So I moved on. Anything to "get away".

At the very least, sensation seekers need caffeine and nicotine to get their system going. This leads easily to substance abuse, commonly with cocaine or amphetamines as both release dopamine in which sensation seekers are low. Chocolate cravings also indicate a need for a caffeine buzz.

Sexual Disorders

Sexual Acting Out

Nothing creates more intense sensation and thrills than sex and you engage in promiscuity, risky sexual behavior, and sexual experimentation.

Learning Disorders

ADHD

If you don't get enough sensation to feed your nervous system, you become frenetic and appear hyperactive and distracted. This is because your cortex lacks sufficient dopamine to engage in the world and you seek activity to boost it.

FASCINATING FACTS: *Ritalin eases attention deficit and hyperactivity by upping dopamine.*

Personality Disorder

Obsessive/Compulsive

You may be a compulsive shopper or gambler, the latter of which entails risk taking.

Sociopathology

Insensitive, poor at reading social cues, and hell-bent on sensation seeking regardless of the other's needs, you appear and may be a sociopath.

AVOIDING – SENSORY DEFENSIVENESS

Sadie has always been hypersensitive to most everything in her environment. Since a child, she has had food and chemical sensitivities, allergies, hypoglycemia, OCD, anxiety, chronic depression, and addictions. For many years, she has been on Prozac and Wellbutrin. They help take the edge off her sensitivity, but when stress builds up, she goes back into overload. To help her cope with her discomfort, her psychiatrist keeps upping her meds but that has never resolved the sensitivity.

Like her doctor, she assumed her hypersensitivities were from anxiety and stress. Only recently did she find out about sensory defensiveness. What relief! Here was the missing piecing of the puzzle she knew existed.

Hypersensitivity or sensory defensiveness creates a constant state of hyper-alertness, agitation, stress, and anxiety. These discomforting states intensify unpleasant emotions and lead to extreme and often uncontrollable behavior. As a result, sufferers manifest a broad range of psychopathology, the depth and scope of which is determined by the degree of hypersensitivity.

Let's explore the slew of psychopathology associated with sensory defensiveness.

Adjustment Disorder

Constantly hyped and hyper-alert, you feel perpetually agitated, tense and stressed. Consequently, you cope poorly with stress and life transitions, such as marriage, divorce, childbirth, changing jobs and so on, and experience ***adjustment disorder.***

Anxiety

Generalized Anxiety Disorder (GAD)

Overwhelmed, hyped, and stressed, you experience constant muscle tension, fidgeting and restlessness, irritability and often angry outbursts, sleep difficulties, concentration difficulties and fatigue— the symptoms generally used to describe people with GAD. These symptoms however come primarily from sensory overload, not from excessive worry as they do in those diagnosed with GAD. The more severe your defensiveness the more severe your anxiety and the more quickly you go over the edge. Writes Temple Grandin in *Emergence: Labeled Autistic,*

> *"The nerve attacks, complete with pounding heart, dry mouth, sweaty palms, and twitching legs, had the symptoms of 'stage fright,' but were actually more like hypersensitivity than anxiety," writes Temple Grandin. "Perhaps this accounts for the fact that Librium and Valium did not provide relief to my trembling body."*

Several research studies conducted by occupational therapist Moya Kinnealey of Temple University support a strong relationship between sensory defensiveness and anxiety in all age ranges.

COMPARISON OF GAD AND SD

Similarities

Both stress responses create sympathetic nervous system arousal, edginess, difficulty concentrating, hypervigilance, avoidance, and lack of control. Both have vulnerability at the core.

Distinctions

Cortex Based

Psychological anxiety is cortex based and triggered from thought. Walking through the mall, you get bumped and fear someone is picking your pocket. The brain flags, "Danger! Get out of here!" and the sympathetic nervous system creates over-arousal. You flee the mall, both body and mind running wild with terror.

Brainstem Based

Sensory defensiveness is brainstem based and triggered from external or internal stimuli that the brain codes as dangerous. Hypersensitive to touch, your body cringes as someone swipes past you in a crowd. The brain interprets the threat, and you think – "I have to get out of here before I kill someone." Here's one man's experience.

"I get extremely violent urges when I get overstimulated. I'm very sensitive to noise, for example, more than one person talking at the same time, or being interrupted by a loud phone when I'm hyper-concentrating. Crowds as well piss me off. Often times I start punching walls, yelling at people, throwing things, and having graphic images in my mind of peeling the skin off my arms or putting nails through my wrists. I'm quite used to it, though I'm not a fan of it. I know I'm a little loopy, but isn't everyone?"

Lacks Dread

As the reaction is physical not mental, you can also feel sensory overload without thoughts of dread. For instance, at a party with pounding salsa music, your body may be jumping but your mood upbeat.

Both Can Interact

At times, sensory defensiveness and mental anxiety interact and become indistinguishable. This can happen when situations both overstimulate and elicit dread, as when your boss, wishing to speak to you about your tardiness beckons you into her bright, cluttered, smoky, and noisy office, or when sensory defensiveness is severe, and you panic when someone touches your highly sensitive neck.

Phobias & Panic Attack

Starting at the moderate level, SDs commonly experience phobias. For instance, glaring light, over-stimulating eye contact, sudden touch and other people's odors may overwhelm you to where you must disengage from social contact, and you appear *socially phobic*. Feeling pain intensely, you freak out when you must get an injection and suffer *needle phobia*.

Space related phobias occur from faulty vestibular integration, and you get easily destabilized from movement experiences, like elevators, escalators, roller coasters, going fast, or spinning and might panic (see chapter one). If sensory defensiveness becomes severe, touch, loud noises or bright lights alone will trigger panic.

> *"I have panic disorder. Once I found out I had SPD, I noticed almost all my panic episodes are sensory related."*

PANIC STAGES BY SEVERITY OF DEFENSIVENESS

<u>Alarm 1</u> *(Mild Anxiety)*: The mildly sensory defensive will feel some alarm as sensory overload starts to build, and feel nervous, tense and butterflies in the stomach.

<u>Alarm 2</u> *(Moderate Anxiety)*: The mildly defensive will experience

moderate anxiety when in overload, while the moderately defensive will quickly get to this point as sensory overstimulation rapidly builds up from ordinary moment to moment experience and you feel uncomfortably tense and aroused. Your heart is beating fast, breathing is rapid, palms are sweaty and muscles tight, but you still feel in control.

Alarm 3 *(Intense Anxiety)*: As sensory onslaught continues to rachet up, the moderate to severe defensive will begin to feel intense anxiety: uncomfortably spacey or light-headed; unsteady on feet; heart pounding or beating irregularly; chest compressed. You worry about losing control.

Alarm 4 *(Moderate Panic Attack)*: If sensory onslaught continues to build, the moderately defensive will experience panic attack, whereas the severely defensive might reach this stage quickly from even mild sensations like a fire alarm going off – recall the movie Rainman with Dustin Hoffman screaming and slapping his hands over his ears in panic from a fire alarm. At this point you are out of control and experience palpitations, difficulty breathing, very tight and compressed chest, and acutely dilated eyes. You feel disoriented, detached and unreal, and go into full blown panic.

Alarm 5 *(Major Panic Attack)*: If you cannot escape the situation and quiet your nervous system, you go into shutdown, a severely traumatized state where you experience exaggerated terror, intense dread, numbness and feel unreal. You fear you are going crazy or dying and you must flee or perish.

> *"The first time I ever panicked I was in an Israeli Dance Club. It happened soon after I entered and I was being hit on all sides by the other dancers. I freaked out and ran out of there screaming. I thought I was going to die I was so scared.*
>
> *The same thing happened at other dance clubs when people got too*

close to me and their bodies hit me unexpectedly. I eventually figured out that if I wanted to dance few if any other people could be on the dance for with me and the second the cigarette smoke became significant I had to leave immediately.

So I am that freak that will start dancing when I like the song but no one else is on the dance floor. It isn't embarrassing for me at all."

Post-Traumatic Stress Disorder

As you can see from these stages of alarm, severe sensory defensiveness is traumatizing. In overload you can easily go over the edge into shutdown, where you become numb and tune out to the world. Such is the on-going reality of the sensory defensive for whom many experiences are connected in memory with irritation, annoyance, distress and even pain. Consequently, you essentially live as if you have PTSD.

"I work in a library with the public and have learned to focus my attention very closely when patrons speak to me. Often I will lean across the desk towards them with my head turned slightly to the side so I don't have to look at faces. I was diagnosed with PTSD as a teen based on my depression and dislike of looking at faces. However, I think this is a sensory filtering issue."

Conversely, those who have experienced trauma are hyper-alert and commonly experience sensory overload. In other words, sensory defensiveness may result from, cause, or contribute to posttraumatic stress disorder.

Agoraphobia

Easily overloaded in public places, the moderate to severe sensory defensive can go over the edge from sensory overload and have a panic attack. To avoid another, you bury yourself in your home and appear agoraphobic, a serious disorder in which the person fears harm in open space, away from the security of the home and a safe person. Here is one woman's experience.

> *"Every time a car backfires, a radio blares, a crowd hums, I feel uncomfortable internally (because, hey, you're wired that way). Too much of this input, and your wiring cannot process the noises properly, so it short-circuits: you have panic attacks, feel dissociated, cry, explode with anger. You don't understand why. Enough experiences like this, and most likely you'll start avoiding the places and situations in which you feel crappy."*

The sensory defensive can also become reclusive because home is the only place where they can reasonably control sensory input.

Obsessive-Compulsive Disorder (OCD)

Tactile defensiveness can make certain sensations on your hands, like dirt or anything gooey or sticky bother you acutely. You may wash your hands constantly, wear gloves when preparing meals, and obsess over getting dirty, and psychologists diagnose you with OCD.

You may also engage in rituals like repetitive rocking or counting as a distraction, and to lower your arousal level as repetition boosts serotonin in the brain to regulate mood and balance neurochemistry. Ordering objects serves a similar purpose, a common compulsion for those on the autistic spectrum who are often neat freaks. And keeping things in order creates predictability that gives the defensive more control and influence over their immediate environment, clothes, food, and activities, so they can be more open to other issues.

FASCINATING FINDINGS: *In a study done by Eric Rieke and Diane Anderson,* *reported in the American Journal of Occupational Therapy in 2009, adults with OCD scored higher than the average on sensory sensitivity and sensation avoiding.*

Substance Abuse

To create a steady flow of pleasurable vibes and blunt feelings of tension, anxiety, and frustration, as well as to blunt the senses, the moderate to severe defensive might develop an addiction to controlled depressive substances, like alcohol or tranquilizers.

Mood Disorders

Depression

"It is an affliction that often starts young and goes unheeded — younger than would seem possible, as if in exiting the womb I was enveloped in a gray and itchy wool blanket instead of a soft, pastelcolored bunting."

~Daphne Merkin, in a *New York Times Magazine* piece about her life-long struggle with depression.

Lonely and anxious, stressed and fatigued, unable to sleep or find comfort in cuddling, the sensory defensive become depressed easily. The extreme stress associated with sensory defensiveness also depletes serotonin. Add to this a profound lack of control in your life that makes you despair of getting what you want, creating learned helplessness, you drag through life. The more severe the defensiveness, the more you feel out of control of your destiny and the deeper the depression.

The restrictions you feel compelled to impose to avoid overstimulation also dampen mood. For instance, you might like cloudy days because you are light sensitive. You might stay home to avoid the overstimulation of crowds, noise, bright lights, and people and feel alienated from others. And the big one: intimacy. If you are tactile defensive, intimate contact might feel uncomfortable. This puts a wedge between you and close human connection. That is profoundly depressing!

Bipolar Disorder II

Moderate to severe SD can mimic bipolar disorder II. Sensory overload causes impulsive, frantic, aggressive, and even violent behavior and you appear manic. Says one woman,

> *"I am bipolar II. Certain food smells, like broccoli make me go manic. I become extreme irritated, angry, and hostile and I must leave the table."*

When you cannot escape the overload, you shut down and appear depressed. At the severe level especially, you vacillate from meltdown (mania) to shutdown (depression).

Auditory processing problems are common in bipolar disorder. Writes Mitzi Waltz in *Bipolar Disorders: A Guide to Helping Children and Adolescents*, "...These patients will describe many normal sounds as affecting them like fingernails scraping a blackboard..."

And not just auditory defensiveness. Waltz believes that under- or oversensitivity to smell, taste, texture, types of touch, and movement are more common than the literature discusses, and change depending on the current stage of the bipolar cycle. During a manic phase, heightened sensitivity may be experienced as pleasurable or in some cases painful.

Bipolar children are especially hypersensitive in a depressed-irritable state, writes Waltz. In fact, the *Juvenile Bipolar Research Foundation* describes symptoms of sensory defensiveness, or hypersensitivity for item five of the "Core Phenotype-Research Diagnostic Criteria" for juvenile bipolar disorder (depression accompanied with episodes of mania).

"Disturbance in the capacity to habituate to sensory stimuli often when

exposed to novel, repetitive or monotonous sensory stimulation. A tendency to over-react to environmental stimuli and to become over-aroused, easily excited, irritated, angry, anxious or fearful when exposed to novel sensory experiences (e.g., vacuum cleaners, ticking clocks, thunder and lightning), and dissonant sensations (e.g., shirt tags, fit of clothes or shoes, perceived foul odors)."

Akathasia/Suicide

If anxiety and tension become unrelenting and maddening, making you constantly wanting to jump out of your skin—a psychiatric condition called akathisia—some severely SDs will attempt suicide. Akathisia happens also in response to drug withdrawal from anti-depressants and has long been linked to suicide as the only means of ending horrific bodily upheaval.

Eating Disorders

Anorexia

Moderate to severe oral defensiveness can be confused with anorexia. Teenagers will refuse to eat, not because they want to be thin necessarily but because eating is an effort. This happens because many food textures feel irritating to the mouth, and anorexic-like starving gets misdiagnosed and mistreated as such. Further, limited food choice can lead to nutritional and vitamin deficiencies that impact the nervous system, intensifying sensory issues, stress and starvation and the likelihood of a misdiagnosis.

Personality Disorders

Avoidant Personality

As sensory issues cause you to withdraw from social experiences and intimacy, you seem standoffish and might be labeled an avoidant personality.

Borderline Personality

Unstable relationships, poor or negative sense of self, inconsistent mood and significant impulsivity characterizes the borderline personality. An intense fear of abandonment interferes with many aspects of your life and often acts as a self-fulfilling prophecy because you cling to others, are very needy, and feel helpless. Further, dependency needs cause you to become overly involved and immediately attached.

As sensory defensiveness intensifies, you may be misdiagnosed borderline from marked shifts in mood, impulsive and unpredictable behavior, and great difficulty in personal relationships, often transitory. You show as well self-destructive addictive behavior, like substance abuse for self-calming. In doing research into sensory defensiveness and borderline personality disorder in England, OT Kathryn Smyth found a high incidence of sensory defensives in people hospitalized for BPD.

Obsessive-Compulsive Personality

Bombarded at every turn by sensations that you cannot control, you take extreme measures to self-calm. This can lead to compulsive activity like eating, shopping, sexual activity and so forth, predisposing you to obsessive and compulsive behavior. The more severe the defensiveness, the more severe are the rituals and compulsive behavior.

"If I am in a crowded room to learn i will not learn anything as i am bombarded with sensory stimuli. One could surmise i have an attention deficit issue. On the other hand, if you put me in a serene environment, i can focus for hours on end, and love to do this. One could surmise i am obsessive-compulsive from this. But i see the root cause for my behaviors,

and it is the sensory sensitivity combined with the lack of sensory filters that initiates these actions."

Dissociative Disorders

Depersonalization/Dissociation

When life inside your body becomes intolerable, you shut out the world and depersonalize, losing sense of self as real, and you feel out of your body. The experience is terrifying as you lose touch not only with the world but with self as an agent in it and you become a floating non-entity.

"Last week, after being forced to go to a basketball game with my boyfriend, I had a disabling sensory overload event — panic attack and then dissociation, hugely upsetting. My boyfriend was sitting next to me. He felt a million miles away. He saw I was out of it and took my hand. I barely felt it. I got up and made my way to the door, mumbling something about a bathroom. I felt as if I were escaping from a war zone."

Some dissociate and lose memory, as in amnesia or multiple personality disorder.

ADD

If you feel overwhelmed by sensory input, you can't attend to the task at hand, what someone is saying to you, or anything else for that matter and may appear as if you have ADD.

"If I am in a crowded room to learn i will not learn anything as i am bombarded with sensory stimuli. One could surmise i have an attention deficit issue. On the other hand, if you put me in a serene environment, i can focus for hours on end, and love to do this. One could surmise i am compulsive-obsessive from this. But i see the root cause for my behaviors,

and it is the sensory sensitivity combined with the lack of sensory filters that initiates these actions."

Putting It Together

To sum up, let's look at the different psychiatric disorders and degree of sensory defensiveness.

Under anxiety disorders, generalized anxiety is experienced at all levels of defensiveness. **Phobias** begin at the moderate defensive level where overload can be quickly achieved; when it becomes severe you panic. As such, those at the severe level basically live in a state of **PTSD.** Those at the severe level will panic easily from what most consider manageable sensation and may become **agoraphobic** as sensory assault is most controlled when at home. The need to control sensory overload leads to ritualistic behavior at the moderate to severe level and you can appear as if you have **OCD.** Moderate to severe oral-motor defensiveness can mask as **anorexia** in adolescence.

Coping with sensory defensiveness can create learned helplessness and varying degrees of **depression** occurs across all levels. The moderate to severe defensive will have meltdowns from sensory overload, which can look like mania, and you may be diagnosed as **bipolar II.** To cope, those at the moderate to severe level may turn to **substance abuse.** When severe sensory defensiveness causes you to want to jump out of your skin and overwhelms coping ability, you may attempt **suicide** to end extreme internal upheaval.

Moderate to severe SD can create **avoidant and obsessive-compulsive behavior** and you may be misdiagnosed as such. Likewise, at the severe level you may appear a **borderline personality** as sensory avoiding creates extreme moods and behavior along with relationship difficulties.

Severe sensory defensiveness can lead to shut down and you begin to **depersonalize.**

Level of Sensory Defensiveness & Psychopathology

	Mild	Moderate	Severe
Anxiety Disorders			
GAD	+	+	+
Phobias		+	+
Panic attack			+
PTSD			+
Agoraphobia			+
OCD		+	+
Mood Disorders			
Depression	+	+	+
Bipolar Disorder		+	+
Suicide			+
Addictions			
Substance abuse		+	+
Eating Disorders			
Anorexia (teens)		+	+
Personality Disorders			
Avoidant		+	+
OCD		+	+
Borderline			+
Dissociative Disorders			
Depersonalization			+

SPD & PSYCHOPATHOLOGY

	Languid	Bold	Defensive
Anxiety Disorders			
GAD	+		+
Phobias	+		+
Panic attack			+
PTSD	+		+
Agoraphobia			+
OCD			+
Mood Disorders			
Depression	+		+
Bipolar Disorder	+	+ (mania)	+
SAD	+		
Suicide	+		+
Addictions			
Substance abuse	+	+	+
Compulsive overeating	+		
Eating Disorders			
Anorexia (teens)			+
Bulimia	+		
Sexual Disorders			
Acting Out	+	+	
Personality Disorders			
Avoidant			+
OCD		+	+
Borderline			+
Dependent	+		
Sociopath		+	

	Languid	Bold	Defensive
Dissociative Disorders			
Depersonalization	+		+
Impulse Control			
Cutting	+		
Trichotillomania	+		
Skin picking	+		
Learning Disorders			
ADD	+		+
ADHD		+	+

SENSORY DISCRIMINATION

If you have SPD, good chance that you may have problems with sensory discrimination. If so, these problems will add to the fire by raising arousal and adding to extreme behavior. Such behavior will result in sensory modulation issues and the mental health issues that accompany them. If you are one, you are likely to suffer:

Learned Helplessness/Depression: As you get easily confused, you feel inept and unable to meet wants. This creates learned helplessness and depression.

Dependent Personality: Needing to rely on input from others to glean appropriate information from the environment and to help get organized, you appear helpless and dependent.

Fear of Dark: Easily disoriented in the dark, you become fearful when robbed of orienting light.

Eating issues: Poor tactile discrimination creates problems with interoception, and you lack cues to know when you are hungry or satiated, resulting in eating too much or too little.

OCD: Because you are confused and easily thrown, you need everything in its place and rigid routines and schedules.

Depersonalization: Out of touch with your body, you may feel unreal and the world distant.

MOTOR PROBLEMS

Walking around not feeling stable on terra firma because of low muscle tone and problems with bilateral integration and dyspraxia makes you feel insecure in your place in space, and fears and phobias are common.

Rachel Simone on her very helpful blog *Coming to My Senses* describes a typical day in Manhattan.

"We are quickly approaching an oddity in the sidewalk: a gap where steps lead up to a plaza and a bank, which I find very disconcerting. After all, if my proprioceptive sense (body in space) is out-of-whack, imagine how the body feels when the supportive buildings give way to a gap. It happens fast, as if someone has pulled the composure clear from my grasp, and I am left naked and shivering. The once reflective beings are now incomprehensible. They are masses I cannot process or predict, and they are everywhere. Sounds flood through my system and my hands shake. In this moment, I am physically present, but cannot compose myself and cannot move; if I can't process the world around me, cannot feel where my body is located in the din, how am I supposed to get on a subway and go home? My walking companion puts me in a cab as the tears start to well up."

Here are the many phobias associated with sensory movement disorder.

Sports: As you are clumsy & uncoordinated, you fear mishaps like getting hit by a ball that you misjudge, or tripping and falling while running, and you dread doing sports.

School: As a child you dreaded school and hated having to go to gym and recess, worried you would be ridiculed for your clumsiness.

Socializing: As a child, clumsiness and other sensory issues interfered with your success in school and your popularity with your peers, creating low self-esteem and social isolation. As you grew up, you became self-conscious about looking awkward when eating and drinking, or writing or signing your name in front of others, and you feel anxious in social situations. You may refuse to go dancing, nervous that others will laugh at your two left feet.

Space: As you easily lose your place in space, you fear flying, heights and wide, open spaces and may panic or develop space related phobias.

Elevators/Escalators: You fear escalators, afraid of not being able to get on or off the escalator on time or without tripping, as well as elevators, worried you will be unable to get in or out before the door closes.

Tunnels: You fear tunnels, nervous that you will be unable to keep your car within its lane in the dark.

Hitting/Getting Hit: You fear getting hit while crossing a street or hitting someone while you are driving because you are unable to determine the speed, position, or direction of moving vehicles.

Crowds: Because you easily lose balance, you fear being in a crowd where you might get jostled and knocked down.

Choking: You fear swallowing pills, worried that you will choke as vestibular dysfunction may un-coordinate normal reflexes.

Agoraphobia: Floppy muscle control creates jelly legs and you fear falling, fainting, getting injured or losing control in public and you fear going out.

CHILDHOOD DISORDERS

In the *Canadian Child and Adolescent Psychiatry Review* in May, 2005, Michael Cheng, M.D. and Jennifer Boggett-Carsjens, OT describe a 9-year old boy who, impulsive and aggressive in school was diagnosed as Bipolar, ADHD, and ODD (oppositional defiant disorder). He was put on antidepressants and psycho-stimulants, and given psychotherapy, counseling and anger management programs.

Fortunately, he was also seen by a pediatric occupational therapist who diagnosed him as severely sensory defensive. His aggression toward other children happened when other children got too close or touched him and his impulsivity and hyperactivity— "mania"—reflected extreme agitation from sensory overload. When too overloaded, his system would shut down and he would appear "depressed." Within weeks of receiving appropriate occupational therapy interventions, he calmed down, became more alert, focused, and able to learn in school, and handled school better.

Occupational therapists often find that children with sensory processing issues have disorders that the DSM IV lists as first recognized in childhood.

Separation Anxiety

Children with sensory defensiveness feel unsafe when separated from parents who have learned the tricks to help regulate their child and the child will often show separation anxiety. The more severe the defensiveness the more extreme is the separation anxiety.

Social Anxiety

Children with sensory issues often feel isolated from other children who enjoy physical activity and playing in mud, getting their hands dirty and wearing school uniforms, and who don't squirm when touched or clap their hands over their ears when the bell rings. Such behavior can make them seem like the odd one out and other children will reject and often bully them, creating social anxiety.

Oppositional Defiant Disorder

Both the bold seeker and the sensory defensive child might get misdiagnosed with *oppositional defiant disorder.* The bold child may become aggressive and defiant if forced to be in a boring, unstimulating situation while children with moderate to severe SD may demonstrate wild mood swings of unpredictable *aggression* when in sensory overload. For instance, the tactile defensive child will tear off her clothes and refuse to get dressed or unintentionally punch someone who bumps into her.

Autism Spectrum (displays all subtypes)

Autism

The vast majority of children with autism, which involves significant delay in language, cognitive and self-help skills have sensory processing issues. These issues are often severe, and most notably that of hearing, touch and vision.

Aspergers

Children with Aspergers, a mild form of autism where you function basically normally but have limited social skills commonly suffer sensory processing issues as well.

Pervasive Developmental Delay

Many children with PDD have sensory processing issues.

Learning Disorders

ADHD (bold; avoider)

Children with ADHD have trouble with focus, attention, impulsivity, and hyperactivity, and show constant, fidgety movement. Inattention, impulsivity, fidgetiness, and constant movement are also symptoms of SPD—as you might recall, as many as 70% of these children have sensory processing issues. And though ADHD and SPD are two distinct syndromes, clinicians believe that many children with SPD are misdiagnosed with ADHD and put on unnecessary medication.

As A. Jean Ayres first noted, a tactile defensive child in overload looks over-alert, distracted, and hyperactive, the symptoms of ADHD. Also, a bored bold seeker might become overly active and impulsive in his quest for sensation and appear hyperactive and distracted. Writes Carol Kranowitz in *Beginnings* from the *National Alliance on Mental Health* (Summer, 2010), "Sensory stimulation—too much, too little or the wrong kind—may cause poor motor coordination, incessant movement, attention problems and impulsive behavior as the child strives to get less— or more—sensory input."

ADD (languid)

Those with ADD have problems with focus, attention, and impulsivity but not hyperactivity. As previously noted, the languid child can seem out of it and distracted and appear as if he is not paying attention.

Now that we've explored all the myriad of mental health issues associated with SPD, let's look at the many ways available to balance the nervous system.

Summing Up

SENSORY MODULATION:

Languid

The **languid** may show the following mental health issues:

Anxiety:
> Generalized Anxiety
> Phobias
> PTSD

Mood Disorders:
> Depression
> Bipolar II
> SAD

Addictions:
> Substance Abuse
> Compulsive Over-eating

Eating Disorders:
> Bulimia

Sexual Disorders:
> Sexual Acting Out

Personality Disorders:
> Dependent Personality

Disassociative Disorders:
> Depersonalization

Impulse Control Disorder:
> Cutting/Hair Pulling/Skin Picking
> Learning Disorders
> ADD

Bold

The **bold** may show the following mental health issues:

Depression
> Mania

Addiction
> Substance Abuse

Sexual Acting Out
> Acting Out

Personality Disorder
> OCD
>
> Sociopath

Learning Disorder
> ADHD

Sensory Defensive

The **sensory defensive** may show the following mental health issues:

Adjustment Disorder Anxiety
> Generalized Anxiety Disorder
>
> OCD
>
> Phobias
>
> Panic Attack
>
> PTSD

Mood Disorders
> Depression
>
> Bipolar II
>
> Suicide

Addictions

Substance Abuse

Eating Disorders

Anorexia

Personality Disorders

Avoidant Personality

Borderline Personality (BPD)

Obsessive-Compulsive Personality

Disassociative Disorders

Depersonalization

Learning Disorders

ADD

SENSORY DISCRIMINATION PROBLEMS

Mental health issues associated with discrimination problems include:

- Learned Helplessness/Depression
- Dependent Personality
- Fear of Dark
- Eating issues
- OCD
- Depersonalization

SENSORY MOTOR PROBLEMS

Many phobias are associated with sensory movement disorder. These include:

- Sports
- School
- Socializing

- Space
- Elevators/Escalators
- Tunnels
- Hitting/Getting Hit
- Crowds
- Choking
- Agoraphobia

CHILDHOOD

Mental health issues and SPD that are first seen in childhood include:

- Separation Anxiety
- Social Anxiety
- Oppositional Defiant Disorder (bold seeker; avoider)
- Autism Spectrum (displays all subtypes)
  - *Autism*
  - *Aspergers*
  - *Pervasive Developmental Delay*
- Learning Disorders
- ADHD (bold; avoider)

Part Two

Balancing Body

5

Sensory Diet

"To keep the body in good health is a duty... otherwise we shall not be able to keep our mind strong and clear."

~Buddha

You've learned much about how *sensory processing disorder* can distort reality and make life a challenge to a living hell. Now it's time to learn how the right sensory input can help heal you.

What *is* the right sensory input?

The right sensory input is that which creates a *"womb with a view,"* as the social scientist Ashley Montagu once quipped. Inside the womb the fetus is tightly contained, joints bent into a fetal tuck (somatosensory—tactile/proprioceptive input) and squeezed (tactile input). The body is swayed and jolted (vestibular/proprioceptive input) as the mother moves, often rhythmically as the mother walks (vestibular input).

The closest we come again to this ultimate serenity, the "oceanic" feeling as Sigmund Freud called it, is being enveloped in a bear hug with one we love, as we gently sway to and fro.

By changing lifestyle to accommodate ongoing vestibular, proprioceptive, and tactile sensations, we would achieve more of the adult version of a womb experience.

Feeling grounded, centered, stable and secure in space is where we were designed to hang out, and always did before modern technology made us sedentary. Children learn about the world by actively exploring. But today the average toddler and preschooler spends hours a day in front of a TV screen as well as a computer, smart phone, and tablet screen. This robs them of synchronizing audiovisual input with tactile, vestibular, and proprioceptive input that forms the foundation for learning.

The Good Old Movement Days

"There are children playing in the streets who could solve some of my top problems in physics, because they have modes of sensory perception that I lost long ago."

~J. Robert Oppenheimer

As short as 75 years ago, heavy work and movement were woven into everyday life: we walked to the store; sprinted to catch the bus; carried groceries home; and walked up and down stairs, often with a baby in our arms who experienced an on-going *womb with a view*. Kids played outside, walked and biked to school and roller skated to the store. They took out the garbage, planted a garden, pushed a lawnmower, and shoveled snow. Farm folks pitched hay, milked cows, and rode horses. They sowed the land, cleaned out the barn and carried water from the well.

What has happened to our bodies in modern, technological life is a travesty: we were never designed to be couch/mouse potatoes. Body and mind totally interconnect. The brain changes from neuroplasticity, the ability of the brain to rewire itself.

Movement and exercise increase brain-derived neurotrophic factor, or BDNF. This protein supports the survival of existing neurons, encourages the growth of new neurons, fosters long-term memory formation, and improves mood.

In other words, new learning is structured in physiology, and especially in movement and multisensory experiences. Those activities done automatically as part of a pre-high-tech lifestyle established a strong neurological base that primed children for successful learning and more stable emotions.

Our sedentary lifestyle, designed around sitting, often slouching in front of a screen has robbed our nervous systems of the organizing sensations needed to regulate our emotions, and to be alert to and learn from the world.

And it's not just a lack of movement, it's also a lack of head change that generates vestibular input. Sitting upright in front of a screen to work at a computer, watching video games, texting or watching a movie keeps the head mostly upright and straight.

How to Change This

Whether you need to calm down, rev up, concentrate, wind down into sleep, or cope with traffic, you will get there quicker if you get your daily dose of intense proprioceptive input (push/pull), vestibular input (balance), and tactile (touch) input. In other words, move your body! And that doesn't mean just a casual stroll through the park. You must break a sweat and do so daily. If not, you cannot develop muscles. Without muscles you cannot support your body against gravity, and you drag through life, literally and figuratively.

Vestibular, proprioceptive, and deep pressure touch changes your neurochemistry and quickly. They are a drug! As such, in designing your sensory diet, think of movement as your main sensory meal. Granted sight, sound, smell, taste all have an effect. But it is shorter and less powerful and thus must be used more as a sensory snack: listening to a favorite song on the radio will keep you in the zone for only minutes; boogey to it and you will stay in the zone far longer.

Still resistant to the thought of moving your body? Let me shake you up by enlightening you about what happens in the brain when you move your body for all its worth.

Magic of Movement

BDNF: As mentioned, *brain derived neurotrophic factor* is released when you exercise or move muscles and joints and serves many purposes.

- **Strengthens** the myelin sheath that surrounds the nerve cell so nerve cells can fire faster.
- **Protects** neurons in areas that control mood and control memory (the hippocampus of the limbic system) against cortisol, the "fight or flight" hormone.
- **Encourages** neurons to connect to one another and grow, making it vital for neuroplasticity and neurogenesis.
- **Turns** on genes to produce more neurotransmitters, like serotonin and neurotrophins.
- **Releases** the neurotransmitters glutamate and ACH, both critical to learning and building memory.
- **Releases** GABA in the cerebellum to turn the volume down on sensations. An inhibitory chemical, GABA responds directly to proprioception (joint input).
- **Releases** just the right amount of dopamine needed for focus, attention, concentration, planning ahead, and resisting impulses when necessary. This is crucial. ADHD, Alzheimer, Parkinson, depression, bipolar disorders, binge eating, addiction, gambling and

schizophrenia all involve dopamine problems. Basically, if we have too little dopamine, we become manic and seek sensation, leading to binge eating, addiction and gambling. If we have too much dopamine, we can become psychotic. Illicit drugs that dump loads of dopamine, including cocaine and methamphetamines, cause euphoria, aggression and intense sexual feelings.

For Your Protection: *Sugar suppresses BDNF so carefully monitor your sugar intake. The wisest course to protect your memory and to stave off depression is to eliminate all processed sugar and get your sugar primarily from eating raw fruit, with a focus on those low on the glycemic index like berries.*

Amygdala: Movement regulates the amygdala in the limbic system so that you don't overreact to new stimuli. That is big especially for the sensory defensive.

Hippocampus: Exercise increases the number of cells in the hippocampus. This is especially important for the depressed who tend to have fewer cells in the hippocampus.

Prefrontal Cortex: Movement helps grow the prefrontal cortex, giving you greater control over impulses and thought processes. Using MRI scans, a 2006 study from the University of IL conducted by psychologist Art Kramer and doctoral student Michelle Voss showed that as little as walking three times a week increased the volume of the prefrontal cortex.

Basal Ganglia: Exercise creates new dopamine receptors in the basal ganglia. Located in the forebrain, the basal ganglia is believed to ensure that actions the cortex plans get executed. It does so because dopamine motivates us to choose behaviors that have rewarded us in the past and to be dogged in their pursuit, pushing the competition—think of the alpha male as a dopamine machine. In other words, exercise makes us happier and more successful. The more you exercise, the more pleasurable it becomes—*and it will once you develop muscles and better coordination*—and the more you will exercise.

What's more, the basal ganglia appear to be looped with the cerebellum to play a role in planning and coordinating specific movement sequences, and to control fine body movements, particularly of the hands and lower extremities—information of great importance to those with dyspraxia. When you are in flight/fight and your capacity for higher rational thinking is diminished, you revert to rote behaviors stored in the basal ganglia. If it's damaged, as it is in Parkinson's disease that results from the death of dopamine neurons, you are thrown off course.

There's more. Growing evidence indicates that dysfunction of the basal ganglia and/or cerebellum may be partly responsible for the symptoms of schizophrenia, obsessive-compulsive disorder, attention deficit hyperactivity disorder, depression, and autism.

Macrophages: The body's immune system warriors, macrophages work better with movement, joint input, and deep pressure touch.

Serotonin: Exercise naturally increases serotonin to keep us calm and focused.

Norepinephrine: Part of the sympathetic nervous system, norepinephrine is a neurotransmitter and stress hormone produced by the adrenal glands that, along with adrenaline (epinephrine) triggers the fight-or-flight response. A buddy of dopamine, its purpose is to create attention to help us flee and aggression to helps us fight the enemy. Over-release is a problem in those with autism, SPD and the fearful. Movement as well as deep pressure touch like therapeutic brushing, massage, and vibration puts the reign on the chemical.

NTs and Neurotropins: Movement and exercise release NTs and neurotropins, the fertilizers of the brain.

Hormones: Exercise normalizes insulin resistance to control mood swings and depression.

Resiliency: Exercise helps you combat anxiety by making your brain more resilient during times of stress, according to Princeton University researchers.

Little wonder sensory integration therapy, which focuses on vestibular and proprioceptive input, has helped improve the lives of so many children with SPD. And while little specific research has been done using sensory integration therapy to reduce anxiety and mental health issues in adults, one study done by Beth Pfeiffer and Moya Kinnealey did find a decrease in both sensory defensiveness and secondary anxiety. The changes happened from providing insight into sensory defensiveness, regular and daily sensory input, and exercise to promote proprioceptive, vestibular, and tactile sensory input.

Now itching to get moving? Great. Let's get moving!

Summing Up

All want a "womb with a view." The right sensory input creates a *"womb with a view,"* in other words, containment, movement, and tactile input. Moving our bodies, along with hugging and holding do the trick.

Designed to move: We were meant to be on the move and, as short as 75 years ago, always were with heavy work and movement woven into everyday life.

Magic of Movement:

BDNF: Releases BDNF which has enormous implications for functioning.

Amygdala: Regulates the amygdala in the limbic system so that you don't overreact to new stimuli.

Hippocampus: Increases the number of cells in the hippocampus.

Prefrontal Cortex: Helps grow the prefrontal cortex, giving you greater control over impulses and thought processes.

Basal Ganglia: Exercise creates new dopamine receptors in the basal ganglia.

Macrophages: The body's immune system warriors work better with movement, joint input, and deep pressure touch.

Serotonin: Naturally increases serotonin to keep us calm and focused.

Norepinephrine: Movement as well as deep pressure touch like therapeutic brushing, massage, and vibration puts the reign on this flight/fight chemical.

NTs and Neurotropins: Movement and exercise release NTs and neurotropins, the fertilizers of the brain.

Hormones: Normalizes insulin resistance to control mood swings and depression.

Resiliency: Helps combat anxiety by making your brain more resilient.

6

*

Moving

"There is more wisdom in your body than in your deepest philosophy."

~Friedrich Nietzsche

PROPRIOCEPTION: Sense of Body Awareness ("Push/ Pull")

The first line of defense for organizing the nervous system is *heavy work*—heavy resistance and input into the muscles and joints (proprioceptive input). Heavy work gets you quickly into your body to ground you, so you feel relaxed alertness. It will do so whether you are overloaded and anxious or bored and need jazzing up. This is because heavy work to muscles and joints stimulates the brainstem and the cerebellum, which is responsible for coordination of voluntary motor movement, balance and equilibrium and muscle tone. Proprioception also raises serotonin, your mood neurotransmitter, organizing your behavior to relax you when hyped and alert you when lethargic.

You get heavy work from strenuous activity, like biking up hill, weightlifting, standing on one leg, pushups, jumping rope, carrying a twenty-pound baby, pushing and lifting furniture, or taking your feisty golden retriever for a walk. You also get it from chomping, chewing, and sucking and helps explain why we eat when we're upset or nervous.

Here are some of the ways to feed your brain "heavy work:"

Crash on a Trampoline

Crashing down on a trampoline is a fun way to get heavy work that you can do in your own backyard. While you jump, you tap into balance, push/pull, deep touch, and hearing if you jump to music. Be sure and follow all the safety guidelines so you don't fall out of the trampoline or otherwise hurt yourself.

You can also get a home rebounder. Though you can't crash down, bouncing up and down still provides heavy work.

Do Tug of War

Try *tug of war*. Find a partner. Stand facing each other, arms outstretched toward the other and hands pushed into the other's palms, feet forcefully press into the ground. With your bodies forming a triangle or upside down "v," push hard against each other until you feel exhausted. Let go. You should feel greater body awareness and relaxation.

I frequently have people do tug-of-war as a quick, hands-on way to experience firsthand the calming power of somatosensory (touch and proprioception) input.

Take Power Yoga

Power yoga encompasses many postures that involve balancing on one leg (half-moon, warrior III, dancers pose), balancing on your arms (crow, side plank, peacock) and inverted postures supported on your hands (handstand), your forearms (feathered peacock), and your shoulders (shoulder stand). These postures offer amazing input into the joints and muscles that very quickly ground and settle you. If you are able to do a handstand against the wall safely without hurting yourself, this is a speed bullet to get into that just right place. In fact, the bliss that people feel at the end of a power yoga class comes largely from intense proprioceptive input, as well as intense vestibular input that I'll describe in the next section. It is no surprise that researchers from Boston University School of Medicine found yoga to be superior to other form of exercise in positively affecting mood and anxiety.

And while power yoga offers intense proprioception, even a basic hatha yoga class involves much joint and muscle input. Take updog, a common pose in hatha yoga. Lying on the stomach, you push up until your arms are straight, engaging the wrist and shoulder joints. The child pose, a basic resting pose, involves curling up into the fetal tuck and provides calming body flexion.

FASCINATING FINDINGS: *A study published in 2011 using a procedure called the rubber hand illusion, induced by simultaneously stroking a visible rubber hand and the subject's hidden hand, found that schizophrenics have a weakened sense of body ownership. "After a while, patients with schizophrenia begin to 'feel' the rubber hand and disown their own hand. They also experience their real hand as closer to the rubber hand." said Sohee Park, the Gertrude Conaway Vanderbilt Chair of Psychology and Psychiatry, who conducted the study with doctoral candidate Katharine Thakkar and research analysts Heathman Nichols and Lindsey McIntosh.*

At the same time, a German study published in 2008 found a 12-week exercise program reduced the symptoms and improved the behavior of a small group of patients with chronic schizophrenia when compared to a control group that did not exercise as well as increasing size of the patients' hippocampus slightly—a smaller-than-normal hippocampus is well-established in schizophrenia. The authors suggested that focused physical exercise involving precise body control, such as yoga and dancing could benefit those with this disorder.

Take a Wild Vacation

Instead of getting smashed in a bar on your next vacation, get your body smashed with white water rafting, downhill skiing, surfing, or horseback riding.

Get Weighted Down

Wear light weights on your ankles as you go about your daily business (around one pound to not put strain on the extremities) and even while you sleep. This will provide traction that increases firing from joint receptors.

Tighten Up

Try progressive relaxation by briefly tensing and relaxing each muscle group—hands, arms, legs, feet, back, stomach, face. When practicing and using PMR, proprioceptive impulses to the hypothalamus decrease and emotional reactivity is reduced, lowering sympathetic nervous system arousal, and calming the body. Your body will relax quickly into an alpha brainwave state (slow brainwaves that occur while daydreaming, meditating, or practicing mindfulness, and to ready you for sleep).

Get Cocooned

The fetal tuck is the most calming position for the body as the limbs are flexed inward, offering much proprioceptive input and deep pressure touch. Here are many ways you can get cocooned.

- **Rest** in the child pose.
- **Curl** up in a yoga silken cocoon like an inversion sling; put on an eye pillow, play some meditative music, and feel your whole being let go and recharge.
- **Curl** up into the newly designed cocoon pod. They come in many

shapes and sizes. One in particular, the Napshell has visual and acoustic effects (MP3 sound-system with speakers/ headphones), along with sound proof doors and a massage system.

- **Sleep** tucked into a body pillow.
- **Sleep** on a firm daybed with your back curled into the surface of the back side of the bed, front body curled into a body pillow.

Do Heavy Work in a Quick

- **Stand** in a doorway in plié, horseback riding position with your knees bent and out and push hard with your hands into the sides of the door. This will intensely engage at once your ankles, knees, hips, shoulders, elbows, and wrists. Hold for 10 to 15 seconds. If you are doing the Wilbarger Protocol that I will discuss soon, this is a good way to get proprioception following therapressure.
- **Stand** about two feet from a wall and push against the wall arms straight. Hold for 10 to 15 seconds.
- **Do** an arm balance sitting in a chair.
- **Push** your hands together in prayer as hard as you can.
- **Jump** up and down a few times with emphasis on the down.
- **Push** hard into the steering wheel while driving.
- **Do** a yoga wide leg downdog. Come onto the hands and knees on a non-skid surface, like a yoga mat so you won't slide. Hands are shoulder-width apart and knees hip-width apart. Lift the hips towards the sky straightening the arms and straightening the legs. Bring the feet to the side and widen the stance, big toes gently face in and heels face out. Lift the tailbone up towards the sky and drop the chest down towards the floor. Take 5 to 10 long deep breaths here.

Sneak in Heavy work

Figure out ways to incorporate heavy work into your daily activities. Here are some ways.

- **Carry** heavy groceries to your car, that you deliberately park far.
- **Push** a heavy grocery cart.
- **Walk** upstairs, two at a time.
- **Carry** a 20-pound baby.
- **Bike** rather than walk to work, the store, or the school. Make some of the ride on an uneven surface like grass or dirt so your muscles need to work harder, and you bounce around a bit.
- **Do** a wall push up in the shower, also known as a half-down dog. Here's how.

Here's how to do it.

- Face the wall in the shower away from the water spray. Stand about 3 or 4 feet away with your feet hip width apart or wider.
- Place your hands on the wall, arms straight out from your shoulders with your index fingers pointing straight up at 12 o'clock. Your torso should be parallel to the ground with your legs straight and your spine maintaining natural curves.
- Press through the base of the index finger and the thumb, your arms strongly pushing into the wall while creating an upward lift from your knees to your hips. The harder you push into the wall, the more you heavily you engage your muscles and the proprioceptors located in your wrists, elbows, shoulders and hip joints.
- If this pose is too difficult, move closer to the wall and move your hands up the wall so your arms straighten.
- If you don't feel a stretch, step further back from the wall and move

your hands lower.

- The stretch is intense so only stay in it initially for 10-15 seconds. Gradually increase the time as the pose becomes more comfortable.
- To get out of the stretch, gradually walk forward toward the wall until your legs are straight.

FYI: *Tilting your head forward and down creates a surge of vestibular input, while pushing into the wall and into the ground creates deep pressure touch, adding to the powerful organizing effect of this pose.*

Do Quick Grounding Tips

When you feel out of touch with your body, here are some quick ways to get back in touch.

- **Lightly** tap your belly.
- **Pull** on your ear lobes.
- **Stick** your index finger in your earlobe and push under your ear with your thumb.
- **Yank** your hair.
- **Stick** your hand out the window if you're driving. The surge of the wind will make your arm come alive.
- **Lift** and lower both heels up and down a few times while standing up straight to physically ground and center yourself.
- **Lean** your body over to one side, bending at the waist and let your corresponding arm dangle down. Push your feel into the ground. Feel how connected to the earth you feel, how wonderfully whole and present.

BALANCE (Vestibular Sense)

In the MOMA atrium in Manhattan, Serbian performance artist

Marina Abramovic sits completely still staring intently at the visitor facing her. She did this for 700 hours at the MOMA 2010 sold out show. Sitting perfectly still is very difficult. How did she do it? Amazing balance.

How's your balance? Could you sit perfectly still even for a few minutes? Few can and especially if you have SPD. Balance is the action of not moving. To stay seated for a long period of time, to stand in line without moving, to sit quietly and converse with someone you must have a well-integrated vestibular system. To achieve this requires befriending gravity by awakening a sluggish balance system.

As the most sensitive of all sense organs, we know that the vestibular system powerfully affects your arousal level, calming you when hyped and revving you up when you feel lethargic, an effect that, depending on quality, intensity, and duration, can last four to eight hours. How often should you engage in strong vestibular stimulation? As long as possible as the more vestibular stim, the better any nervous system functions, and especially one that is starved.

This doesn't mean you should ride a merry-go-round, or roller coaster daily unless this is what your nervous systems demands to settle. It means taking every opportunity to move your body, through exercise, household chores, gardening and so on. Remember, every change in head position stimulates some of the vestibular receptors in the inner ear. When you bend down to pick up crumbs from the floor, the downward bend of your head nudges the vestibular system. If you stay bent forward for a bit, as you do in a yoga class, you get a vestibular punch and after you feel noticeably more settled.

BE MINDFUL: *If you get dizzy or queasy, start out rocking, spinning, swinging and swaying slowly and gradually increase vestibular input. The more you feed the balance system, the less adverse reaction you will have. You can also modulate vestibular input by adding proprioception. Jumping on a trampoline, for instance, entails both up and down movement and the effort to propel your body stimulates* *joint and head compressions. Bouncing up and down on a therapy ball, in contrast, does not heavily engage joint receptors.*

Different medical conditions create vestibular imbalance. If you suffer vertigo or get quickly dizzy from everyday activities, get your balance system checked out by an ENT physician, preferably one at a balance center.

Yoga

If you were to ask a yogi what makes yoga so calming and organizing, they will likely say it's a spiritual thing. If you were to ask an occupational therapist the same question, he would tell you that it's all that vestibular and proprioceptive sensation.

Head Change

In yoga, you go through a series of poses or asanas that combine awareness of alignment with breathing and movement. Doing so involves continual head change from neutral to up, down, back, sideways and so forth and especially in vinyasa flow yoga. Many yoga asanas also force you to lift your body against gravity, such as the boat, the bow, superman, bridge, cobra, side plank, and wheel. Several positions in yoga, like the camel pose require bending backward and are called "fear" poses because so many people get an uncomfortable surge when the head is bent back.

Building Core

Yoga builds core and we need core to move successfully. Your body has 29 core muscles located mostly in your back, abdomen and pelvis. Strengthening these muscles helps protect and support your back, makes your spine and body less prone to injury, and helps you gain greater balance and stability. Examples of yoga postures helpful in building core are downward dog, cobra, and tree pose, all of which when done with proper alignment and breathing engage the core muscles wonderfully.

Adding Up

All in all, yoga postures help with sensory integration by providing core development, antigravity control, postural control, midline development, coordination, and regulation of breath.

One of my yoga teachers, a true sage with whom I take a form of yoga called "Raja," has low muscle tone and some hypersensitivity. He credits yoga for giving him a body that he can live with and a viable, pleasurable life.

To meet his special challenges, he does not touch anyone to adjust their postures (physically adjusting the student's body is a standard procedure in yoga practice) but verbally instructs people on how to get into the posture correctly. He constantly confuses right from left. You need to second guess his instructions to get into the correct position, but no one seems to mind. The room is heated to 93 degrees as he does not like the cold ("hot" yoga is a common and popular form of yoga), kept dark as he does not like light, and filled with new age music as he is not a fan of boom, boom. As a classic avoider, I find this atmosphere sacred, calming, and organizing. His students accept all his quirkiness and attend his classes in droves enamored of his wisdom and marvelous sense of humor.

HEADS UP: CRANIAL WORK. *Though doing the activities that I describe will help awaken a sluggish vestibular system it will not greatly alter poor posture that may be driving vestibular issues. If you have poor posture, slouch, and also have facial asymmetry, headaches or TMJ, the likely cause is a misaligned skull from birth trauma or any blow to the head that you've experienced. To correct this, you will need cranial therapy such as cranial/sacral therapy or the far more powerful and permanent neurocranial restructuring (NCR) or biocranial therapy. For information on these therapies, see* **Too Loud, Too Bright, Too Fast, Too Tight, and**

Anxiety: Hidden Causes.

Go for the G Force

If you seek movement, go for it. Ride the roller coaster, dive from the high dive, go bungee jumping.

If you are hypersensitive to movement and gravitationally insecure, don't get bamboozled into zooming down the aerial skytram in Costa Rica's rainforest, as you observe the monkeys and parrots. It will terrify you. Instead, observe from a slow stroll along the bridge.

Forget the Car

Save on gas and bike to the store. Walk heel-to-toe to a friend's house.

Trade Bumpy for Smooth

Forget concrete. Walk on sand or grass.

Hang Like a Bat

Hang upside down for a quick way to get intense, long-lasting input. Many props exist to help you hang freely like Batman, including an inversion table that gives the back traction and helps with back pain, and yoga props. These include:

Yoga inversion sling: This requires muscles and a well-developed core to manipulate your body into the postures.

Yoga hanging wall: This is a sling attached to the wall and easier than the inversion sling as you can use the wall to get in and out of postures.

Yoga headstand bench: This allows you to do a headstand without your head touching the floor. It requires some core to get into a headstand and stay there and may be initially difficult if you have low muscle tone and little musculature.

*BE MINDFUL: If you get dizzy doing an inversion, go slowly and build up the time you stay in them. The **Relief Band for Motion Sickness** is a great device to help with dizziness, vertigo, car sickness and sea sickness.*

Create Balance Challenges

Look for other ways to challenge your balance, like walking around curves. Be creative:

- **Brush** your teeth and take out the garbage with an eye pillow on top of your head.
- **Make** your bed while standing on tiptoes.
- **Cross** the midline to reach into a bowl of popcorn.
- **Walk** heal-to-toe.
- **Rather** than just say 'yes' or 'no,' shake and nod your head to give the balance system a nudge. In turn, this will help alert you.

Rock and Roll

Endless ways exist to pleasurably oil the vestibular system. These include:

- **Rock** in a rocking chair or glide on a glider.
- **Sway** to music.
- **Cat** nap in a hammock, especially prone.
- **Sleep** on a waterbed.
- **Hold** and sway a baby.
- **Sit** in a ball chair at your computer.

- **Swivel** in a chair while watching TV.
- **Bounce** on an exercise ball.

Jump Start the Day

Skipping rope first thing in the morning or jumping up and down on a trampoline offers intense balance and proprioception that may keep you alert and together through to the afternoon.

Return to the Womb

Roll back on forth on your belly on a large exercise ball for fifteen minutes in the morning and you will set off a vestibular pow that may get you through the down afternoon time. This powerful, long lasting vestibular effect results from how the position replicates the rocking movement in utero.

Super Challenge Your Brain

Walk heel to toe down a hallway, preferably barefoot. When you can manage this without teetering over, add variations.

Head Weight: Place an eye pad or bean bag on top of your head and walk heel to toe.

Crossed Arms: Leaving the weight balanced on your head, cross your arms, and walk heel to toe down the hall. Cross your arms the other way and walk back down the hall in the other direction.

Hand Weights: With the weight balanced on top of your head, add a one-pound hand weight in each hand and walk heel to toe.

Look to the Side: With the weight balanced on top of your head, walk down the hallway looking to the right for a few steps and then looking to the left for a few steps.

- **Weights**: Repeat the above sequence carrying weights in your arms.
- **Cross Arms**: Repeat the above sequence and add crossing your arms, first one way and then the other.
- **Nodding**: Take the weight off your head and walk down the hallway heel to toe nodding your head yes. Repeat nodding your head no. Next, try the nodding carrying a one-pound weight in each hand.

Do this exercise outside on grass, sand, or concrete. This will add tactile sensation.

Is your head spinning, pun intended? It's okay. Expect this exercise to be hard if you have vestibular challenges. Welcome the challenge! Walking heel to toe alone will improve balance. Adding each variation causes the brain to make slight variations. This extra work creates a wider branching out of synaptic connections to rewire the brain to cover a broader and more generalized territory. This will not only help you feel more stable in space but also think more clearly and abstractly, focus better, and remember more. Remember, the more integrity in the brainstem, the better the higher brain works. So take off your shoes and get earthy, literally.

Try Earthing

Walk barefoot. Everyone should. Throughout history humans always walked barefoot until modern lifestyle necessitated wearing shoes. This has disconnected us from the Earth's energy which vibrates at a specific frequency, known as the Schumann Resonance. All of life is composed of frequencies and vibrations and our bodies were designed to coincide with earth's rhythms.

When our bare skin touches the surface of the earth, or if we are immersed in a natural body of water we tune to this vibration and experience profound healing. Some of us sensitive folks feel the vibration as a pleasant warm, tingling, sensation when trodding barefoot along the water's edge at the beach or on a stretch of dew-moistened grass.

There are about 5,000 nerve endings in the bottom of each foot. As our feet touch the ground, the feedback creates a light, natural stride in the body contrary to the impact and joint torque in a shoe. This stride reawakens muscles atrophied from wearing shoes and reawakens our balance system as nerve endings on the bottom of our feet tell us that we're leaning or tilting forward, or that we're bending forward at the waist.

Such feedback stimulates new neural connections and remaps the mind for greater balance. With practice, walking barefoot will translate into running, walking, and even standing with better posture, more mobility, a stronger body, and less joint pain. And there's more good news. Studies show that stimulating the nerve endings on the bottom of the feet can decrease blood pressure and reduce sympathetic activity, reducing stress and inflammation.

Maximize "Earthing"

Walk barefoot outdoors whenever possible and especially after it rains when you get even more of the earth's healing energy. Sit, stand, or walk on grass, sand, dirt, or concrete as these surfaces transmit the earth's energy while wood, asphalt, rubber, plastic, glass, and synthetic materials block it.

When you must wear shoes, wear natural fabric shoes like leather or canvas as the popular rubber- or plastic-soled shoes disconnect you even further from the earth's vibrations.

Sleep, work at the computer, or relax watching TV in contact with conductive sheets or mats that transfer earth's energy to your body (see www.earthing.com) and notice the difference when you don't. For me it's immediately evident. Working at the computer quickly drains me, and I have to take frequent breaks and recharge. When I put my bare foot on an Earthing mat under my computer, I don't get quickly drained and can work far longer. I also sleep more soundly and wake up more relaxed with an Earthing mattress that I always take with me when I travel.

To increase the power of bare skin to earth even further, I take daily barefoot walks along the grassy knoll behind my house as I joyfully pick the fruit of the season off the trees, such as avocados, mangos, loquats, and sapoté, and indulge.

FOR THE TACTILE DEFENSIVE: *Try wearing* ***fivefinger footwear***. *These are flat shoes that fit around the foot and each toe and allow you to move through the world in a more connected way without uncomfortable sensation, while at the same time providing the same sensory feedback critical to balance and agility as does walking barefoot.*

Do a Somersault

Do a few somersaults. This will give you vestibular input, proprioceptive input, and deep pressure.

Whirling Dervishes

Spin around like a whirling dervish. If you get dizzy, stop, hold onto something and stare at something stationary until your head stops spinning.

Get Tipsy on Balance Board

For an economical and convenient way to make a huge difference in your balance system, purchase a balance board. Widely used in occupational therapy, a balance board is a simple wooden platform with a pivot underneath that works with the proprioceptive and the vestibular systems to improve balance.

When we stand on a balance board, sensations travel up our body from our toes, through our joints to the cerebellum in our brain. When we move any part of our body, our balance shifts and our body automatically will make corrections so that we do not fall off the board. This action requires using both hemispheres of the brain. When both sides of the brain are working together, we process, file and store information more efficiently, leaving us with a more organized brain.

Try standing on the balance board when you are at the sink brushing your teeth or when talking on the phone. Listen and move to music to enhance the experience.

Whole Lot of Shaking Going On

Creating a similar but more powerful effect as the balance board is the body vibrating machines. These machines have become the rage for an amazing and quick home workout. All you do is stand on an oscillating platform that produces vertical vibrations with a side-alternating rocking movement, similar to walking or balancing on a balance board. The movement creates a pleasant rocking and rolling action that causes the brain to tell the muscles of your body to actively contract to maintain its equilibrium and results in a therapeutic and muscle toning workout.

Take Up NIA

Combining many movement modalities, including Tai Chi, Tae Kwon Do, Aikido, jazz dance, modern dance NIA is a sensory-based movement practice that works directly on head movements to tap into the vestibular system and cultivate body-centered awareness. Try it out.

Dance the Night Away

If you love to dance, take advantage of the many ways it feeds the movement system. To begin, moving in rhythm with the music enhances input into the vestibular system. And you are moving your whole body, using both sides of the body, and crossing the midline, along with sequencing moves that makes it a great activity to increase bilateral integration, praxia, and body-centered awareness.

Let's now explore the different activities we can do to use our mouth to modulate.

Summing Up

PROPRIOCEPTION: Sense of Body Awareness ("Push/ Pull")

Ways to get it:

- Crash on a Trampoline
- Do Tug of War
- Take Power Yoga
- Take a Wild Vacation
- Get Weighted Down
- Get Cocooned
- Tighten Up
- Do Heavy Work in a Quick
- Sneak in Heavy work

VESTIBULAR: Sense of Balance & Movement

Ways to get it:

- Yoga
- Go for the G Force
- Forget the Car
- Trade Bumpy for Smooth
- Hang like a bat
- Create balance challenges
- Rock & Roll
- Jump Start the Day
- Return to the Womb
- Super Challenge Your Brain
- Try Earthing

- Do a Somersault
- Whirling Dervishes
- Get Tipsy On Balance Board
- Whole Lot of Shaking Going On
- Take Up NIA
- Dance the Night Away

*

7

Mouthing

"One man's meat is another man's poison."

~Roman poet Lucretius

What does the newborn do to calm when in distress? She turns to her side, pulls into the fetal tuck, searches for her fists (and later her thumb), and sucks away. The strong suck provides intense somatosensory (tactile and proprioceptive) input into the jaw muscles, one of the strongest muscles in the body and is and forever remains our first line of defense. As adults, the minute we feel unregulated, our first tendency is to chomp, chew, and suck away.

Unknowingly we also self-stim with oral motor input every time we drink, smoke, chew gum, bite our fingernails, lick our lips, chew on pencils, drink through a straw, use a toothpick, electric toothbrush, or floss, chatter, laugh, hum, or breathe deeply.

How much you will engage in oral/motor input varies by sensitivity. If you are hyposensitive to oral/motor input, you have low muscle tone in your mouth and need more oral/motor input. As a result, you may not chew your food well and overeat to get more sensation. You need to constantly have something in your mouth and often lick, taste, or chew inedible objects, like a pencil or your hair.

And while over-eating is bad as are habits like smoking, oral-motor input used correctly can be highly instrumental in changing your state of being, both by revving you up and calming you down. Let's look at how you can do this through choice of the food you eat and drink and by using oral/motor input to deepen breathing.

FOOD

When we get anxious or bored, we often turn to comfort food to wake us up or calm us down. The conventional wisdom is that food makes us feel better because of the biochemistry inherent in the taste and smell. But what is often overlooked is the effect of food texture and even temperature on our state. As the jaw is one of the main joints in our body, chewing, chomping and sucking apply pressure to the proprioceptors to help get us together. Take chips. In addition to the salt and the fat, we get addicted to chips because crunchy food employs strong input into the jaw joint and raises our endorphin level.

Of course, while chewing, sucking, chomping and crunching is good to alter state, it's bad when it makes us fat, sick, anxious, depressed and spacey, as it will if you choose the *wrong* foods. So be cautious in your food choices. Food manufactures know well how to get you to use your jaws: develop the crunchiest, saltiest, most sugary, fatty food. High in calories, nutritionally deficient of vitamins, minerals, amino acids and fatty acids, loaded with artificial ingredients and toxins, and hard to digest and assimilate, such food creates cravings, digestive problems, allergies, and a slew of physical ailments that will further destabilize your nervous system.

And it robs the brain of sufficient nutrition to produce neurotransmitters, resulting in anxiety, depression, fatigue and moodiness. Such food includes white grains, white sugar, white milk products, high allergen food (gluten, pasteurized dairy, peanuts, soy, corn), food additives, food dyes, artificial sweeteners, and processed meat. Bottom line: if your brain is not getting fed the nutrition it needs, all other interventions to organize the nervous system will have little effect.

True, it's hard to give up junk food. And for good reason. Our brain is programmed to desire sweet, fatty foods to help us survive in the climate of feast or famine in which we evolved. Eating this food raises the endorphin level in the brain and creates cravings. So when we need a quick fix, we wolf down these foods as the quickest, easiest, most pleasurable way of modulating our nervous system.

Don't. You can do all the sensory diet changes in the world, and nothing much will change if you don't feed your nervous system and body the nutritional food it needs to function. And that is primarily whole, plant based nutritionally dense food, organic whenever possible to avoid the effects of pesticides, chemicals and genetically modified organisms, or GMOs. Remember, SPD is synonymous with digestive issues and sensitivity. If you wish to stabilize your nervous system, eliminating toxic foods and eating a whole, organic, plant-based diet is not a choice, it's an imperative.

IMPORTANT INFO: *If you eat meat or dairy, it should be from pastured animals or else you will be ingesting pesticides, herbicides, antibiotics, hormones and other chemicals.*

FOOD FOR MODULATION

Below is a list of whole, healthy foods divided by taste, texture, and temperature. Choose what foods work best for your system. In general, wake-up foods tend to be cool to cold, crunchy, salty, bitter and spicy, while calming foods tend to be warm to hot, smooth or sweet. Foods that entail heavy work to the jaw and cheek muscles, like chips, can be either calming or alerting depending on what you need at the moment.

ALERTING FOOD

"I think we love bacon because it has all the qualities of an amazing sensory experience. When we cook it, the sizzling sound is so appetizing, the aroma is maddening, the crunch of the texture is so gratifying and the taste delivers every time."

~Alexandra Guarnaschelli

Taste: Intense to wake up the mouth

- *Sparkling water**
- *Kombachu (sparkling probiotic drink)*
- *Kevita (sparkling probiotic drink)*
- *Cocobiotic (fizzing probiotic drink)*
- *Ice chips*
- *Sour fruit popsicles*
- *Cloves*
- *Lemon*
- *Pure cranberry juice*
- *Pickles*
- *Radishes*
- *Wasabi peas*
- *Cajun spice*
- *Hot peppers*
- *Cloves*
- *Grapefruit Juice*
- *Urban Moonshine Organic Bitters***
- *Spicy Salsa*

- *Peppermints (natural sugar)*

*Carbonation leaches out minerals and can cause sleep problems, irritability and upset stomach. So use sparingly.

Bitters to wake up the mouth and to stimulate digestion (order from **http://www.gapsdiet.com).

FASCINATING FINDINGS: *Eating spicy foods helps stimulate endorphins. According to research at the University of Buffalo, stimulation occurs when the spicy part of the food comes into contact with the taste buds on your tongue. The brain reacts similarly as it would to pain, triggering the release of feel-good endorphins. This may be why eating spicy foods seems so addictive.*

CAUTIONARY ADVICE: *Before going to sleep, avoid stimulating substances like caffeine, including cola and chocolate, or smoking a cigarette in the evening, or spicy foods, high carbohydrate foods, and alcohol, all of which can disrupt sleep all night.*

Texture: Heavy Work to Jaw

Crunch, Chomp

- *Mary's pretzels (non-gluten)*
- *Mary's crackers (non-gluten)*
- *Nuts, especially walnuts*
- *Seeds*

ESSENTIAL FATTY ACIDS: *Both walnuts and seeds are high in essential fatty acids. Essential fatty acids and especially Omega 3's, are brain food. The myelin sheath across which messages transmit is fed by water and omega 3's; the thicker it is, the faster an impulse can transmit. Deficiency causes brain cells to malfunction and can result in anxiety. For instance, panic attack has been linked to a deficiency of alpha-linolenic acid, the essential omega-3 fatty acid found in high* concentrations in flaxseed oil. Omega-3's also regulate mood: the more omega-3s in your diet, the less likely you will be depressed. Fish oil, high in omega 3 fatty acids effectively helps treat manic depression or bipolar disorder, and even schizophrenia. This is because omega 3's, along with vitamin D affect serotonin level in the brain.

REGULATING DOPAMINE: *Sesame and pumpkin seeds make a great snack and help regulate dopamine levels. Tahini, a paste made from sesame seeds, is an excellent source for the amino acids needed for dopamine production.*

CRUNCH AWAY: *To get both crunch and essential fatty acids throw seeds into your salad or cereal. This includes flaxseeds (ground or pre-soaked), hemp seeds, pumpkin seeds, sunflower seeds, sesame seeds or chia seeds (pre-soaked) that you vary daily. You can also throw them into your morning smoothie. Using an herb or coffee grinder, grind together all but the chia seeds.*

- *Raw vegetables (carrots, celery, kale, asparagus)*
- *Cole slaw*
- *Raw zucchini spaghetti (zucchini put through a spiral vegetable slicer)*
- *Popcorn (air popped preferably; no butter or oil)*
- *Apples*
- *Chips*
- *Granola*
- *Rice cakes*
- *Raw sauerkraut (probiotics)*
- *Kimchi (probiotics)*

IMPORTANT INFO: *Over the past 10 years, numerous studies have linked insufficient gut flora to a range of behaviors, including mood and emotion, and appetite and satiety. Having healthy gut flora is not only essential to help maintain brain function but also to decrease the risk of psychiatric and neurological disorders, including, anxiety, depression, and autism. Probiotics have become a major* *component of the GAPS dietary protocol that has shown much success in treating autism (**http://www.gapsdiet.com**).*

- *Raw broccoli*

FOLIC ACID: *Broccoli contains folic acid that boosts serotonin levels and improves mood. Other vegetables that contain folic acid include spinach, corn, beets, parsnips, and Brussels sprouts.*

Chewing

- *Gum (preferably with xylitol in place of sugar)*
- *Popcorn (preferably air popped)*
- *Raw, dehydrated kale chips*
- *Seaweed snacks ((high in L-tyrosine, boosting dopamine in the brain)*
- *Collard greens*

B6: *Leafy green vegetables contain B6 which elevate serotonin to "feel good" levels. Vitamin B6 or folate deficiency is commonly found in the bloodstreams of those diagnosed with clinical depression.*

Sucking

- *Clove*
- *Green olives*
- *Cinnamon stick (helps control blood sugar)*
- *Hard ginger candy (digestion)*
- *Organic chocolate, dark and preferably raw*
- *Chocolate mousse from chocolate (try raw cacao mousse)*
- *Drinking smoothies through a straw*

CHOCOLATE POWER: *Chocolate from the cacao bean acts as a natural anti-*

depressant, balancing mood, reducing PMS symptoms, and increasing focus and alertness. It is high in L-tyrosine, boosting dopamine in the brain. Chocolate also contains phenylethylamine or PEA, a stimulant that causes the release of norepinephrine and dopamine. The "love" molecule, PEA gives you that head-over-heels, elated part of love.

Tugging/Biting/Pulling (More punch):

- *Licorice (Zagarize-pure licorice extract)*

BE MINDFUL: Licorice (DGL) helps with digestion. Licorice candy is not real licorice and has no health benefits. Take a pass.

- *Fruit leather*
- *Goji berries*

GOJI POWER: *Goji berries offer brain, and neurological support and increase resistance to stress. Try them covered with organic chocolate!*

Temperature: Cold

- *Fruit Popsicle**
- *Frozen grapes***
- *Frozen bananas****
- *Banana ice cream*****
- *Frozen peas or diced carrots*
- *Ice cold drink*
- *Fruit flavored ice cubes (organic fruit)*

*Juice organic berries—strawberries, blueberries, raspberries, blackberries—and freeze. These berries supply nutrients that trigger dopamine release.

** Must be organic as commercial grapes are loaded with pesticides.

***Bananas are a major source of L-tyrosine to help stimulate dopamine. The riper the banana the more tyrosine it contains.

****Put frozen bananas through a homogenizer like the Champion or Omega juicer for a great, healthy "ice cream" snack.

CALMING FOODS

Taste: Sweet *(eating sugar is deregulating and the following list does not contain foods with cane sugar):*

- *Raisins*
- *Dates*
- *Fruits*
- *Dried Fruits*
- *Sweet potatoes*
- *Applesauce*
- *Mango*

Texture:

Soft

- *Warm oatmeal for breakfast**
- *Soaked chia seeds*
- *Soft boiled eggs (free range, organic)*
- *Bananas*
- *Goat cheese*
- *Rice pasta with cooked tomatoes*
- *Melon (not watermelon)*
- *Baked salmon (high in omega 3 fatty acids)*
- *Baked, mashed beans*

- *Cooked quinoa*
- *Cooked buckwheat (kasha)*

*Oats are high in L-tyrosine, boosting dopamine in the brain and they reduce stress hormones, upping serotonin and calming you.

Smooth

- *Mashed potatoes*
- *Avocados (a healthy fat that should be eaten often for brain function; also increases dopamine levels)*
- *Papaya (green papaya contains papain, a digestive enzyme)*
- *Bananas*
- *Coconut ice cream*
- *Coconut milk shake**
- *Goat yogurt (probiotics)*
- *Buttered (organic, non-pasteurized milk) Ezekial toast or Ezekial bagels*
- *Oatmeal (fiber)*
- *Almond butter***

*Blend coconut water & meat (preferably young coconuts), raw cacoa beans if you can handle caffeine, and a tsp. vanilla.
**Almond butter is an excellent source for the amino acids needed for dopamine production and it contains tyrosine for alterness.

Sucking

- *Yogurt (probiotics)*
- *Applesauce*
- *Mangos*

Temperature: Warm

- *Soup*
- *Bone broth (chicken or beef)**
- *Tea*

*A staple on the GAPS diet, bone broth contains a rich concentration of nutrients to help "heal & seal" the gut lining, playing a critical role in soothing the gut and allowing the body to absorb and assimilate critical nutrition.
(http://www.gapsdiet.com/).

ORAL DEFENSIVENESS

If you are oral defensive, certain food textures feel irritating. A picky eater, you confine eating to specific textures, such as chomping food, like chips or crackers, or soft food, like a banana, spaghetti, or ice cream, or hot or cold food. Such eating habits create a restricted diet that potentially may have nutritional and vitamin deficiencies and affect behavior and development.

In adolescence, it is especially dangerous because oral defensiveness can lead to anorexic like starving and be misdiagnosed and mistreated as such.

Many interventions exist to alleviate oral defensiveness by getting into the mouth and providing normalizing sensation. Explore these and do them so you can eat a wider variety of food. In *Too Loud, Too Bright,* I describe Serena, a young woman who was oral defensive and diagnosed as anorexic. Two days after starting a simple intervention to combat oral defensiveness devised by Patricia Wilbarger, she was eating soft, mushy foods, like ice cream and bananas, for the first time in her life.

POWER OF BREATH

How are you breathing? Deeply? Shallowly? Fast? Slow? Most likely if you have SPD, it's fast and shallow. This is especially so if you are hyper-responsive or if you have poor posture as the lungs cannot inflate fully. Slouching clenches the diaphragm, and you don't take in as much life-sustaining oxygen when you inhale, or expel as much of the potentially hazardous carbon dioxide when you exhale. This inhibits oxygen to the brain and creates fatigue, forgetfulness, and anxiety.

One of the most powerful stress management techniques, and your first line of defense when discombobulated is to change your breathing. When relaxed, you breathe slowly and deeply. When stressed, you breathe fast and shallowly. By consciously slowing and deepening your breathing, you can willfully relax your body. Here are the many ways you can do this.

Blow Gabriel Blow

Blow through a straw, a wind instrument (flute, recorder, clarinet, saxophone, etc.), a whistle, a respiratory breathing "whistle" or blow up a balloon. These are all good activities to deepen the breath.

Laugh Away Tension

Do anything that makes you laugh, giggle, and even cry as all change respiration and release endorphins that help balance the nervous system. Sex does as well. Indulge!

Breathe Deeply

Deep breathing exercises will teach you to slow down breathing and to breathe fully from your abdomen, or diaphragm. This will increase the amount of oxygen getting to your brain and muscles and stimulate the calming parasympathetic nervous system to override the arousing sympathetic nervous system.

This calming effect happens as well because deep diaphragmatic breathing, with a long, slow exhale stimulates the vagus nerve and slows heart rate and blood pressure, and especially when stressed. As you recall, high vagal tone links to physical and psychological well-being, while low vagal tone links to inflammation, anxiety, and depression, as well as heart attacks. Healthy vagal tone is indicated by a slight increase of heart rate when you inhale, and a decrease of heart rate when you exhale.

QUICK BREATHING TIP: *For a quick way to immediately breathe deeply, stick out your tongue and hold it for a few seconds. The result will be a very deep breath regardless of what state you're in.*

Here are some yoga breathing exercises to train you to breathe deeply and fully.

Ujjayi Breathing

A yoga breathing technique, *Ujjayi* breathing is deep-chest breathing that strengthens breath by slightly constricting the throat and producing a hissing sound—think Darth Vadar. Ujjayi breathing is employed throughout a yoga practice to energize the body.

Here's how to do it.

- **Lie** down, so you're not fighting gravity and close your eyes.
- **Place** one hand on the upper abdomen just below the base of the sternum, your power spot and the other hand on your chest.
- **Place** the tip of your tongue behind your bottom front teeth.
- **Slightly** purse your lips and breathe out through your mouth making a "hah" sound. Slowly push the stale air out of your lungs and let your whole body go, as if sinking into the floor. Exhaling stimulates vagal

tone, relaxing you.

- **Place** the tip of your tongue against the back of top front teeth.
- **Inhale** slowly and deeply through your nose, creating a yawning sensation in the back of your nose and throat and expanding your abdomen, ribs and back like a balloon.
- **Pause** briefly at the end of the exhalation and let your next inhalation begin on its own, without "grabbing" for it. Pausing following exhalation extends parasympathetic arousal, which will prolong a feeling of calm and slows your breathing even further, while holding your breath at the end of inhalation extends sympathetic arousal.

Take at least ten full abdominal breaths slowly and smoothly, prolonging exhale. Slowly increase to forty cycles a session. Take a few regular breaths between each ten-breath cycle.

Alternate Nostril Breathing

One of the most powerful breathing exercises for those with sensory issues is alternate nostril breathing. ANB involves breathing through one nostril at a time and alternating between sides. Researchers believe that right nostril dominance stimulates the arousal-producing sympathetic nervous system and left nostril dominance elicits the relaxation-producing parasympathetic system. Doing this exercise balances the two sides of the brain.

Here's how to do ANB.

- **Sit** comfortably in a chair or cross-legged on a cushion.
- **Close** the right nostril with your right thumb.
- **Exhale** completely through the left nostril.
- **Inhale** slowly and evenly through the left nostril.
- **Hold** the air for a few seconds, closing the left nostril with the left thumb.

- **Release** the right nostril and exhale slowly through it.
- **Inhale** through the right nostril.

This completes one cycle. Continue for up to 20 cycles and finish by exhaling through the left nostril. Once you get the knack, try counting on each inhalation and exhalation with even counts. This will help your mind focus. Start with a low number, such as four, and gradually build it up.

FASCINATING FINDINGS: *A research study conducted in 1997 using alternate nostril breathing to deepen and slow breathing found increased spatial memory in 10-to 17-year-olds. Increased spatial awareness relates to field independence, the ability to accurately orient and maneuver in space, in other words to be centered and grounded in space. This makes practicing ANB an important opportunity to enhance body awareness for those with SPD.*

If you spend three to ten minutes a day (10 to 40 breathing cycles), twice a day doing deep breathing, you will strengthen the muscles that support breathing and gradually enhance their flexibility and resilience. This will reset the rhythm and rate of your breathing and with regular practice of deep breathing, will increase lung capacity to enable you to breathe more deeply. Conversely, if you slow down your brain waves through biofeedback, meditation or therapeutic listening, all of which I will discuss, you can slow your heart rate and respiration.

COACHING TIP: *When you are in overload, you may be unable to deepen and slow down breathing. Don't despair. Use other sensory tools to get yourself better organized, like therapressure, a quick proprioception handstand against the wall, or whatever works for you. It also helps to retreat to a quiet, dark place to chill out.*

Let's now explore the different activities we can do to use touch to modulate.

Summing Up

Good/Bad food: Processed refined food makes us anxious, spacey, depressed and sick and exacerbates sensory issues. Whenever possible, eat whole food from the earth, organic as much as possible.

Regulating arousal: What food you eat can help you regulate your arousal level.

ALERTING FOOD

Taste: Intense to wake up the mouth

Texture: Heavy Work to Jaw

- Crunch, Chomp
- Chewing
- Sucking
- Tugging/Biting/Pulling (More punch):

Temperature: Cold

CALMING FOODS

- Taste sweet
- Texture soft
- Temperature warm

Oral Defensiveness: If you are oral defensive, certain food textures feel irritating, and you are a picky eater. There are interventions to help stimulate your mouth so you can eat a wider variety of food.

Power of breath: One of the most powerful stress management techniques, and your first line of defense when you begin to get discombobulated is to change your breathing. When relaxed, you breathe slowly and deeply. When stressed, you breathe fast and shallowly. By consciously slowing and deepening your breathing, you can willfully relax your body.

Here are the many ways you can do this.

- Blow Gabriel Blow
- Laugh Away Tension
- Deep breathing
- Ujjayi Breathing
- Alternate Nostril Breathing (ANB)

8

*

Touching

"Touch comes before sight, before speech. It is the first language and the last, and it always tells the truth."

~ Margaret Atwood, *Der blinde Mörder*

Oh, the magic of touch. And oh how wonderful when we have an affectionate, loving partner at hand, willing to gives us calming, pleasurable warm, deep pressure touch when we desire it and fire those serotonin and dopamine receptors to launch us into a fuzzy, peaceful oblivion.

If you are not one of those people, don't despair. Many ways exist to get your daily tactile fix. In so doing, you will reduce tactile defensiveness, become organized, and feel more of the relaxed alertness needed to engage fully in the world.

Sensitivity Threshold

How you respond to touch will vary according to sensitivity. If you are tactile defensive, you need more calming than alerting touch. That means rhythmical, slow, even, continuous, prolonged, and steady deep pressure touch, like you get from a massage. And you need textures that are more silky, soft, and smooth.

If you are hypo-responsive, you can enjoy both calming touch to relax you, and stimulating touch to arouse you. Arousing touch is more arhythmical, light, fast, short, uneven, and intermittent like vibrating, tapping, or light stroking. You are also likely to seek more of a rough, gritty texture.

The following factors influence also how one responds to touch.

Place: What body part is touched—the back or more sensitive neck for instance.

Context: What is the situation in which the touch occurs—at home, in a crowd?

Relationship: What is the relationship between the persons involved? Lovers? Strangers?

Arousal: What is your current level of arousal? You will react differently to touch depending on whether you are drowsy or alert, calm or excited, aroused or in overload.

Control: Who's in control? Touch is more easily accepted if you initiate when, where and how long than if you are unexpectedly touched.

Touch Experiences

Any kind of skin stimulation will release tension, even if briefly—rubbing your skin with a terrycloth washcloth, rolling a wooden roller up and down your thigh, fidgeting with your jewelry. Deep pressure touch though is the "heavy work" of touch and will last far longer. It will help prepare your nervous system for stressful events, enabling you to tolerate what otherwise might be a punishing experience.

Deep Pressure Touch

The Magic Brush

The Wilbarger therapressure protocol is a powerhouse if you are tactile defensive as it quickly settles and calms you. The protocol involves pushing with *very* firm pressure across your skin with a soft and densely bristled plastic brush (the Therapressure Device by Clipper Mills, San Francisco, CA) to the hands, arms, feet, legs and back. The protocol must be taught by someone trained in its administration as it must be done correctly for therapeutic effect.

Therapressure is followed by joint compression to joints of the arms, legs and trunk. For me, the easiest way to do this is to stand in a doorway with knees bent in plié and, with bent elbows, push my hands into the door frame. This gets ankles, knees, hips, wrists, elbows and shoulders at once.

Initially, the protocol is done every two hours or so to maintain modulation. When your system feels more organized, you can use it as needed. As you can easily carry around the small brush with you, it's your best friend when you're out and about and need a quick fix. It makes my skin tingle wonderfully and come alive and I find it intensely pleasurable.

Try doing the Wilbarger therapressure protocol before activities that involve light touch, like walking on sand at the ocean, or playing around in the water as the waves splash.

Preventing Self-injury

Deep pressure touch, whether with therapressure or with a hug is a useful intervention to prevent self-injury, as described by this woman.

A few months before I was diagnosed with SPD, I had one of those days when all I could think about was cutting or otherwise hurting myself. I began to hit myself, and my partner grabbed my hands to stop me and

pulled me against him and wrapped me in a hug so tight I couldn't
move... At first I resisted, but the longer he held me like that, the more I
relaxed. The pent up emotions that had made me want to cut just came
pouring out, and it was the best I had felt in a long time.

Now, whenever I feel myself starting to lose control of my emotions
to the point of wanting to cut, I ask my partner for a "full body" hug, and
it's amazing how quickly I begin to feel better.... It's probably the deep
pressure of cutting that helps most, more than anything else... and as you
have found, it is possible to find other ways to fulfill that need ... that do
not involve self-injury.

Get Kneaded

If you can tolerate human touch, getting a massage is one of the most
pleasurable tactile experiences. Be sure and request "firm touch."

Get a Squeeze Machine

If you can't tolerate human touch, you can get your hugs from Temple
Grandin's hug machine that is available for purchase.

Wear a Bear Hug

Wear a "bear hug" vest that fits snugly next to the body, with
adjustable straps and body wrap to adjust the amount of pressure. For
proprioceptive input, you can also add weights.

Self-Massage

Take advantage of wooden body and foot rollers, tappers,
compressors and mechanical vibrators and massagers. Lie in a massage
chair for calming, or on a vibrating mat for alerting.

Shower Away the Jitters

Unless you are tactile defensive and it would irritate you, use shower attachments that spray, needle, massage or pulse to alert and awake you. Stand under the shower head, close your eyes and feel the water pellets pounding your skin, putting you in touch with your body. The thumping, pulsing, beating pellets provide calming deep pressure touch making you feel alive and energized.

HELPFUL TIP: Before turning on the water spout, exfoliate your skin. Using a vegetable fiber brush, make circular and long strokes towards your navel. Brush for three to five minutes before taking your shower. This will slough off dead skin cells, stimulate acupressure points, activate lymphatic drainage, and keep your skin soft and healthy.

FOR YOUR INSPIRATION: Feel your shower as a "baptism" as the way to start a new day and a new life. Picture the water washing away your worries and woes. See those unwanted dark feelings and thoughts going down the drain.

In truth negativity is being washed away. Taking a shower fills the air with negative ions. Negative ions are created in nature by water, air, and sunlight as it impacts the Earth's inherent radiation. That blanket of good feeling that falls over your body at the ocean's edge, near a waterfall or after a storm comes from the saturation of negative ions. When you take a shower, the stream of hot water and steam also produces negative ions. That's part of why you feel so refreshed and awake after.

Body Rolling

Try body rolling. Lying on specially designed balls into specific areas of the body, body rolling creates intense deep pressure and proprioception to stretch fascia and release tension and stress. The effect lasts around two hours. As an added advantage, the body rolling balls are small enough to carry with you when traveling. You can find classes in your area or buy *Body Rolling*, by Yamuna Zake and Stephanie Golden (Healing Arts Press), and follow the instructions or purchase the DVD.

Get Weighted Down

For a more restful sleep, lie under heavy quilts, or a weighted blanket when going to sleep. During the day, try wearing a weighted vest. While sitting at your computer, put weight on your lap. As a rule of thumb, occupational therapists recommend weight that equals 10% of total body weight plus one pound. More can be used in lap pads though if you can tolerate it. Try watching TV with an aromatherapy neck wrap filled with flax seeds.

"In high school, I loved being playing goalie in hockey. The gear weighed at least 50 pounds. It felt great!"

Walk in Water

Walk in water in rhythm to music with a strong drum beat. The pressure of the water against your body offers deep pressure touch. The drumbeat will give you vestibular input. The deeper the water the greater the pressure against your body. Underwater swimming and especially deep-sea diving are great ways to create the feeling of a pressure cooker.

QUICK DEEP PRESSURE TRICKS: *Roll across the floor. Yank and twist your hair by digging into the roots for deep pressure to your scalp.*

Vibration

Some powerful vibrators provide a deep pressure massage with long lasting effects. Vibrators cause the bones to vibrate and stimulate the gravity receptors as well. Some people are calmed by leaning against a washing machine or dryer, or by resting their heads against a train or bus window to feel the vibration. Vibration is best at 100hz or higher.

If you have problems waking up in the morning, sleep with a vibrating mat and turn it on when you awake.

Texture

Brush Away

Stimulate your skin with a loufah brush, bath sponge, a terrycloth washcloth, a hairbrush.

Try Terrycloth

Sleep on a terrycloth beach towel. Roll up a terrycloth towel and put it under your neck for a pillow. Throw a wet towel over your shoulders or whole body to quickly calm, both from the texture and the weight.

Hot & Cold

Some like hot, some like it cold. Some massage pillows can be heated up in a microwave for calming or cooled in a freezer for alerting, offering both temperature preference along with deep pressure touch. Typically filled with flax or buckwheat seeds, lavender and other fragrant flowers, they are available for the eyes, neck, shoulders or back.

For quick alerting, hold ice in your hand or to your face.

Warm Bath

When you're bent out of shape, take a warm bath. You can vary the bath water temperature to alter blood flow. Cold water stimulates by constricting surface blood vessels and sending blood toward the internals organs which helps them to function more efficiently. Conversely, hot water relaxes by dilating blood vessels and increasing blood flow to the skin. A warm bath is great when you feel too restless to fall asleep.

Add Epson salts, or Dead Sea salts to detoxify, soothe sore muscles, and relax the body.

HELPFUL TIP: Here's how to mix your own: Mix Epsom salt (1 lb or 500 g) and sea salt bath (1/2 lb or 250 g) into a warm bath. Lie in it for 20 minutes and add hot water as you wish. After your bath, wash the salts off your body with a refreshing cold shower. Going from a hot bath to a cold shower is healing and invigorating.

Infrared Sauna

Try an infrared sauna for relaxation, detoxification, and soothing warmth. Though costly, home units are available and can fit snugly into a corner space.

Flotation Tank

Try a flotation tank and float in a warm and dark, salt-water filled, soundproof and lightproof water tank. Without light or sound, it is so quiet you can hear your heartbeat. The extreme buoyancy of the water lends the environment an almost zero-gravity quality and you feel as if you are floating in a womb.

Touch Therapy

Visualize energy coming down from above and flowing through your body. Hold the palms of your hand a few inches from your body and sweep them slowly from head to toe or on specific areas that need healing. Feel the pull of your energy field and how it gets stuck in various places on your body where you feel imbalance.

Tap Away

Lightly place your fingertips on your forehead, about an inch above the eyebrows—your third eye—and tap your fingers. Breathe deeply and stay focused for two to five minutes as the blood circulates in your forehead. Note strong pulses under your fingertips or hands. This is both energizing and relaxing, especially after working at the computer when your forehead is all scrunched up. It's a quick way to get into meditation and I'll talk about that in chapter fourteen.

If engaged in a boring conversation, take your finger and draw the figure eight on your forearm. This will help integrate both sides of the brain and perk you up. If you are tactile defensive, do it firmly.

Fidget Away

Fidgeting is a nice tactile snack to get more focused and centered. You can fidget with jewelry, your hair, a paper clip or whatever works for you.

Try Chinese Balls

Chinese stress balls come from the martial art tradition of the East. As you roll two chimes around in the palm of one hand, which is not as easy as it might seem, you build agility, and relax and exercise your hands. I find it a wonderful, quick stress relief. As my hand opens up, I feel a relief in my jaws which are bent out of shape from years of TMJ.

Get Handy

Knead dough or clay; knit and crochet. All creates rhythmic movement that will relax you.

Pet Away

Pet your cat or dog to release serotonin instantly!

Let's now explore the different activities we can do to use vision to modulate.

Summing Up

Sensitivity Threshold

Of course, how you respond to touch will vary according to sensitivity. And this will vary according to:

- *Place*
- *Context*
- *Relationship*
- *Arousal*
- *Control*

Touch Experiences

Deep Pressure Touch: Here are different ways to create calming deep pressure touch.

- *The Magic Brush: Wilbarger therapressure protocol.*
- *Get Kneaded*
- *Get a Squeeze Machine*
- *Wear a Bear Hug*
- *Self-Massage*
- *Shower Away the Jitters*
- *Body Rolling*
- *Get Weighted Down*
- *Walk in Water*

Texture: Here are ways to use texture to modulate.

- *Brush Away*
- *Try Terrycloth*

Hot & Cold: Here are ways to use temperature to modulate.

- *Warm Bath*
- *Infrared Sauna*
- *Flotation Tank*

Touch Therapy: Here are tactile experience to help modulate.

- *Tap Away*
- *Fidget Away*
- *Try Chinese balls*
- *Get Handy*
- *Pet Away*

9

*

Seeing

"I love hot red and yet I am always in drab gray clothing. I use green sparingly in my paintings yet a large field of green grass brings tears to my eyes."

~Harley Brown

Vision is our on-off sense. Unlike movement, touch, sound and smell, we can close our eyes and turn off what we see and, in our own environment control our ambience to a large extent. This gives us more power over how we react to it. For instance. Consider the experience of blasting the car radio as we belted out our favorite tune, and then startling as we turned on the ignition and got hit unexpectedly by the same loud, screeching volume.

If you are photosensitive, exerting control over visual input will help stop the amygdala from sounding the alarm bell and make life more bearable. You can do this by modifying the light and color in your environment, by engaging in relaxing visual activities, by using color therapy, and of course by avoiding visually overstimulating ambiences.

If you are hyposensitive to light, you might get easily depressed when there's too little light and need more, specifically sunlight, or full spectrum light to balance your nervous system.

If you have visual processing problems, you will need to see a developmental optometrist for evaluation and treatment. It's also wise to see a developmental ophthalmologist to rule out any ophthalmological disease.

LOOKING

Scenery

Enjoy beautiful vistas or, if unavailable, close your eyes and imagine looking out at a scene that calms or excites you, like the vast ocean, a sunset, a star-filled sky, or fireworks.

Avoid visual pollution both in your home and in your workplace as it makes it hard to concentrate.

Movement

Our brain is programmed to focus on movement for survival so we can quickly notice a snake slithering in the grass. This is why we glue our eyes to the TV.

Jazzing Up

If you need jazzing up, go for movement that is quick, multidirectional and disjointed, like the TV and videos. Quickly alerting, they work wonders to calm hyperactive kids. Why? These kids are low in dopamine and move about to rev up as they need more not less stimulation. This is the reason why the stimulant Ritalin is the drug of choice for these kids.

Brightness and flickering movement especially mesmerizes. Those on the autistic spectrum will stare for hours at a spinning disco ball. If you are one who gulps light, the visual pyrotechnics of a rock concert is sensory utopia.

Chilling Out

If you need to quiet your world, trade in Lady Gaga's Monster Ball for Sarah Brightman's Dreamchaser concert of liquid, slow moving, rhythmic pyrotechnics.

Watching slow, steady, smooth movement also hypnotizes to help you calm. This is why gazing at fish swimming in an aquarium, at the sunset, the clouds, or water streaming in a lake is so peaceful. For a similar hypnotic effect, try peering into a kaleidoscope, gazing at a lava lamp, staring at a candle, or watching a slowly spinning windcatcher. Even visualizing these scenes will create calmness as the visual cortex will light up as if you were seeing something with eyes open. In the last chapter, I have several visualizations to try.

When overloaded, you may need to close your eyes, put a lavender eye pillow on them for calming pressure, and retreat to your bed or a dark closet.

LIGHT

"The human body when kept in an indoor environment of low lux light will not realize that it is daytime, as it cannot sense the increasing levels of daylight that the genetics are accustomed to. As such, by late morning your body may start sending a signal for you to sleep!"

~ Steven Magee, *Electrical Forensics*

Sunlight

Sunlight is the purest healing force for life on this earth.

As light enters through the eyes, it travels through the hypothalamus in the limbic system, the master controller of the nervous system and the stress response. To optimize nervous system functioning and reduce stress, you need the sun's full spectrum of solar radiation:

- **Visible** color spectrum (red, orange, yellow, green, blue, indigo, violet;
- **Infrared** (heat just beyond red that we feel when sunburned)
- **Ultraviolet** (UV) wavelengths (just beyond violet)

Lack Sufficient Sunlight

Largely indoor creatures, few of us get enough full spectrum light because it is lacking or minimal in indoor lighting. Even if we wished to be outdoors more, we are advised to stay out of the sun to avoid skin cancer. This concern has been debunked. We now know that skin cancer comes not from sunlight but from sunburn. Unless you are allergic to sunlight, it's safe to be out in the sun, as long as you avoid direct sunlight between 10:00 A.M. and 2:00 P.M. to minimize burning.

Getting Enough Sunlight

We all need at least 30 minutes of exposure daily to natural spring or summer sun without sunscreens or sunglasses. This is the bare minimum to produce adequate daily levels of vitamin D3, that are necessary for healthy teeth and bones, and for the functioning of the brain and the immune system. Ideally, some experts believe we should get two hours of direct sunlight.

Nature light also increases serotonin, upping your mood. If you don't get the sun's full spectrum of solar radiation, you are more likely to feel agitated, fatigued, drained, spacey, and depressed. You will also be more prone to viral and bacterial infections. And photosensitivity will *increase* as your nervous system will be unbalanced.

Here's how to get more of the full spectrum of the sun's rays.

- **Increase** outdoor activities and take greater advantage of backyards and porches.

- **Keep** windows clean and open when possible, unobstructed by drawn curtains or blinds.
- **Install** non-tinted skylights and create atriums and sunrooms where you can.
- **Dress** bedroom windows with sheer or semi-sheer curtains or blinds to let in early, diffused morning light.

If you are photosensitive, you can block sunlight by wearing a cap or visor, anti-glare glasses, or Ott full-spectrum sunglasses. Unlike regular sunglasses, Ott sunglasses allow all the color wavelengths of natural light to come through, while eliminating glare and distortion.

Healthy Artificial Light

Another way to get the sun's benefits is to use full-spectrum light bulbs, the nearest thing to the sun's spectral distribution and brightness, and without heat and glare. UV light in contrast is virtually absent from the old incandescent lighting (lightbulbs), shielded in standard fluorescent bulbs, and virtually blocked by normal window glass, including that on our automobiles and eyeglasses. Even on a rainy morning, it is brighter outside than inside with the lights on.

Light distortion from incandescent, fluorescent, and halogen lights create eyestrain within twenty minutes of exposure, even if you have normal vision. Full-spectrum lighting in contrast is far easier on the eyes, eliminating glare and color distortion, and colors are more accurately and easily perceived. Exposure to full spectrum lighting also feeds your nervous system benefits similar to sunlight.

Many people with SPD are photophobic and suffer anxiety or panic in the presence of bright or unnatural lights. Here are some ways to modulate hypersensitivity.

- **Replace** overhead fluorescent lights with full spectrum fluorescents or an Ott floor lamp.
- **Replace** all incandescent bulbs with full-spectrum bulbs or LED lights as neither flicker. LED bulbs are available that work with dimmer switches and come in many shapes, sizes, and colors, even replacing the commercial fluorescent bulbs we commonly see in stores and schools. LED lights are however in the blue spectrum and may be harder on the eyes if you are visually defensive. Warm white, pink or peach bulbs are good choices for decorator lighting as they put out light from the part of the spectrum which is long wavelength light and is much easier on the eyes.
- **Use** a bright Ott bulb for computer work, reading, artwork or drafting. It emits an uplifting white light, without glare or heat that enables you to see the screen or objects more clearly and accurately, and it provides the benefit of sunlight while working.
- **Wear** UV filter glasses if you have normal vision and must work under cool fluorescent light, especially if you suffer from late-day headache or eye strain. UV filter glasses filter out the harmful ultraviolet, violet and blue light waves emitted by the tubes overhead. For indoor use most people prefer clear or light yellow glasses of the type made by NoIR, Corning or SolarShield.
- **Replace** bathroom lights with full spectrum bulbs as it will help wake you up in the morning, and your body will receive the same effect as natural sunlight. And the whiteness of the light makes you look more natural, as you do in sunlight.

IMPORTANT FINDINGS: *In comparing 33 controls to 24 patients with panic disorder, researchers from the University of Siena in Italy found that whereas the controls were slightly attracted to bright light, those with panic disorder showed medium to high levels of aversion to bright lights.*

COLORS

I am an artist and my walls are filled with my paintings. A colorist, I paint in vibrant hues of orange, purple, pinks, yellows, and blues. I can't imagine my life without my images. When I look at a blank wall, I feel sensory deprivation. If that wall happens to also be white, beige, tan or taupe, I am acutely bored and become fidgety.

I am in love with my paintings. A bit of an exaggeration? Actually, not. Viewing art or anything we consider beautiful triggers a surge of the feel-good chemical dopamine into the orbitofrontal cortex of the brain, the same part of the brain that is excited when in love. Such were the findings of Professor Semir Zeki, a neurobiologist at the University College London, who scanned the brains of volunteers as they looked at 28 pictures. Much of the visual pleasure comes from the colors.

An underused mood changer, colored light, strategically placed, profoundly affects our emotional state. Each color of light vibrates at a different wavelength or frequency and sends a different vibration into the energy system of the body: one color excites, another calms.

Red, Yellow, Orange: The red end of the light spectrum has the longest wavelength and slowest frequency of vibration and energizes you. Red, yellow and orange are warm, energizing, and uplifting, while pink is calming. Decorate your home with red roses to perk you up. Wear a pink dress or red shirt to ward off the blues.

Be cautious about too much red though as it can easily overstimulate and make you nervous and irritable because it causes your body to pump out more adrenaline. Research conducted during the 2004 Olympic Games in Athens found that when evenly matched Olympic athletes competed, those wearing red won significantly more than their blue-wearing opponents. If you want to feel inspired but not wired, add just a touch here and there, like a vase of red roses or an orange sculpture in a corner.

Green: In the middle of the spectrum, green is the most balanced color. Boosting serotonin, it relaxes and speeds up the body's own healing mechanisms, recuperating body and mind.

When you're down in the dumps, walk among green grass and trees. Doing so will not only release serotonin to uplift your mood but dopamine as well from the natural tracking of your eyes from left to right as you take in nature's bounty. Load your home with greenery. In addition to uplifting and energizing you, you will add healing oxygen to the air and detoxify toxic chemicals. Areca palm, Dracaena Janet Graig, Peace Lily, English Ivy, Boston Fern, pothos and spider plant are some of the top detoxifying plants.

Blue: The color of the sky and the sea, blue is on the cool end of the spectrum, calming the mind and helping sleep. Looking out at the blue of water or the sky relaxes and calms. Be careful though in painting a wall blue as blue can also drag you down.

Violet: With the shortest wavelength and the quickest vibration, violet is the most cooling. It helps balance both sides of the brain, harmonizing your thoughts and emotions, and induces a deep, relaxed sleep. Said Leonardo de Vinci, "The power of meditation can be ten times greater under violet light falling through the stained glass windows of a quiet church."

Many ways exist to use color to paint a different self-interior. And though logically seekers should prefer warm colors and avoiders cool colors, this is not set in stone. A consummate avoider, I not only paint in vivid colors but love orange walls, while my neighbor, a consummate seeker has her home decorated in off-white, beiges and browns with only occasional pops of red or orange. You will need to experiment with your emotional response to different colors, and especially if you are photosensitive to see what works best for you.

Here are some ways to add color to your world.

- **Light** a room with colored light bulbs.
- **Illuminate** natural light through stained glass (think of the impact of the light streaming through stained glass windows in a cathedral), a colored blind or sheer curtain, or through a colored lampshade lit with a white light bulb.
- **Paint** a room a particular color.
- **Wear** certain colored clothes.
- **Imagine** colors shining upon you while sitting still with eyes closed.
- **Eat** fruits and vegetables of certain colors.
- **Avoid** white or blue walls for visual comfort and glare reduction. The best wall colors are salmon, pink, peach, and warm beige. Textured walls are better than smooth, shiny ones. Painting and other wall hangings will help soften highly-reflective wall areas.

BATHE IN COLOR: Picture yourself lying in a warm bath with healing colors swirling around. You can do this with specially mixed color tints that you pour into the bathwater. As absorbing light through our eyes has a therapeutic effect, so will absorbing color through our skin help to balance or sustain our body's energy level.

- *A red bath energizes.*
- *A yellow bath boosts mental energy.*
- *A green bath balances.*
- *A blue bath de-stresses.*
- *A purple bath frees your creative muses.*

What color is best at any moment? As a rule, the color you reach for spontaneously is likely the right hue at that time to regenerate your body, clear your mind, or soothe your anxieties.

To energize you, install a shower head with colored LED lights for a colorful rainfall, at once mesmerizing and relaxing.

LIGHT THERAPY

While looking at a green wall or wearing a purple sweater will help rev you up or calm you down, to dramatically change your nervous system you need to shine color directly into your eyes. You can do this for a mild effect by wearing colored eye therapy sunglasses that will help change your mood: the cool colors—blues, greens, violet—calm you; the warm colors—reds, oranges, yellows—stimulate you.

Syntonic Light Therapy

For a profoundly transforming effect, physically and emotionally, try syntonic light therapy. Syntonic light therapy flashes different portions of intense colored light into your eyes, each with a specific effect on the brain and the nervous system that helps re-establish the body's rhythms and balance the body. Color shined into your eyes goes to the hypothalamus gland then to the pineal gland, which directs it to the pituitary gland, the master gland for hormone production. The brain processes this information, which causes cellular and hormonal changes to occur to bring the body into balance.

Raising endorphin levels, stabilizing brain waves, lowering heart rate, respiration and blood pressure, syntonic light therapy will help you sleep better, breathe deeper, and feel more settled. Twenty-minute daily sessions for 20 days straight or close to that will reduce anxiety, clinical depression, stress, light sensitivity, chronic fatigue, thyroid problems, PMS, migraines and jet lag and expand the visual field and improve other visual problems.

As one who uses a home machine, I can confirm these results. In fact, I feel energy surge throughout my body within minutes of looking through the machine's cylinder.

Syntonic light therapy is best done under the care of an optometrist, or colored trained psychologist who will determine the appropriate colors for your needs. Incorrectly used, red can produce tension, while blue can produce depression. You can also purchase a home machine as I did and experiment. For more information, see **http://www.visualdifference.net)**.

Light for SAD

Does lack of light make you anxious and depressed? If so and you suffer SAD (seasonal affective disorder), the solution is light— lots and lots of light. First, get as much sunlight as you can. Morning sunlight with its higher concentration of ultraviolet rays is best, as long as you avoid sun exposure after 10 a.m. As light enters through the eyes, not the skin, don't defeat the purpose by wearing sunglasses, as they block UV light. If sunlight is too bright and you need to wear sunglasses, wear Ott full-spectrum sunglasses.

Next, try a full spectrum light box screen designed by John Ott, the classic intervention for SAD. The light box will expose you to light equal to the full-spectrum of the sun, including a small amount of ultra violet (UV) radiation.

Generally, SAD sufferers sit in front of the light box for about a half hour each morning. Such exposure alleviates the symptoms of SAD in 80 percent of sufferers. Amount of exposure needed however need varies individually and should be determined and monitored by a trained health professional. Light stronger than 2,500 lux has potential side effects including anxiety, nervousness and even eye damage. In some susceptible people, light therapy can generate mania.

HELPFUL TIP: Yoga Eye Therapy: *Yoga moves involving the top of the head, such as headstands, may also help with SAD as it stimulates the pineal gland. The pineal gland produces serotonin and melatonin and helps regulate circadian and seasonal rhythms.*

IMPORTANT FINDINGS: *Researchers reported in a Finnish report in BMC Psychiatry in 2014 that sticking simple LED's in your ear for 12 minutes at a time could reduce SAD by 50% in several weeks.*

Crystal Therapy

Coming in varying color frequencies, crystals have a unique internal structure that causes them to resonate at a certain frequency to give them healing abilities. Expand your sensory menu by wearing crystal necklaces, bracelets and rings; carry a crystal in your pocket, or place them throughout your home.

Crystals in the red, yellow and orange tones, like garnet, yellow topaz, amber and citrine are stimulating. Blues and purples, like lapis, sodalite and amethyst are calming. Green stones, like turquoise and jade create a peaceful feeling, while clear quartz crystal energizes you, and rose quartz creates a serene calmness.

YOGA FOR THE EYES

Like the rest of the body, the ocular muscles of the eyes tighten up and constrict from chronic stress and emotional tension. Yoga exercises that only take a few minutes a day can help relieve the tension to improve functioning of the eyes.

Exercise One:

1.   Begin with eyelids open, head and neck still, and entire body relaxed.

2. Picture a clock face in front of you and raise your eyeballs up to 12 o'clock. Hold them there for a second, then lower the eyeballs to six o'clock. Hold them there again.

3. Continue moving the eyeballs up and down 10 times, without blinking if possible. Your gaze should be steady and relaxed.

4. Once you finish these 10 movements, rub your palms together to generate heat and gently cup them over your eyes, without pressing.

5. Allow the eyes to relax in complete darkness. Concentrate on your breathing, feel the warm prana emanating from your palms, and enjoy the momentary stillness.

Exercise Two:

Follow this exercise with horizontal eye movements—from nine o'clock to three o'clock—ending again by "palming" (cupping your hands over your eyes).

Here's how.

1. Focus your gaze on the tip of your nose without blinking. Remain like this for as long as you can. Then close your eyes and relax.

2. Focus on your "third eye" without blinking. This is the area between the eyebrows above your nose. Then close your eyes and relax. It may feel uncomfortable or hard to do at first, but do not let yourself become frustrated. Keep your focus on that area and with time, you will find this posture easier to do.

3. Without turning your head, focus both eyes on your left shoulder. Remain like this for as long as you can. Then close your eyes and relax. Repeat this sequence with the right shoulder.

4. After you are finished, place the palms of your hands on your closed eyes and rest for as long as you would like.

Let's now explore the different activities we can do to use hearing to modulate.

Summing Up

Looking

Scenery: Enjoy or imagine beautiful scenery. Avoid visual pollution.

Movement: Brain programmed to focus on movement for survival. Those who need jazzing up go for movement that is quick, multi-directional and disjointed, and bright. Those who need to quiet seek slower, more rhythmic moving.

Light

Sunlight: Sunlight is the purest healing force for life on this earth. To optimize nervous system functioning and reduce stress, you need the sun's full spectrum of solar radiation:

- **Visible** color spectrum (red, orange, yellow, green, blue, indigo, violet;
- **Infrared** (heat just beyond red that we feel when sunburned)
- **Ultraviolet** (UV) wavelengths (just beyond violet)

Lack Sufficient Sunlight

Because we are largely indoor creatures, we lack sufficient full spectrum light. We all need at least 30 minutes of exposure daily to natural spring or summer sun without sunscreens or sunglasses. Avoid the sun between 10 am and 2:00 pm.

Healthy Artificial Light: Optimize use of full-spectrum light bulbs.

Colors: Take advantage of colored light as it profoundly affects our emotional state.

Light Therapy

Syntonic Light Therapy: For a transforming effect, physically and emotionally, try syntonic light therapy. Syntonic light therapy flashes different portions of intense colored light into your eyes.

Light for SAD: The solution to seasonal affective disorder is light. Get as much sunlight as you can and use a full spectrum light box.

Crystal Therapy: Coming in varying color frequencies, crystals have a unique internal structure that causes them to resonate at a certain frequency to give them healing abilities.

Yoga for the Eyes: Yoga exercises that only take a few minutes a day can help relieve the tension to improve functioning of the eyes.

*

10

Hearing

"If you want to find the secrets of the universe think in terms of energy, frequency, and vibration."

~ Nikolas Tesla

All things in nature vibrate with sound, light and color. Our bodies too are a musical instrument, composed of energy at various frequencies.

Sound begins with movement that shakes up surrounding air molecules, that in turn stir other molecules, creating a ripple effect to form fields of vibrating energy. As these vibrations hit our body, we entrain to them, and they subtly alter our breath, pulse, blood pressure, muscle tension, skin temperature, brain wave and other internal rhythms.

If the sounds are healing and accord to the body's natural rhythms, entrainment will influence internal rhythms and override internal disharmony, producing changes in the autonomic, immune, endocrine and neuropeptide systems. Think of how, when you dance, the music takes over your body and you automatically adjust to the pace, pulse, and rhythm.

This makes the right sound a powerful healing modality. Listening to

Benedictine Monks chanting, for instance, normalizes adrenaline levels, brain wave pattern and lowers cholesterol levels. Singing, chanting, drumming, playing a singing bowl, playing a musical instrument, and listening to music all create vibrations to re-balance the nervous system and heal us physically and emotionally.

Sound waves can even help us learn better because they are imbued with internal order and symmetry, rhythmic patterns and repetition, ideal mathematical form and harmony. For this reason, music helps us memorize and retain information longer.

Listening to an interview with Bob Dylan, who is presumed to have Asperger's, is excruciating because speaking for him is like walking in mud and you wait for him to utter an awkward sentence. But let him twang and pluck away and poetry flows out from his lips like molten lava. Likewise, people who stutter will often sing with clear speech. If you saw the movie *The King's Speech*, you may remember the therapist, Lionel Logue using this technique with Prince Albert.

MUSIC

"That innate love of melody, which she had inherited from her ballad-singing mother, gave the simplest music a power which could well-nigh drag her heart out of her bosom at times."

~ Thomas Hardy, *Tess of the D'Urbervilles*

Music transports us, purifying and strengthening the energy of any space. The late musicologist Don Campbell described sounds as opening and expanding space, as when listening to a flute, or closing space as when assaulted by leaf blowers; as expanding time, as when listening to the thump, thump of the drum beat, or collapsing time as when listening to dripping water. As the present moment always consists of expanded space and time, and the past and future of shrunken time and space, the right sounds can ground you in the present—exactly where we want to hang out!

Our body entrains to external rhythms and our physiology reacts. Loud, harsh, grating, raucous sound accelerates heart rate and breathing and shifts our brain waves into the high beta stress mode (beta brain waves govern normal waking consciousness, alertness, logic and critical reasoning but translate into stress, anxiety and restlessness when too high).

Soft, rhythmic, flowing, smooth, silky sounds lower heart rate and breathing and shift our brain waves into the relaxing alpha brain wave mode (alpha brain waves govern deep relaxation, well-being and euphoria, as when slipping into meditation, a lovely daydream, or peaceful sleep). Music that pulses at about 60 beats per minute, as do lullabies and New Age music synchronize breathing and create alpha waves to help regulate serotonin and dopamine functions.

How lucky to live in the I-Pod age when we can play music we enjoy at will. Of course, what is right for you may bore someone else or drive them into a tizzy. Choose the sounds you need at any given moment to serve your unique nervous system. If you are high on the arousability scale and you go ballistic when assaulted by "sonic bullies," use the many strategies in this chapter to help you learn to block out the sound assault, to create healing sounds, and to reduce auditory sensitivity.

If you are low on the arousability scale and you are the one who's pushing the dentist's or hard hat's drill, barely reacting to the din, you still need relaxing music at times to change state of being.

Use headphones to listen to soft, calming music as they help integrate both sides of the brain. Avoid listening to charging music with headphones as music with heavy bass will damage your hearing. If you wish to listen to upbeat music on headphones, play the music softly.

VOICES

You entrain not only to external rhythms but to the healing power of your own voice. Chanting, humming, and singing create vibration in the upper body that deepens breathing. This in turn increases oxygenation, relaxes the jaw and throat, and releases tension. Simply softening your voice when you speak lowers blood pressure.

Humming or singing quietly is calming. Humming or singing loudly is alerting.

Vowel Power

Chanting that emphasizes vowel sounds—EEEEE, AAYYYY, OOOOOO (as in go), OOOHHHH (as in goo), AAAHHHH—boosts serotonin and releases endorphins in the brain, inducing a trance like state. By chanting you also create an inner white noise that blots extraneous noises. You can use chanting as a self-help tool in a noisy environment, and to launch into a meditative state.

Mantra

Select a mantra (a word or sound such as "om" or "ieng") and utter it silently or out loud as you exhale. A minute or so of the "ah" sound, which you produce when you yawn, will relax your jaw, open up your breathing, and help regulate the supply of pure blood from the heart to various part of the body. High notes (vowels "aye," and "eee") localize in the sinus cavities and skull and wake up the body. Three to five minutes of "aye" or "eee" will keep you alert when you're sluggish and clear your sinuses to boot.

Power of "Om"

Perhaps the most powerful common chant is repeating "Om." Start with the lips shaping the "ah" sound, slowly change to the "o" sound, and end with the closed-lips, "mmm" humming sound. Chanting OM out loud increases vagal tone, the body's ability to successfully respond to stress. In a few minutes, you should feel a relaxed, energized alertness. After ten minutes or longer, chanting "Om" slows down brain waves to a deep state of consciousness.

Group Chanting

Chanting in a group creates an invigorating sound bath and a feeling of connection and support. The repetition stills the everyday mind and frees the creativity of the unconscious mind, giving rise to bliss and in some visions. A mantra or spiritually significant word or phrase is often used. Particular mantras will stimulate specific chakras (energy centers according to Eastern philosophy), to open them up and move energy from one center to another.

Chant & Move

Moving to music enhances and prolongs the sensory experience. Try chanting while sitting cross legged, or in lotus and moving your upper body around in circles to coordinate with the rhythm of the chanting. Doing so enhances both vestibular and proprioceptive input. Move your body in one direction and then in the other.

SOUND & COLORS

There are seven notes in a scale and seven colors in a rainbow. Do the frequencies coordinate? Indeed. The seven primary colors coordinate with the major chords: red/root; orange/second; yellow/third; green/fourth; blue/fifth; indigo/sixth; violet/seventh.

Consider artist Neil Harbisson. Born completely color blind, he wears a prosthetic device attached to his head—his "eyeborg"—that turns color into audible frequencies. Instead of seeing a world in grayscale, Harbisson can *hear* a symphony of color, even those beyond the range of human sight, and even listen to faces and paintings.

To create a similar experience, try listening to *Chakra Chants* by Jonathan Goldman while wearing color therapy eyewear to match each chant. In a booklet with the audio, Goldman matches chants and colors for you.

RHYTHMS IN OUR BONES

Move to the Beat of Your Own Drum

We not only hear music but feel rhythms in our skin and bones. Drumming creates vibrations that tap bone conduction and penetrate the body's core. It is through vibration that the deaf hear and dance to music.

Drums, crystals, and gongs have powerful frequencies that reverberate throughout your body. They change brain wave frequencies to alpha to match that of the earth's frequencies and connect you with the deeper rhythms of life. When playing drums in sync with the body's rhythms, we feel the pulse of the earth beating inside us, grounding us as we move our body to the beat. Such experience creates deep relaxation, euphoria, and extraordinary aliveness.

Join a drum circle from your local meet-up and beat away. Listen to drums with a heartbeat rhythm when practicing yoga.

Gong Away

Taking up little space, gongs are a convenient means for a quick tune up. I purchased a large gong (about the size of a tire) at a house sale a few years ago and gong almost daily. I feel the vibrations like waves of energy trickling up and down my body and especially in my eyes. This is my most vulnerable area as I have a damaged retina from an accident and circulation is poor there.

A friend who had throat cancer was healed by having a shofar blown down his throat. He feels it was the prayers chanted during the healing that did the trick. I feel it was the powerful vibrations that reverberated throughout his throat and into his whole body at a cellular level that rejuvenated him, buttressed by the energy of the healer's beliefs.

Stroke Crystal Bowls

Crystal bowls, also called crystal singing bowls, are made from quartz crystal that was crushed and heated to very high temperatures. When sounded, the clear tones move through the body in vibrant waves into each organ, cell, and atom. This powerful vibration immediately puts the brain into the alpha state, calming, aligning, and healing the body.

Crystal bowls come in varying sizes and resonate specific notes—C, D, E, F, G, A, B—that correspond with human body energy centers (chakras). The vibration of a specific sound works to unlock the blockages in a specific body area.

Though most crystal singing bowls are made from quartz crystal (clear or frosted finish), you can also find crystal bowls made from rose quartz, celestite, amethyst, and citrine that bring their own unique properties to the healing sound of the crystal bowl.

Try Toning

Toning involves vocalizing a pure sound and requires no singing ability. The vibrations massage the vocal cords and spread throughout the whole body, making it hum with life. The mind is also refreshed and clarified by being cleared of its usual distractions. If you can't sing and feel self-conscious, tone in a group for an invigorating sound bath.

Try a Tuning Fork

If you have an area of your body that needs healing, and has not responded to traditional medicine, try a turning fork. The sound waves of tuning forks vibrate and travel deeply into the body along energy pathways, accessing sense of motion, balance, space, memory, and healing. The experience fills you with vitality and aliveness.

THERAPEUTIC LISTENING

Therapeutic Sounds Programs

If you have auditory processing issues, auditory defensiveness and vestibular issues, therapeutic sound programs can help you heal. You listen to specifically programmed compact discs of psycho-acoustically modified classical music through a pair of good headphones to maximize the integration of sound in both ears.

Unexpected sounds on the CD wake up the brain and force you to listen and process the music. As sound vibrates the inner ear, it will create vibration and feed the vestibular system. This stimulation will in turn impact a wide range of abilities, such as reading, communication, learning and memory.

Several programs exist. To choose the best for you, a pediatric OT, speech therapist or audiologist who is trained in therapeutic listening should set up a program to meet particular needs. Each CD is modified for different purposes, such as for self-regulation, body awareness, auditory processing, and cognitive skills. When listening to the CDs, you need to use good headphones like Sennheiser for optimal effect.

If your therapeutic listening program is right, you will experience greater internal harmony. Breathing slows and sleep is more restful. Focus and concentration are better, and coordination and balance improve. Even handwriting is better. You will feel less over-arousal and sensory defensiveness to sound, touch, movement, and so on.

Masking Noise

If sound goes against our natural rhythms, it throws off the body's rhythms and causes discomfort. Unfortunately, this happens all too often in the modern world of noise pollution. You must do what you can to block out disruptive sound. When you want silence, mask noise with headphones, ear protection earmuffs, or with noise reducing earplugs, and close a window.

Many white noise machines exist to help you mask noise in your home and in your office. Sleeping with one at night, or just turning on a fan helps many people nod off into sleep. Start out with the fan or noise making machine at a low volume and increase gradually until you can tolerate the louder sound. You can also try the infant Sleep Sheep.

Sounds to Nod Off To

White noise will help you wind down into sleep. Try also listening to meditative CDs that change your brain waves to an alpha state to slide you into a restful, restorative sleep. Insulate your bedroom against sounds also with carpeting, insulated curtains, or by closing the door. If necessary, use ear plugs.

To unwind before bedtime, listen to relaxing music. Listening to a relaxation or meditation tape will naturally get your brain into the delta state of deep sleep.

Sounds to Wake Up To

No need to wake up to a jarring alarm clock. You can awaken gradually with soothing chimes from a Zen clock, or the sound of nature with a nature clock.

Nature's Symphony

Open your window or take a walk and listen to nature sounds. The varying sounds of the birds chirping, squirrels flying up a tree and wind blowing open up space and alert you. The swishing sound of the ocean's waves or listening to cascading water with an indoor fountain will calm you.

Let's now explore the different activities we can do to use smell to modulate.

Summing Up

Music: Music transports us, purifying and strengthening the energy of any space.

Voices: Chanting, humming, and singing create vibration in the upper body that deepens breathing to increase oxygenation, relaxes the jaw and throat, and releases tension.

- **Vowel Power:** Chanting that emphasizes vowel sounds – EEEEEEE, AAAAAYYYY, OOOOOO (as in go), OOOHHHH (as in goo), AAAHHHH — boosts serotonin and releases endorphins in the brain, inducing a trance like state.
- **Mantra:** Try chanting your own mantra.
- **Power of "Om":** Perhaps the most powerful common chant is repeating "Om."
- **Group Chanting:** Powerful experience.

Sound & Colors: The seven primary colors coordinate with the major chords: red/root; orange/second; yellow/third; green/fourth; blue/fifth; indigo/sixth; violet/seventh.

Rhythms in Our Bones: We not only hear music but feel rhythms in our skin and bones. Ways to experience this are drumming, gonging, crystal bowls, toning and the tuning fork.

Therapeutic Listening

Therapeutic Sounds Programs: For those who have auditory processing issues, auditory defensiveness and vestibular issues, therapeutic sound programs can help you heal. And it's easy.

Masking Noise: Do what you can to block out disruptive sound. When you want silence, mask noise with headphones, ear protection earmuffs noise reducing earplugs or white noise to help you wind down into sleep.

Winding Down to Sleep: Listening to a relaxation or meditation tape will naturally get your brain into the delta state of deep sleep.

Sounds to Wake Up: Try awaking gradually with soothing chimes from a Zen clock, or the sound of nature with a nature clock.

Nature's Symphony: Try listening to nature's sounds for a calming experience.

*

11

Smelling

"The fragrance of white tea is the feeling of existing in the mists that float over waters; the scent of peony is the scent of the absence of negativity: a lack of confusion, doubt, and darkness; to smell a rose is to teach your soul to skip; a nut and a wood together is a walk over fallen Autumn leaves; the touch of jasmine is a night's dream under the nomad's moon."

~ C. JoyBell C.

Do your spirits rise from the scent of jasmine floating through the air? Do you perk up with delight from the scent of coffee brewing?

Smell as we've learned is a direct shot into your limbic system, making it a powerhouse for changing emotions. Use this power for all its worth. Take a moment to breathe in nature's scents, like freshly mowed grass, the gardenias in the backyard, fresh fruit, and exhilarating fresh herbs.

And take full advantage of aromatherapy. Smelling the scent of aromatic plants creates instant enjoyment and vitality. As odors make a beeline from the nasal cavity to the limbic system in the brain, they stir emotions, set mood, lower stress, boost energy, and enhance sensuality. This makes aromatherapy, the science of using essential oils from plant extracts for healing body and mind, one the easiest and quickest ways to profoundly affect anxiety, fear, depression, anger, joy euphoria and all other emotions.

Make inhaling invigorating, uplifting scents an essential dish of your sensory diet. Some aromas will wake up your senses and help energize you, others will calm you and help you rest or sleep. Indulge throughout the day to match your moment to moment needs.

Here are the top essential oils for alleviating anxiety, stress, and depression and for boosting learning, focus, concentration and memory. Yes they really can do all that!

LAVENDER

The "universal oil," lavender is the most popular and versatile of all essential oils. Its lightly sweet and freshly floral scent has been used for thousands of years as a calming and soothing herb, and has proven effective in treating tension, depression, headaches and insomnias.

An excellent anti-depressant, lavender boosts serotonin and dopamine, making it both uplifting and calming. Inhaling lavender is also a great stress buster as it increases the brain's alpha wave activity, relaxing you, and it decreases cortisol, the stress hormone secreted by the adrenal gland, reducing anxiety, stress and headaches. Unlike drugs, it does all this without sedating.

If you suffer PMS, and women with SPD commonly do, consider lavender essential oil in place of the Prozac your medical doctor will likely suggest. Japanese researchers found lavender essential oil to alleviate premenstrual emotional mood changes. The markers were increased heart rate variability, indicating improved moods and reduced stress, and a higher score on the Profile of Mood States compared to the two control groups.

If you have SPD, it's almost certain you have digestive issues as well. Lavender oil helps digestion by stimulating gastric juices and bile to increase the mobility of food within the intestine.

Tips for Use

Place a few drops of lavender essential oil into the palms of your hands, cup over your mouth and breathe deeply. In the morning, diffuse your car with lavender, which will both calm and energize you, setting up body and mind for the day.

Before sleep, rub a few drops of lavender on the bottom of your feet to distribute the oil to every cell in your body in approximately 20 minutes. To add even more pleasure, dab your bed linens and pillow with some lavender essential oil before nodding off. Lavender also helps serotonin to make melatonin, the sleep hormone.

FRANKINCENSE

An ancient herb with origins in Egyptian, Persian, Babylonian, Roman and Christian culture, Frankincense gets the prize as the most valuable essential oil for slowing and deepening breathing, and for helping to allay fear, anxiety, nervous tension and stress. Endlessly versatile, it also relieves depression, enhances memory, clears brain fog, and acts as a psychoactive substance to expand consciousness.

In studies conducted at Vienna and Berlin Universities, researchers found that sesquiterpenes, a natural compound found in essential oils of Frankincense as well as Vetiver, Patchouli, Cedarwood, Myrrh and Sandalwood can increase levels of oxygen in the brain by up to 28 percent. Increasing oxygen in the brain leads to heightened activity in the hypothalamus and limbic systems of the brain, altering not only emotions but learning, hormone balance, and energy levels. This is a great oil for everyday use to help maintain overall cellular balance, and quell stress and anxiety. When in doubt, use Frankincense.

Tips for Use

Diffuse, inhale, or rub 1-2 drops on the bottom of your feet and back of your neck to alleviate jumpiness and uplift your spirit. Mix with lavender in a carrier oil to increase the effect of both.

HOLY BASIL

The "Queen of Herbs," Holy basil, or Tulsi has been revered in India for over five thousand years to focus the mind while relaxing the body.

A rich source of antioxidants that protect cellular health, Holy basil is an amazing stress buster. Scientific research found that ingesting holy basil normalized quantities of epinephrine, norepinephrine and serotonin in the body, the neurotransmitters that the body uses to cope with stress. The herb contains rosmarinic acid and eugenol, along with triterpenoic acids that work together to lower cortisol and reduce the adverse effects of stress. Lower levels of cortisol improve mental clarity and memory, assisting with learning and healthy aging. Holy basil functions also as an adaptogen, enhancing the body's natural response to physical and emotional stress.

Tips for Use

Holy Basil or "tulsi" is ingested as an herbal tea.

ROSEMARY

Do you have rosemary in your garden? If so, you know its invigorating scent and power to create alertness and clarity.

Rosemary lowers cortisol levels, calming the nerves, relaxing the muscles and relieving the physical effects of stress. Over time, rosemary may be able to help maintain low stress levels by producing carnosic acid in the body, a protein vital to cell growth and maintenance of nerve tissue. With regular rosemary use you can handle higher levels of stress in your day-to-day life. Rosemary also boosts blood flow to the brain to help us think more clearly while improving memory.

Tips for Use

If you have rosemary in your garden, indulge in its invigorating, pungent fragrance in food preparation. Diffuse or dilute it in carrier oil and apply to your skin or bath water.

Diffuse rosemary while you work, or while in your car if you need sprucing up.

TAKE HEED: Rosemary essential oil may irritate those with sensitive skin if applied directly. Avoid if you have high blood pressure.

LEMON

Radiant, uplifting, reviving, and stimulating, lemon essential oil boosts serotonin and like lavender does double duty to both relieve anxiety and uplift the spirit. Both lemon and lavender contain linalool, a chemical known to soothe away emotional stress.

Tips for Use

First thing in the morning drink ½ fresh lemon squeezed into pure water to set your pH to more alkaline, the range necessary for optimal health. Add 1 drop of lemon essential oil to a glass of water and drink throughout the day.

Inhale lemon essential oil or place a few drops on a cotton ball to replenish your mind, body, and spirit. Mix with carrier oil if you have sensitive skin and rub on your wrists when you need reviving.

TAKE HEED: *Lemon essential oil may irritate those with sensitive skin if applied directly. Avoid using on skin exposed to direct sunlight or UV rays. Do not use near fire, flame, heat or sparks.*

PEPPERMINT

My friend Stella is a classic hypo-responsive languid who, without a huge pow of sensation can't engage in the world and get her fleshy body to move. She has been depressed her whole life as a result. After dragging around for weeks and feeling too depressed to even open the blinds and let in badly needed light to wake her up, she agreed to try an experiment.

I told her to dab a drop or two of peppermint essential oil on the bottom of her foot when she awoke in the morning and to inhale the scent throughout the day. Suddenly, she was able to get out of bed, open the blinds, take her shower and her Prozac, go to her morning water aerobics class which she hadn't taken in ages, and cheerfully go about the rest of her day. She made the peppermint oil a part of her daily regimen and has stayed chipper and productive without a relapse of the depression. An over-eater with a long-time bout with obesity, she was also delighted to learn that research done by Dr. Alan Hirsch found that peppermint oil makes you feel satiated when you've eaten enough and you eat less. Inhaling it also improves taste and smell.

Peppermint oil is jam packed with oxygen and, as with Stella a whiff sharpens the senses, instantly waking you and getting you going. With a soothing and stimulating effect on the brain, it makes you alert but not hyperactive, boosting thinking, memory, and focus. The Japanese pipe peppermint, pine, and other uplifting scents through the ventilation systems in most work areas to get better productivity from their wonders. It's also good for depression, headaches, and for clearing the sinuses.

Tips for Use

Inhale to improve concentration and alertness. Add to carrier oil and apply on the back of the neck and shoulders to keep energy levels up during the day. Diffuse in an aromatherapy diffuser or on cotton pads placed around the room.

Add a drop of peppermint essential oil to herbal tea to help aid normal digestion. Diffuse or inhale peppermint essential oil mid-morning to curb the desire to snack.

Rub one drop of peppermint essential oil on the temples, forehead, over the sinuses (avoid contact with your eyes), and on the back of the neck to relieve head pressure.

TAKE HEED: *Some may be sensitive to direct application on the skin. Do not apply to a fresh wound or burn.*

PATCHOULI

Patchouli draws me like a magnet, and I grab whatever has its addictive scent, essential oil, lotions, soaps, shampoos, incense.

With its earthy, musky fragrance, Patchouli grounds and stabilizes the mind, making it excellent for those who feel spacey, dreamy and detached from their bodies. If you suffer depersonalization, a common problem for those with severe sensory defensiveness or balance issues, carry some Patchouli essential oil around with you. When you begin to feel as if you are viewing the world from a long telescope, inhale some to help you re-connect.

Stimulating the release of pleasure hormones like serotonin and dopamine, Patchouli's strong, pungent scent also diminishes depression, eases anxiety and helps you recover from nervous exhaustion, stress and stress-related conditions.

Tips for Use

Apply 2-3 drops to the base of the skull and breathe in the aromas to calm and ground you. Dilution is not required, except for the most sensitive skin. Diffuse up to one hour three times daily.

VANILLA

The closest in fragrance and flavor to mothers' milk, the pure scent of warm vanilla makes you feel at home and may stimulate warm, pleasant memories. At once soothing and stimulating, this rich aroma creates tranquil relaxation and mental clarity, and uplifts mood. In a study conducted in 1994 at Manhattan's Sloan-Kettering Hospital, the scent of vanilla helped reduce stress related to claustrophobia 63% during MRI scans. It will help you get a good night's sleep and, if you have a weight issue, reduce cravings for sweets. And it has a longstanding reputation as an aphrodisiac.

Tips for Use

Vanilla essential oil can be safely applied on the skin. Drip a little vanilla oil into some bath salts and take a warm bath to beat the blues. As it is very thick, don't diffuse it in an oil nebulizer. Don't use before bedtime as it can be stimulating.

BERGAMOT

Bergamot essential oil is highly versatile, relaxing, energizing and uplifting us. The presence of alpha pinene and limonene, which improves blood circulation, makes it both an antidepressant and stimulant, while its flavanoids make it able to soothe nerves and reduce nervous tension, anxiety, stress and sleeplessness.

Bergamot's powerful effect on the nervous system comes in large part from its role in stimulating hormonal secretions. These hormones help to maintain proper metabolic rates and to increase the secretion of digestive juices, aiding digestion, proper absorption of nutrients, assimilation and decomposition of sugar and the resultant lowering of blood sugar.

Relaxing us, uplifting us, helping us digest our food better, Bergamot is ideal nourishment for your sensory menu.

Tips for Use

Diffuse or apply to temples, forehead, wrists, feet, and back of neck.

TAKE HEED: *Bergamot is very photosensitive. Do not apply it to skin that will be exposed to direct sunlight or ultraviolet light within 48 hours. Bergamot contains bergaptene, a dominant photosensitizer, and can cause severe reactions.*

GRAPEFRUIT

Grapefruit's very light but tangy citrus scent increases dopamine and norepinephrine levels, refreshing the mind and energizing and motivating you. It's a great way to prepare for a stressful day or as a pick-me-up during a mid-afternoon slump to revive you.

Tips for Use

- Dilute 1 drop with 1 drop of carrier oil and apply to desired area.
- Diffuse up to 1 hour three times daily.

TAKE HEED: *Avoid direct sunlight or UV rays for up to 12 hours after applying product.*

ROSE

The scent of rose is exhilarating. It is used to increase concentration, regulate the appetite and provide relief from both stress and depression.

Tips for Use

As rose essential oil is very costly, it is most commonly sold with carrier oil or mixed with other oils.

JASMINE

The sensual scent of jasmine is a natural anti-depressant, boosting serotonin and your spirits.

Tips for Use

Jasmine can be applied directly on the skin. Apply 2-4 drops to a desired area. Diffuse up to 1 hour three times daily.

GERANIUM

With its strong, floral, intoxicating scent, geranium oil is energizing, uplifting and balancing, relieving stress and depression. Often used to balance female hormones, it is especially helpful for PMS or during menopause.

Tips for Use

Geranium is wonderful alone or blended with other essential oils like lavender, palmarosa, jasmine, rose, neroli, or rosemary. Add a drop or two to a tissue and inhale or apply 2-4 drops to your skin.

I am in love with its strong, rose like scent and I frequently add it to carrier oil like jojoba or almond and wear it as a perfume.

SANDALWOOD

Sandalwood is high in sesquiterpenes that stimulate the pineal gland to release melatonin, the hormone that regulates sleep, making it a wonderful sleep remedy. The deep relaxation it creates has made it used for centuries to enhance meditation.

Tips for Use

Apply 2-4 drops directly to desired area. Diffuse up to 1 hour three times daily.

NEROLI

Extracted from the flower petals of the bitter orange tree, Neroli is one of the more precious and expensive of the essential oils because it takes literally 100 pounds of blossoms to generate just one pound of the oil. If you've ever walked among orange trees with their flowers in bloom, you know how hypnotic the scent is.

Both calming and uplifting, Neroli's fresh, delicate, sweet floral aroma treats both anxiety and depression. Found only in Neroli oil is phenylethyl which has sedative properties to help you relax and has shown some success in calming down hyperactive children.

Tips for Use

Apply 2-3 drops to the base of the skull and breathe in the aromas to calm and ground you. Add to bath salts. Sprinkle a few drops onto a cloth or tissue, or diffuse up to one hour three times daily.

TAKE HEED: *Don't take neroli essential oil internally as it could have toxic effects.*

ESSENTIAL OILS & AUTISM, ADD & AHDH

The use of essential oils may be one of the most effective, non-drug approaches to treating ADD and ADHD and to improve the lives of those with autism.

In a study conducted in 2001 by Dr. Terry Friedman, the effects of lavender, vetiver, and cedarwood essential oils were compared in improving focus and learning in ADD and ADHD kids.

- Vetiver essential oil was found to be the most effective in observations and brain wave scans, showing improvements in 100% of subjects.
- Cedarwood essential oil was 83% effective.
- Lavender essential oil was 60% effective.

Excited about the results of the study, some parents of autistic children began using these oils with astonishing results. Children were calmer, happier, less "cranky," less anxious, better focused, happier, slept better and made more eye contact and social engagement.

SUGGESTION BOX: *Some with autism are particularly sensitive to smell and may resist the use of oils. Applying to the feet, even after they are asleep, can circumvent this problem.*

Here are some of the ways parents have found essential oils to help their autistic child.

- **Peppermint** essential oil helps with concentration.
- **Neroli** essential oil helps quell obsessive behaviors.
- **Roman chamomile** and sandalwood essential oils reduce hypersensitivity and aggression, to prevent tantrums and to ease transitions.
- **Frankincense** oil helps them regain focus and calm.

- **Lavender** oil or other relaxing oils helps the child wind down into sleep and is applied as a foot massage.

HOW TO USE ESSENTIAL OILS

Essential oils are extremely concentrated — one drop of peppermint essential oil is equal to 28 cups of peppermint tea! A little bit goes a long way so only use 2-4 drops for an application.

Only buy 100 percent pure, organic essential oil made from plant materials. The higher quality, the more potent and smaller amounts are required. My bias is *Young Living Essential Oils*, long considered the Rolls Royce of aromatherapy.

In addition to the information for use for each of the above essential oils, here are the many ways to apply the oils.

Dab on skin: A few oils like lavender can be applied directly to the skin but, as they are extremely potent in their pure form most should be blended with carrier oil, like jojoba, sweet almond, or avocado before use. Add touch by getting a massage using your favorite essential oils.

Diffuse them: Add 3-4 drops of an essential oil onto a diffuser to quickly deliver its therapeutic scents throughout the room. The best diffuser disperses the oils without heating them so they retain their therapeutic benefits. An easy diffuser is a clean crumpled tissue, a handkerchief, or a pillow. When going to the dentist, dab some calming essential oil like lavender onto a cotton ball and place it on your chest to lessen your anxiety.

Add to Shower: During your shower, drop 2-3 drops of essential oil on the floor in front of your feet and shower with soap, shampoo and conditioners made with essential oils.

Add to Bath: Fill up a bath and mix 3-5 drops each of essential oil to Epsom salts or dead sea salts before putting into water. Place oiled salts into bath water and soak for 20 minutes. If you just add essential oils to the water they will float on its surface and possibly cause skin irritation.

FYI: Epsom salts and dead sea salts are excellent for those with SPD as they provide magnesium, an essential mineral for the nervous system and one in which most people are low. Another way to get quick transmission of magnesium into your body is with magnesium oil.

Soak in a warm bath with soothing essential oils, like lavender, rose or geranium before retiring to bed. The hot water causes your body temperature to rise about 2°F. In response to a sudden rise in temperature, the pineal gland produces melatonin, which decreases and normalizes body temperature and lulls you to sleep. Lavender oil also produces melatonin.

Add to Steam & Sauna: Throw eucalyptus, tea tree or pine oils onto heat source of a sauna or steam source in a steam bath.

Dab on Feet: Add a small amount to the soles of the feet or to the back of the neck to disperse the oil quickly into the cells of the body.

PRECAUTIONS

Skin: Never use essential oils near sensitive skin, around the eyes, broken skin, or near mucous membranes.

Pregnancy: Though essential oils are not harmful, most practitioners feel it best to not use them while pregnant or nursing.

Children: Do not use essential oils for aromatherapy on anyone under the age of five. Don't use directly on the skin of anyone under the age of twelve.

Sun: Some oils are photosensitive meaning they react to radiant energy or light such as natural sunlight, sunlamps, or other sources of UV rays. An adverse response appears within minutes, hours, or days after first application and exposure. These oils are primarily citrus oils and include angelica, Bergamot, Grapefruit, Lemon, Lime, Orange, Wild Orange, and tangerine. The result is a dark pigmentation or a rash on the skin. Follow the instructions on how to properly use each oil.

Allergies: You will not get an allergic reaction to an essential oil but you may get one to the carrier oil like almond oil.

Defensive Reaction: Some people react defensively to essential oils, even lavender. The explanation appears to lie not in the properties of the essential oil but in inner toxicity. Essential oils vibrate at a much higher frequency than the toxins we harbor within. When you find the scent of something as healing and innocuous as lavender irritating, you are reacting to the toxins stirring up within you.

If you get a skin rash or other allergic-like symptoms such as headaches or nausea, this is also not likely an allergy but a detox reaction. You will know this because while allergic reactions worsen with each exposure to the allergen, detox reactions reduce with each exposure to an essential oil until it disappears completely once the toxins are cleared from the system.

Nevertheless, if you react negatively, it's best to back off from using the oils for a while as the oils are detoxing too rapidly for the colon and kidneys to handle it and so the toxins release through the skin. Instead, increase your water intake and follow a cleansing, detox routine to rid your body of toxins.

A defensive reaction is especially likely if you have ADD/ADHD, Asperger's, or autism. These conditions go hand in hand with gut issues and poor ability to excrete heavy metals due to a poor glutathione system. If you do react negatively, welcome it as a red flag to let you know that you must do some heavy detoxifying. My book *Anxiety: Hidden Causes* contains much information on how to detoxify internally and externally.

Now that we've explored the many different ways to modulate the senses, let's now look at the other piece of the puzzle for modulation: the mind.

Summing Up

LAVENDER: The most versatile of all scents, it treats tension, depression, headaches and insomnias.

FRANKINCENSE: Slows and deepens breathing, and helps allay fear, anxiety, nervous tension and stress.

HOLY BASIL: Focuses the mind while relaxing the body.

ROSEMARY: Lowers cortisol levels, calming the nerves, relaxing the muscles and relieving the physical effects of stress.

LEMON: Boosts serotonin to both relieve anxiety and uplift the spirit.

PATCHOULI: Grounds and stabilizes the mind.

VANILLA: At once soothing and stimulating, this rich aroma creates tranquil relaxation and mental clarity, and uplifts mood.

BERGAMOT: Relaxes, energizes and uplifts us.

GRAPEFRUIT: Increases dopamine and norepinephrine levels, refreshing the mind and energizing and motivating you.

ROSE: Increases concentration, regulates appetite and provides relief from both stress and depression.

JASMINE: Natural anti-depressant.

GERANIUM: Energizes, uplifts and balances, relieving stress and depression. Especially helpful to balance female hormones.

SANDALWOOD: Sandalwood is high in sesquiterpenes that stimulate the pineal gland to release melatonin, the hormone that regulates sleep, making it a wonderful sleep remedy.

NEROLI: Extracted from the flower petals of the bitter orange tree, it has a hypotic scent to calm and balance the nerves.

Essential Oils & Autism, ADD & AHDH: Studies have found the use of essential oils may be one of the most effective, non-drug approaches to treating ADD and ADHD and to improve the lives of those with autism.

HOW TO USE ESSENTIAL OILS

- Dab on skin
- Diffuse them
- Add to Shower
- Add to Bath
- Add to Steam & Sauna
- Dab on Feet

Precautions: There are precautions you need to know about before using essential oils.

*

12

Getting In Sync

"Happiness is not a matter of intensity but of balance, order, rhythm and harmony."

~Thomas Merton

Now that you know what sensations are most calming and what are most alerting, your next task is to figure out how much, how often, how long for, and what qualities you need of individual sensation for your unique sensory diet.

Once you do and you implement your sensory diet, you should notice dramatic changes and feel more in control of body and mind. In time, this will translate into feeling more upbeat and energetic, focused and productive, loving and joyful. Your moment-to-moment existence will be one less of distress and discomfort, and more one of "enthusiastic serenity."

Different Strokes for Different Folks

If you have a modulated nervous system, you self-regulate by "self-stimming" automatically and relatively effortlessly to maintain a calm, alert, and focused state.

If you have sensory modulation problems, you will need considerably more or considerably less intensity, frequency, and duration of sensation to achieve balance, and need to work harder to get to and stay in the comfort zone: when hyped, you might have to go to an extreme to quiet and focus; when bored, you might have to go to extreme to get enough sensation to engage in the world and to focus on the task at hand.

To feel most calm and relaxed, focused and energetic, stable and upbeat, seekers tend to need more alerting sensation and avoiders more calming sensation.

ALERTING SENSATION	CALMING SENSATION
Cold	Hot
Fast	Slow
Spicy	More bland
Loud	Quiet
Irregular rhythm	Regular rhythm
Jarring, rough	Subdued, soft
Intense, complex	Simple
Novel & surprising	Predictable, familiar

What's Right for You?

We know that people can both seek and avoid sensation. So how do you know what is correct for your nervous system? It's simple. If sensations are right for you, they feel safe, interesting, and not too much or too little. If sensations are wrong for you, they feel dangerous, uninteresting, and too much or too little.

Respect your intuition and be careful about following generic advice. Folks who don't know about sensory processing, and that's most people, take a one-size-fit-all approach for all nervous systems.

For instance, many will advise a generic exercise program for all such as the popular intermittent exercise. This involves briefly engaging muscles very intensely, resting briefly and repeating this pattern for a specific time.

If you are easily hyper-aroused, this may not work for you as brief fast, intense movement may be too exciting and further stress you. This is also the case with fast moving sports, such as basketball, hockey, soccer, and racquetball. Moreover, competitive, confrontational sports may exhaust your nervous energy and further tense you. Exercises that provide calm and focus, like yoga, swimming, or dance, may be more beneficial.

If, however, you jump from low to high arousal, fast moving sports may better thrust your system into an optimal zone.

Activity Dynamics

For modulation, you need to know not only the correct *kind* of sensations but also *when* to do them, *how much* to do them, for *how long* and so forth.

For instance, you may know that your system requires intense exercise but if you only work out in the morning, or in the evening, you will not keep your system regulated all day. Likewise, if you need a 20-minute run around the block but only sprint for five minutes, you will not achieve the balance you need for optimal alertness.

In setting up your sensory diet, pay attention to:

- Intensity
- Frequency
- Duration
- Rhythm
- Timing
- Sameness/Novelty
- Enjoyment

Intensity (how much)

Activity Intensity. Power comes from the intensity of the individual activity. How much of a wallop the nervous system receives determines intensity: riding in a speed boat is more vigorous than rowing in a canoe. Getting deep into the tactile receptors, the Wilbarger therapressure protocol is more powerful than a loufah brush massage. Likewise, jumping on a trampoline provides more intense vestibular sensation than rocking in a rocking chair, while diffusing jasmine essential oil has more smell input than smelling a jasmine flower.

Sensory Involvement. The intensity of your sensory experience varies by how many senses are involved: the more senses the greater the impact on your nervous system. You will perk up quicker during mid-afternoon downtime if you infuse rosemary essential oil, play rhythm and blues, brush your skin with a loufah brush, and move gently back and forth on your exercise ball as you sit at your computer than if you just infuse rosemary oil. Likewise, you will chill out more quickly at night if you do the Wilbarger therapressure protocol, dab some geranium essential oil on your wrists, and lie in your hammock watching the sunset with serene Tibetan bells playing in the background than if you only do one of the sensory activities.

For the most intensity, engage in sports that offer the widest and strongest sensory input. Horseback riding, for instance, taps into vestibular, proprioceptive and deep pressure touch, odor, vision, and hearing, as does surfing, mountain and water skiing, mountain biking, and deep sea diving.

Intensity & Learning. Using multiple senses peaks interest and attention to learning, making it easier for the brain to match new information to existing knowledge. The more senses involved during learning, the more likely the brain will receive and process information. For instance, thinking skills develop better when intertwined with music and movement as music develops spatial reasoning, skills that can be transferred to mathematical understanding.

Multisensory Power Activities

	Balance	Push/Pull	Touch	See	Hear	Smell
Trampoline	✓	✓	Crashing whole body			
Horseback Riding	✓	✓	Pressure lower body	Nature	Nature	Nature
Skate-boarding/	✓	✓		Nature	Nature	Nature
Surfing	✓	✓	Water, Wind	Nature	Nature	Nature
Deep Sea Diving	✓		Pressure Whole body	Nature	✓	
Skiing /mountain	✓	✓	Wind	Nature	Swish/ Wind	Nature
Skiing /water	✓	✓	Wind	Nature	Water/ Wind	Water
Mountain Biking	✓	✓	Pressure lower body	Nature	Nature	Nature
Mountain Climbing	✓	✓		Nature	Nature	Nature
Power Yoga	✓	✓	Partner yoga		Music	

How Much Intensity Do You Need?

Individual Arousability. You need to learn what intensity you need for modulation.

If you are a sensation seeker, you will need a pow of sensation to charge your system enough for the world to register and wake up your brain. For instance, first thing in the morning you may need to smell peppermint oil, blast rock music, and take a cold, pounding shower.

If you are a sensation avoider, you will need less sensation for the impact to register, and a bit of light into your eyes will do the trick.

Age. How much intensity you need varies by age.

To maintain optimal arousal, the young child needs considerable sensorimotor input and may need to be rocked strongly (intensity), for a half-hour (duration), several times a day (frequency).

As we mature, we require less input for organization, and unconsciously moving around in our seat or stretching may do the trick.

At the same time, the more disorganized the nervous system, at either the high or low end, the more sensory nutrition needed to feed and regulate it. For some, that might mean as much input as for the young child—daily, on-going, frequent, and vigorous exercise.

Frequency (how often)

To maintain optimal arousal and organization, sensorimotor activities should happen at specific intervals and throughout the day. This is necessary as the nervous system continually changes throughout the day according to circadian rhythms, temperature and arousal, annoying sensation, daily hassles, hurt feelings, conflict and other stresses. These stressors constantly destabilize the nervous system, and it needs to be rejuvenated. At the end of the chapter, you will fill in a daily chart to use for your sensory diet (this can be downloaded off my website, www.sharonheller.net as can all the charts presented in this book).

Duration (how long)

Activities vary in time spent doing them and in length of effect. Choose activities with long-lasting effects. For instance, specific treatment interventions, like the Wilbarger therapressure protocol is short but effective for 1 to 2 hours. Likewise, twenty minutes of swinging or bouncing on a rebounder could keep you together for up to eight hours. Others, like fidgeting in your seat or chomping on chips act as brief mood changers.

You also need to know for how long you need to do a particular activity. Some people get organized with five minutes on the trampoline, while others need a half hour of jumping and bouncing.

Rhythm

In general, familiar, slow, and even repetitive activities boost serotonin levels in the brain and lower arousal level, while novel or fast and uneven non-rhythmic activities boost dopamine and perk you up.

Avoider

If you are an avoider and need much calming, opt for slow, rhythmic new age music and a walk through the park. Even taking a break from the computer to wash dishes or fold towels will calm you.

Seeker

If you are a seeker, repetition can be overly sedating and you might have to play some salsa music while washing the dishes or walking through the park, lest your arousal dip too low.

Timing

Our body's rhythms change throughout the day. As arousal is lowest first thing in the morning, you should start the day with intense heavy work, like fifteen minutes on the rebounder, and some tactile stimulation, like the Wilbarger therapressure protocol as strenuous physical activity along with tactile input will feed your system for two to eight hours.

To prevent tension from escalating, incorporate frequent quick heavy work throughout the day, like standing up to stretch, pushing against the wall, bending forward to touch your toes and so forth.

Try to do this for twenty-one days or three weeks straight as this is the amount of time proposed for a habit to form. If you have a family to care for, you can make activities like play wrestling or jumping on a trampoline in the morning a family affair.

To slough off excess stress chemicals ideally repeat heavy work or some movement at noon, in the late afternoon or early evening, or anytime stress escalates. If your schedule does not permit a workout during the day, early morning vestibular input like swinging, that can last 6-8 hours, will sustain you. As tension rises during down times, employ little pick-ups.

Particular sensations also work better at different times. For instance, moving up and down, which provides powerful vestibular input, is alerting and we would not want to do this when winding down to sleep.

Biorhythms

Schedule your activities at the right time of day for you. High arousal introverts are early birds and are alert in the morning but reach their edge early and start to wind down by evening. In the morning, rock music on the car radio may increase alertness. At the end of a long day, the same boom, boom is cacophonous.

Low arousal extroverts, in contrast, are owls and tend to be drowsy in the morning and increasingly alert as the day goes on. To become alert in the morning, you need intensity like loud music, cold water splashed on the face, jumping jacks, and caffeine.

Knowing your style will allow you to vary the intensity, frequency, duration, and rhythm of sensorimotor input throughout the day. At one point, you may need to run around the block to get organized, at another munch on a carrot.

Sameness vs. Novelty

Pay attention to sameness or novelty. Generally, we want novelty when bored and sameness when overwhelmed to cut down on confusion. Repetition seems to calm, for instance rocking or chanting in religious ceremonies, while novelty seems to perk us up.

Sensation seekers, who get quickly bored, seek novelty more often than sensation avoiders who tend to want more sameness and repetition. Everyone is different!

Enjoyment

Choose activities you enjoy. If you dislike Zumba, don't force yourself to gyrate through a class because it's the latest craze. Know your body and respect its reaction or you won't exercise.

If you'd rather poke needles in your eyes than do any exercise, o figure out how to transcend this as you must move your body for a happy, productive life. Here are some things to get motivated.

Buddy Up: Find an exercise buddy and motivate each other.

Reward Yourself: Set up an exercise plan with a reward system. For instance, if you walk for 30 minutes daily every morning for one week, you will pamper yourself with a manicure; every day for 2 weeks, you will in indulge in a manicure and pedicure; every day for 3 weeks, the time it takes to change a habit, you will indulge in a manicure, pedicure and facial.

Imagine: Visualize the body you want. In chapter fourteen, I have some visualizations for you to follow.

Self-Talk: Tell yourself that exercise will become enjoyable once you develop muscles and retrain your balance system.

Identifying Your Organizing Strategies

To figure out what gets you going, what slows you down and what sends you over the edge, you need to know what strategies comfort and alert you and what strategies bother and disorganize you. The sensory preferences on the following chart will help.

MODULATING SENSATION

	Calming Sensation	Alerting Sensation
Mouth – Food *Texture*	Crunchy, biting	• Smooth, creamy, • Sucking
Mouth – Food *Taste*	•Sour, bitter, salty, spicy •Coffee •Spicy herbal tea	• Sweet foods • Bland foods • Herbal tea (chamomile, lavender)
Mouth – Food *Temperature*	•Cool/cold drinks •Cool/cold food	• Warm drinks • Warm foods
Mouth *Heavy Work*	•Crunching •Biting •Sucking smoothies- w/straw •Water bottle w/straw – (lemon; ice)	• Chewing gum • Chewing foods • *Sucking
Touch *Pressure*	•Light or jerky touch •Bug bite •Staccato touch •Stroking with feather •Rubber band wrist snapping •Tickling	• Rhythmic pressure • Massage • Bear Hug • Wilbarger protocol • Holding/petting a pet • Wrapped in heavy blanket • Body Rolling
Touch *Temperature*	•Cool ambient temp •Cold/cool shower •Holding/rubbing ice on hands, face •Wrapped in cool bed sheets •Cold wraps	• Hot shower/bath • Fireplace • Warm towels • Warm wraps
Touch *Texture*	•Rough, prickly materials/fabrics •Dry w/textured towel, fast movements •Clothing with rough textures •	• Smooth/soft materials/fabrics • Soft terry towel • Clothing w/soft textures, natural cotton
Touch *Vibration*	Vibration mat	

	Calming Sensation	Alerting Sensation
Move *Movement*	• Fast or jerky • Hip/hop movement	Smooth, rhythmic movements
Move *Joints* */Muscles*	• Aerobic exercise • Power walks	• Isometric exercises • Yoga
Move *Heavy Work* *Body*	• Bumpy car ride • Exercise bands • Weighted vest during work out	• Rocking in rocking chair • Swinging on swing
Move *Balance* *System*	• Merry-go-round • Spinning on swing • Roller coaster • Fast movement • Jerky movement • Rotary (spinning movement) • Sit on exercise ball	• Rocking in rocking chair • Swinging on swing • Slow rhythmic motions • Rocking on glider • Linear movement
See *Lights*	• Bright lights • Flashing lights • Neon lights • Lightning	• Soft, low lighting • Lite-cutting visors • Hats • Sunglasses
See *Colors*	• Bright colors • Colorful, busy patterns	Cool colors – violet, purples, blues, greens, aqua
See *Scenes*	• Colorful, busy patterns • Mobiles	• Aquariums • Lava lamp • Sunset, sunrise
Hear	Loud, arrhythmic, fast, continually changing sounds;	Soft, rhythmic, slow, ambient
Music	• Fast paced, upbeat • Irregular rhythms (jazz) • Low heavy bass • Plays drums	• Slow, rhythmic • Humming • Singing quietly • Crystals
Sounds	• Alerting sounds of nature (birds; crickets; heavy rain; thunder) • Strident voice • Loud voice	• Slow, rhythmic music • Humming • Singing quietly • Crystals • Quiet voice • Modulated voice • Wear headphones, white noise

	Calming Sensation	Alerting Sensation
Smell	• Heavy perfumes • Chemicals – bleach • Sharp smells – kitchen spices… • Rosemary, cloves, lemon, peppermint, cinnamon, patchouli, Frankincense	Lavender, geranium, jasmine, neroli, rose, vanilla

*Starred activities both calm and alert to optimally organize the nervous system.

SENSORY QUALITY EVALUATION

Using the above chart as a guideline, fill in the following self-evaluation. Again, you can download all charts, lists, self-tests and evaluations from my website and fill it in to guide you (**www.sharonheller.net**). OTR Angie Voss on her website, www.asensorylife.com also has a helpful self-test on what you can use to self-regulate.

SENSES

Touch

Organizing: _____

Disorganizing: _____

Temperature

Organizing: _____

Disorganizing: _____

Movement

Organizing: _____

Disorganizing: _____

Sounds

Organizing: _____

Disorganizing: _____

My favorite music is:_____

Lighting

Organizing: _____

Disorganizing: _____

Colors

Organizing: _____

Disorganizing: _____

My favorite colors are: _____

Smells

Organizing: _____

Disorganizing: _____

My favorite scents are: _____

ENVIRONMENT

Organizing: _____

Disorganizing: _____

Environment needed to wake up (alarm, soft music, chit chat, sunlight, dark):

_____

Environment needed to fall asleep ((dark, quiet, soft music, or low steady hum):

_____

REJUVENATION ROOM: When the world becomes too much, it's crucial to have a hideaway to retreat to and regroup. It can be a corner of a closet, a nook in the bedroom hidden by a beautiful screen, or an area up in the attic. Here are some thoughts in choosing a space.

- *It should be small enough to allow you to feel contained and safe, softly colored and textured to encourage relaxation, and quiet.*
- *You should be able to darken the space for meditation or light therapy.*
- *It should include something that moves, rock or sways such as a rocking chair, hanging hammock or movement cushion.*
- *It should not have anything that will do you harm—toxic materials, stressful lighting, and unnerving noise, like a ticking clock.*

PEOPLE

Organizing: _____

Disorganizing: _____

FOOD

Organizing: _____

Disorganizing: _____

My favorite foods are: _____

I prefer foods that are,

_____Crunchy

_____Chewy

_____Cold

_____Hot

_____Mushy

_____Spicy

_____Bland

DAILY ROUTINE

Morning Activities

Organizing: _____

Disorganizing: _____

Afternoon Activities

Organizing: _____

Disorganizing: _____

Evening Activities

Organizing: _____

Disorganizing: _____

Sleep Activities

Organizing: _____

Disorganizing: _____

Part of day you feel most

Organizing: _____

Disorganizing: _____

I tend to be:

_____An owl and gain alertness as the day goes on

_____A lark and feel most alert in the morning

GETTING IT TOGETHER

You are now ready to set up a detailed sensory diet.

SENSORY DIET

To wake up in the morning, I need to

Move _____

Mouth _____

Touch _____

Look _____

Listen _____

Smell _____

To perk up during down times, especially midday, I need to:

Move _____

Mouth _____

Touch _____

Look _____

Listen _____

Smell _____

To concentrate, I need to:

Move _____

Mouth _____

Touch _____

Look _____

Listen _____

Smell _____

When I'm frustrated or upset, I need to:

Move _____

Mouth _____

Touch _____

Look _____

Listen _____

Smell _____

To calm, I need to:

Move _____

Mouth _____

Touch _____

Look _____

Listen _____

Smell _____

To go to sleep, I need to:

Move _____

Mouth _____

Touch _____

Look _____

Listen _____

Smell _____

You are now ready to fill in your daily sensory diet. This will vary according to day, so you may want to download more than one copy from my website, www.sharonheller.net. Be sure and read over chapters five through eleven carefully to help you fill this in. There's a ton of information in these chapters to help every nervous system. Take full advantage!

DAILY SENSORY DIET

	Wake Up	Mid-a.m.	Noon	Mid-day	Wind down	Go to sleep
Move						
Mouth						
Touch						
Look						
Listen						
Smell						

Summing Up

Different Strokes for Different Folks: If you have sensory modulation problems, you will need considerably more or considerably less intensity, frequency, and duration of sensation to achieve balance and therefore you will need to work harder to get to and stay in the comfort zone.

What's Right for You?: If sensations are right for you, they feel safe, interesting, and not too much or too little. If sensations are wrong for you, they feel dangerous, uninteresting, and too much or too little.

Activity Dynamics: For modulation, you need to know not only the correct *kind* of sensations but also *when* to do them, *how much* to do them, for *how long* and so forth.

In setting up your sensory diet, pay attention to:

- Intensity (how much)
- Frequency (how often)
- Duration (how long for)
- Rhythm
- Timing
- Sameness/Novelty
- Enjoyment

Identifying Your Organizing Strategies: To figure out what gets you going, what slows you down and what sends you over the edge, you need to know what strategies comfort and alert you and what strategies bother and disorganize you.

13

*

Setting Up Environments

"Experience of self is profoundly connected with the existence of life in buildings and in our surroundings."

~ Christopher Alexander, *Luminous Ground*

Now that you you've set up your sensory diet, you might be wondering how to modify it in specific environments, like when you are driving in your car, at work, or travelling. This is especially important for the sensory defensive.

Here are many helpful ways.

WORK ENVIRONMENT

Many people who are hypersensitive find it impossible to work outside their homes. If you must, here are some suggestions.

Auditory: Wear earplugs with music to drown out the background noise and to organize your brain. Choose music that will alert you when you are drowsy, and calm you when overstimulated.

Visual: Get a divider for your desk or computer so you can't see anything from the side. Put a lava lamp in your cubicle for you to stare at when you need to get organized. Place small paintings in your cubicle to stare at and raise serotonin.

Tactile: Sit with a weighted lap cushion to feel more grounded (see southpawenterprises.com). Have fiddle objects with you to play with. Retreat to the bathroom to do the Wilbarger therapressure protocol. Keep your bare foot on an Earthing mat under your desk to keep you settled and grounded (Earthing.com).

Pressure: Try wearing a weighted vest or a bear hug for grounding.

Scent: Keep vials of essential oils like rosemary and lemon to perk up and organize you, or lemon or geranium to relax you. Put a low light plant on your desk to help refresh the air.

Oral/motor: If you need alerting, drink cold drinks of peppermint tea or lemon water through a straw. Chew gum or suck on a lemon or lime. If you need calming, drink some warm chamomile tea.

Vestibular: Sit at your desk on an exercise ball or get an exercise chair. This will keep you moving all day long, greatly help organize you and give you the vestibular input you need. Take a break and go into the bathroom and do a forward bend.

Proprioceptive: Do an arm balance in your chair.

DRIVING IN THE CAR

Driving in your car can be an amazing opportunity for your sensory diet.

Auditory: Listen to the music that you need at that time to either perk you up or calm you down and sing along with it. Turn off the music and chant, or listen to the sound of raindrops or falling snow. Open the window and listen to nature's sounds, especially if you are driving along the ocean.

Scent: Infuse essential oil with a device that you plug into your cigarette lighter. Choose the oil you need to either perk you up or calm you down. If you're lucky to be driving through an orange, cherry or apple grove in bloom, open up your window and inhale deeply.

Tactile: Use a vibrating mat behind your back that plugs into the cigarette lighter. Massage parts of your body with wooden rollers. Open up your window to feel the warmth of the sun on your body or the refreshing cold of lightly falling snow. Stick your arm out the window and let the grounding surge of the wind against your skin perk you up for amazing body awareness. If you are drowsy, rub something with rough texture against your skin to perk you up.

Pressure: Put weight on your lap.

Oral/motor: Drink cold drinks of peppermint tea or lemon water through a straw to alert you and especially if you are driving while drowsy. Also, chew gum or suck on a lemon or lime. Drink warm chamomile tea to calm you.

Proprioceptive: Push into the steering wheel at a light.

Vestibular: Driving in your car naturally gives you vestibular input and especially on a bumpy road or going up or down hills.

TRAVELING: THE HOTEL SENSORY NIGHTMARE

If you are fussy about your sensory world, travelling can be an unmitigating nightmare. Here are some things to help you tolerate the experience.

Auditory: Listen to meditative music in ear plugs while winding down to sleep. Take your Zen clock with you so you don't have to wake up to a screaming phone.

Scent: Carry a small diffuser with you and diffuse the room with lavender to help you sleep, to clean the air of the all too common musty odor, and to provide white noise. Take a warm bath with some essential oils.

Tactile: Bring your own pillow and sheets, at least the top sheet and your own towel. Massage parts of your body with a wooden roller before going to sleep. Do the Wilbarger therapressure protocol. Sleep with an eye mask. Bring your own soaps and shampoo with you.

Pressure: Do body rolling before going to sleep. For added weight, sleep with the bedspread on top of your comforter.

Oral/motor: Bring filtered water with you so you don't have to drink the water provided by the hotel or motel.

Proprioceptive: Do progressive relaxation before going to sleep.

Visual: Place a nightlight in the bathroom to help you navigate in a strange environment if you wake during sleep.

Now that we've explored the many different ways to modulate the senses, let's now look at the other piece of the puzzle for modulation: the mind.

Summing Up

WORK ENVIRONMENT: Many people who are hypersensitive find it impossible to work outside their homes. Modifying lighting, sitting on an exercise ball, wearing earplugs or headphones, putting weights on your lap and using essential oils are some of the ways around this.

DRIVING IN THE CAR: Driving in your car can be an amazing opportunity for your sensory diet. Listening to music, diffusing essential oil, using a vibrating mat, putting weight on your lap and drinking drinks to modify your alertness are some of the things you can do.

TRAVELING: THE HOTEL SENSORY NIGHTMARE: Travelling can be a nightmare. Many things can help you tolerate the experience including bringing your own sheet, pillow, towel, and soap, listening to calming music, and putting lavender on the bottom of your feet to help you go to sleep.

Part Three

Balancing Mind

14

Change Your Brain, Change Your Life

Watch your thoughts, for they become words.
Watch your words, for they become action.
Watch your actions, for they become habits.
Watch your habits, for they become character.
Watch your character, for it becomes your destiny.

~Anonymous

Andy's sensory defensiveness resulted from head trauma. I encouraged him to get cranial work to correct his skull misalignment to feel more balanced, physically and emotionally. "I'll never do it," he said. "It's over an hour drive. I don't have the time."

Marisol is a classic languid with low muscle tone, lethargy, and depression. I encouraged her to do daily exercise to build muscle so she will feel more grounded and connected to her body. Her energy and motivation would increase, and her mood would improve. "I hate exercise," she said, "I know I'll never do it."

Don't these people want to get their sensory issues under control? Don't they want their lives to be easier and more joyful? Of course they do. But they're stuck. Reasons abound, from time constraints to financial constraints, from fear of failure to fear of succeeding and people will expect more than they can deliver. These are thoughts in their minds.

The primary cause of the inertia though lies in their bodies. There life is lived largely in the survival mode, and they do what they must to get through the next minute. Who cares about tomorrow?

Get Me Out of Here Now!

If your brain shouts "danger" from sensory overload, calming your nervous system takes priority. You might leave the mayhem of the party early even though there were interesting people you wished to talk to. Or you might retreat to a quiet corner and wolf down a handful of chocolate chip cookies because carbs boost serotonin and calm the nervous system. Who cares that processed sugar will quickly drive up your sugar level and soon put you in worse shape? You need that sugar now!

Conversely, you will feel jumpy if you need *more* sensation. At the party, you rudely turn away from your elderly uncle, who is boring you with useless advice, and grab a cigarette and a coke as fast as your legs can take you. Never mind that your father will be on your case. That's tomorrow.

Revise Your Inner Script

How do you step aside from your sensory issues and take control of your behavior? You train yourself to take control of your thoughts. In this way, the thinking brain can learn to over-ride the survival brain.

But there's a glitch. To do so *you must believe that your actions will make a difference.* If your life has been a school of hard knocks no matter how hard you tried to succeed, this is difficult. Years of experiencing frequent failure, constant disappointments, intense frustration, lack of understanding and validity, and poor self-esteem created *learned helplessness,* and you feel that what you do doesn't get you what you want. Why try and feel devastated?

For instance, say you are at a loss for words when trying to ask out a girl because you worry that she won't be interested in anyone as nerdy as you are—you, with your flabby torso, slouched posture, and thick glasses. To add fuel to the fire, you've been frequently rejected. After repeated failures, you stop trying because the rejection is too painful. Learned helplessness has crippled your ability to take charge of your life and you are doomed to loneliness and despair.

Scientists have documented brain changes during learned helplessness: decreases in norepinephrine, serotonin and dopamine; less GABA, a neurochemical that dampens excitement to lower anxiety; increased activation in the amygdala in the limbic system.

To get rid of the naysaying that cripples you from taking action, you must change the narrative that streams constantly through your head and learn to light a candle rather than curse the darkness. This will allow you to make a different choice and take action that is intentional and aligned with your purpose, your values, and your goals. Maybe some outgoing girl will feel attracted to you because she likes to dominate the conversation and you'll live happily ever after. Of course, if you decide it will never happen, you won't talk to her *at all*.

You Are in Charge

You must believe you are the captain of your own ship. If you believe outside forces rule your behavior, like doctors, priests, parents, children, god, you won't take action to change.

Take Maddy, a senior languid woman suffers depression and many health problems in large part because of her unhealthy lifestyle. Though she has significant health problems, she continues to eat the processed, refined food that, high in calories and low in nutrition makes her sick, fat, spacey, and depressed. She knows that she should be eating whole plant based organic food but chooses to continue her self-destructive eating patterns because, "My fate is pre-ordained by God. Nothing I do will change that."

Her belief that a higher force, not her own actions determine her fate results in large part from having grown up with SPD. Clumsy, not knowing right from left, unable to cross the midline, having poor binocularity and poor body awareness, she felt inept and unable to do the simplest things that most did without thinking, like tying your shoe, riding a bike, or hitting a ball. This left her stuck in a what-I-do, doesn't-accomplish-my-goal mindset. The obvious solution was to relinquish her power to a benevolent higher force that would take care of her needs.

Will Changing My Thoughts Eliminate Sensory Problems?

Changing your thinking is not going to eliminate sensory issues. Sensory issues are neurological, not cognitive. Smiling and saying, "I'm happy!" when inside everything is jumping, thumping, burning, and screaming "Get me out of this body!" will have little immediate effect. It takes a bit for the message to get to the prefrontal cortex where you can analyze it and tell yourself, "calm down."

Nor will positive thinking change being unable to walk across a room without tripping over a chair because you have sensorimotor issues; or being unable to make sense out of what your boss is rambling on about because you have auditory issues; or feeling too lethargic to get out of bed in the morning because you have sensory modulation issues; or being forever late for an appointment as it takes forever to find your shoes, your glasses, and your keys because you have sensory discrimination issues.

What changing your thinking will do is to change how you *respond* to your sensory issues and empower you to take action. Thinking positively will turn things around and free you from the shackles of learned helplessness that keep you stuck and afraid to move on, literally. When you are bouncing off the walls and hit a brick wall, change direction.

By convincing yourself that you *can* make your life better, you will do what it takes to stabilize your nervous system so you can think more clearly, feel more upbeat, and have more energy. You will implement a sensory diet, eat whole, plant-based food as nature intended, clean out the toxins in your body and in your environment, and employ interventions to straighten out your posture. You will meditate, breathe deeply, and do some yoga, tai chi or qi gong. You will evolve! In so doing, you will dethrone SPD as the CEO of your body and brain and replace it with your true essence. It may never go away. But it no longer has to define and rule you.

Rewiring Your Brain

When thinking the bottle is half full rather than half empty becomes a habit, you will change the neural circuitry in your brain to become more engaged and creative, motivated and energetic, resilient and productive. That in turn will change your behavior out of the learned helplessness mode, and motivate you to continue on an upward path because your own volition can effect change. This isn't just New Age pep talk. This discovery has been repeatedly borne out by rigorous research in psychology and neuroscience.

Neuroscience has a saying: *neurons that fire together, wire together.* This means that the more you think and rethink about certain experiences, the stronger the memory and the more easily activated the related feelings become. If those thoughts are negative and resign you to suffering, this negative belief will remain in the loop.

Let's say a young girl tells her mother that she doesn't want to go to the birthday party because the pop of the balloons hurt her ears and startle her. Her mother says, "Stop being such a scaredy cat. I bet none of the other little girls are afraid of balloons. You're going and that's it." She goes to the party and the popping balloons become further etched in her memory of parties-as-unsettling. Anticipatory anxiety sets in as the amygdala cannot distinguish between the threat coming from sensory input and the imagination. Worry gets added to actual sensory overload and for the rest of her life she cringes even at the thought of going to a party.

Even more important, the emotional pain of not being understood may become linked with any number of thoughts or beliefs: "No one understands." "I don't know how to protect myself." "No one cares." "It's dangerous to expect love and understanding." "I hate her."

The more the child gets this response from her mother—or even *imagines* getting this response—the more the need for the mother's understanding and interest. This need becomes paired with the belief that she will be refused, and accompanying feelings of fear, hurt, or anger. Years later, she may hesitate to even try to explain how she feels, expecting rejection or even ridicule. Or, if she does explain, and the other person so much as pauses or looks distracted, the old feelings instantly take over and she becomes enraged, or withdraws inward, blocking her feelings altogether.

Positivity to the Rescue

To change this pattern, she needs to create a different feedback loop in her brain by feeding it positive thoughts. For instance, instead of thinking all parties equal noise she tells herself that parties mean meeting potentially interesting people. Going to the party is no longer seen as a problem but as an opportunity. As a result, she will take action to increase the likelihood that she will go to parties. She will get a good night's sleep the night before. She will feed her nervous system first before going to the party to reduce the intensity of her sensitivity. She will not eat the junk food that she knows will further destabilize her.

She will take with her a bag of tricks if she starts to feel overwhelmed: she will take her magic brush and retreat to the bathroom to do the Wilbarger protocol; she will move to the quietest area to converse; she will stay only as long as she feels comfortable, and not allow herself to go into overload.

Over time, she will reprogram her brain to equate parties more with pleasure than with discomfort. As sensory issues are exaggerated by stress, this mindset will in turn reduce their intensity and further motivate her to take action to alleviate her distress.

Of course, if you can't control something, you accept it and work around it. If the party is for young people and a band will be playing music with a pounding bass, you go early and leave when the traumatic din starts, or you don't go at all. Know your limits and respect them.

Encouraging Neurogenesis

Changing the neurocircuits of your brain can be done in many ways, including cognitive behavioral therapy, affirmations, NLP, and mind/body techniques like meditation, visualization, neurofeedback and the SCIO machine. Let's explore these techniques.

Think Empowering Thoughts

"A man is but the product of his thoughts. What he thinks, he becomes."

~Mohandas Gandhi

The first step in taking better control of your brain, and subsequently your life is to not allow negative beliefs to hijack your mind. Once they do, negative thinking will create turbulent emotions that will keep you in a negative feedback loop. To do this you must catch the negative thought as it happens and replace it with a life affirming thought. For instance, if you catch yourself saying, "I can't learn to play tennis, I'm a clutz." replace it with, "Tennis is not my sport. I enjoy swimming."

Granted, changing your mental chatter isn't easy because the same self-demeaning script has likely run through your head your whole life. You know it. "I'm dumb." "I'm clumsy." "I'm weird." "I annoy people." On and on. But if you deliberately change this script by focusing on your good points, by convincing yourself that things can get better and by showing self-compassion when you fail, your brain will create new neural circuitry and rewire and reshape. You will now approach life with more confidence and hope. This in turn will give you the motivation to take the steps needed to change your nervous system.

From this day on, vow to banish negative thoughts by replacing them with a positive one. Wear a rubber band on your wrist and when your inner critic starts to nag, flick the rubber band, and change your thought to a positive one. When you do, your body automatically lets go. Follow this up with something physical, even if it's just briefly bending forward to touch your toes or stretching to the side.

Try This Exercise on Thoughts & the Body

To gain insight into how thoughts affect the body, draw a line down the center of a piece of paper. Write on the left side all the things that are not so great in your life. Write on the right side all the things that you're happy about.

Cover up the right side. How does looking at all the bad things in your life make you feel? Tense and lousy.

Now cover the left side. How does focusing your attention just on the positives in your life make you feel? Quite different no doubt. Doesn't it make sense to put your energy into the positive forces in your life than to focus on all those life sapping negatives?

Say Affirmations

Affirmations help build powerful mental images in the conscious mind that lessen the power of unconscious memories, experiences, habits and thoughts that unknowingly dictate your behavior.

Start each morning with this affirmation in front of a mirror out loud:

"I accept myself unconditionally right now," suggests Dr. Christianne Northrup, the world's leading authority in the field of women's health and wellness. If it helps, try placing your hand over your heart, as though it were the heart of a precious child. This will help you learn to perceive yourself as worthy of self-love.

This might seem silly to you. It did to me until I read *The Message from Water*, by Masaru Emoto, a creative and visionary Japanese researcher. Emoto discovered that crystals formed in frozen water change depending on what thoughts you direct toward them. Clear water and water exposed to loving words show brilliant, complex, and colorful snowflake patterns, while polluted water, or water exposed to negative thoughts, form incomplete, asymmetrical patterns with dull colors.

Here are some affirmations to choose from although it's best to devise your own:

- *I am master of my fate, not my SPD.*
- *My clumsiness does not define me.*
- *I won't let SPD rule my life.*
- *I can calm my body when I need to.*
- *I love my body and will do whatever is necessary to nourish it.*
- *I am willing to grow and evolve.*
- *I am excited about my life.*
- *I love, approve of, and nurture myself.*
- *I am confident.*
- *I create my life.*
- *I deserve success.*
- *I see beauty in my life.*
- *I am a gift to the world.*
- *I am strong.*
- *Being me is beautiful.*

Learn EFT

Emotional Freedom Technique is a form of psychological acupressure that utilizes simple tapping with the fingertips. Such tapping is believed to input kinetic energy onto specific meridians on the head and chest while you think about your specific problem and voice positive affirmations. By both tapping the energy meridians and voicing positive affirmation, you clear the emotional block from your body's bioenergy system, restoring your mind and body's balance. Many people swear by EFT.

Try Biofeedback

An amazing tool for change is the **EPFX-SCIO,** a quantum biofeedback machine. The EPFX-SCIO scans the body for 9000 frequencies, compares them to a norm and ranks them in degree of reactivity, identifying both acute and chronic imbalances, both physical and emotional. The machine then uses energetic therapy to balance or harmonize any aberrant frequencies. After, you feel more relaxed and less stress. The effects are cumulative over time as the SCIO gets into the cell and changes cellular memory.

Keep a Gratitude Journal

Too often we focus on what we don't have rather than on what we do have. For instance, you might bemoan the fact that you have two left feet but forget to appreciate your thick, shiny hair. If you can reflect on all the positive things in your life, rather than what you don't have, your life will take on different meaning and perspective.

One of the most effective ways to capture all the good in your life is to keep a daily *Gratitude Journal*. Each night before you go to bed, write down three to five things that you feel grateful about that day. They don't have to be groundbreaking. Even simple joys will do like "I am grateful to see my rose bush bloom."

Practice Self-Compassion

Okay, so you had a meltdown waiting in line at the supermarket and left your cart and stormed out. You had a bad day. True, you have more bad days than the average person. But if you get in the car and start lambasting yourself for being such a moron as to go to the supermarket at the busiest time of day, you will add fuel to the fire. When you have a bad moment, stroke your chin kindly and say, "Calm down. This too will pass. Things will get better. I promise myself. Let me take a moment, push into the steering wheel, put a drop of lavender essential oil on my wrist, and do some deep breathing." This will help you regroup, forgive yourself and calm your nervous system.

Control What You Can

Many things in life are beyond your control and you must work around that. Rather than stress out over them, try different strategies. For instance, take those supremely annoying landscapers with their loud motors that spew fuel into the air. You can curse the leaf blower and feel like jumping out of your skin. Or you can arrange to not be home on the day they come to mow the lawn. Of if you must be home you can think of ways to block out the noise, like taking a long shower, wearing your headphones or ear plugs, or hanging out in the part of the house furthest from the noise. And you can feed your nervous system to tone down your reaction.

See a Therapist

Psychotherapy is often necessary for those with SPD to work on changing negative thinking and eliminating learned helplessness. Talking things out will also help you feel less emotionally fragile and better about self.

Sensory defensiveness especially creates chronic, ongoing agitation, anxiety, and hyperarousal—essentially PTSD in those who suffer SD severely—and you cannot tolerate even minor stress. Psychotherapy can be helpful.

If your therapist is not familiar with SPD, lend her a book or two on the topic.

Try Neurolinguistic Programming

NPL is an approach to psychotherapy and organizational change that seeks to educate you in self-awareness and effective communication, and to change behavioral patterns. Many people embrace it as a useful, life changing tool.

Another way to change your "mind," is with mindfulness meditation. Let's now explore that in depth.

Summing Up

Get Me Out of Here Now!: Sensory issues cause you to lose control of your behavior.

Revise Your Inner Script: To take control of your behavior, you need to take control of your thoughts. To do so *you must believe that your actions will make a difference.*

You Are in Charge: To feel in charge, you must believe that you are the captain of your own ship. If you believe that your behavior is ruled by outside forces – doctors, priests, parents, children, God — you won't take action to change.

Will Changing My Thoughts Eliminate Sensory Problems? No. What changing your thinking will do is change how you *respond* to your sensory issues and empower you to take action.

Rewiring Your Brain: When you get into the habit of thinking positively, you will change the neural circuitry in your brain to become more engaged, creative, motivated, energetic, resilient, and productive at work. That in turn will change your behavior out of the learned helplessness mode and motivate you to continue on an upward path because your own volition can effect change.

Encouraging Neurogenesis

- *Think Empowering Thoughts*
- *Say Affirmations*
- *Learn EFT*
- *Try Biofeedback*

- *Keep a Gratitude Journal*
- *Practice Self-Compassion*
- *Control What You Can*
- *See a Therapist*
- *Try Neurolinguistic Programming*

*

15

Being Present

"Life can be found only in the present moment. The past is gone, the future is not here, and if we do not go back to ourselves in the present moment, we cannot be in touch with life."

~ Thich Nhat Hanh, *The Heart of Understanding*

Life can be found only in the present moment. The past can't be changed and causes depression. The future creates worry and anxiety. Only in the present moment can you experience joy, bliss, ecstasy, serenity.

What does being "present" mean? It means being *in the flow, in the zone* where you feel neither anxious nor bored but "just right;" in short, *modulated*. Problem is, if you have SPD, modulation and balance, steadiness and stability are fleeting at best. Most of the time, you're trying to escape the moment, not embrace it.

Before you give that a second thought, consider this. Thinking is a left brain activity, the logical, language producing part of the brain that keeps up trapped in the past or obsessing about the future. Hanging out there results in too much thinking, not enough time *being*.

Ideally, you want to hang out in the creative right brain as much as possible. There, you live in the present moment, with the parasympathetic nervous system activated. The PNS overrides the adrenaline releasing sympathetic nervous system and translates into less stress and therefore better modulation.

How can you get there? One quick way is to practice mindfulness meditation. Mindfulness meditation is purposefully paying attention to the present, neutrally and non-judgmentally. In so doing, you can catch your thoughts in the "magic quarter-second" between thoughts and actions so you can learn to stop running, anticipating and planning, and instead pay attention to what is around you and inside you in the here and now. When thoughts enter your mind, you accept and observe them neutrally and then let them fly away like clouds, thus not triggering an emotional or "automatic" reaction. This process takes time. You need to be patient and practice self-compassion when your thoughts start to pull you away from the present.

Meditation is a powerhouse. Study after study shows that on-going practice can change the neural circuitry of the brain, and you feel calmer, more balanced, more energetic, more organized, and even smarter. When we meditate our brain waves slow down to alpha and theta waves and we become at once restful and deeply relaxed, and more alert and focused, improving concentration and creativity. Regular meditation also increases mood altering chemicals such as serotonin, relieving anxiety, stress and hyperactivity and enhancing quality of sleep.

If you are hypo-responsive, it's easy to meditate because you easily shut out sensory stimulation. If you are hyper-responsive it's difficult because you are too distracted by sensation to let it go. With practice you can slowly train yourself to get into a meditative state. With the right brain now in charge, you become less aware of sensory information stemming from the external environment, even if it's only fleeting initially.

You can practice mindfulness every second of your life, wherever you are or whatever you are doing. Establish contact with body and breath and feel the aliveness present in the moment.

When you feel hyped or bored and thoughts about the future or the past distract you from the present, focus on your breath or movement of your diaphragm, or on pleasing outside sensations, like the woosh of the wind, or the scent of jasmine outside your window. Eventually you will learn to become a witness to your thoughts and emotions and physical sensation, rather than a slave under their control.

Daily, set aside a specific time for formal meditation in a sacred space without distractions. Allow at least 15 to 45 minutes.

It takes time to cultivate mindfulness meditation but if you stick with it, you will learn how to control your thoughts and emotions rather than have your thoughts and emotions control you.

Mindfulness Meditations

Let's explore a few different meditations. You may try them all, depending on your needs for the moment, or you can choose to focus on specific meditations.

Object Meditation

In the object meditation, you keep your eyes open and focus on an object out in the world such as a candle flame, tip of your nose, a photo, a symbol a vase or something that evokes the divine. Or you can close your eyes and visualize in your mind an object to focus on such as the sun, a star, a crescent, a cross, symbol of Om, a lotus flower, your personal deity or whatever you wish. It is your practice. Some yoga practitioners focus on the third eye, the space in the middle of your forehead.

As a start, try the following exercise.

Look at the palm of your hand. Feel it as you look. Now imagine that it is getting warmer. Keep looking and focus on it getting warmer; see the color becoming redder. If you maintain focus on this intention, your palm will in fact grow warm and red. Tibetan Buddhist monks use this simple biofeedback loop (an advanced meditation technique known as *tumo*) to warm their entire bodies. So effective is it that monks can sit in freezing ice caves meditating overnight while wearing nothing more than their thin silk saffron robes.

Once you create a simple feedback loop like this that totally engrosses you, you will be amazed at what you can induce merely through intention. You cross a frontier. If you can voluntary lower your heart rate, you are in control of your body's mechanisms and your body's thoughts and emotions.

Guided Visualization

Guided visualization is a powerhouse for changing your thoughts and actions. Visualizing something in your mind lights up the same neurons in your brain as when the image is seen and elicits the same feelings. A study reported in *Psychological Science* in 2013 found that conjuring up a visual image in the mind, like a sunny day or a night sky has a corresponding effect on the size of our pupils, as if you were seeing the image. This means that when you can "see" the images in your mind, your body begins to physically "feel" the benefits it seeks to change.

FASCINATING FINDING: VISUALIZATION & RELIGIOUS BELIEF: That the same areas of your brain light up when you see something and when you visualize something is probably the power behind religious belief. When you pray to Yahweh, or Jesus, or Allah, you see them in your mind's eye as if they actually exist, as research has documented, and therefore believe they are real. Interestingly, if you tell an atheist to talk to "god," the visual cortex does not light up because there is no belief of the existence of this other being.

To practice guided visualization, find a quiet place devoid of distractions, close your eyes and imagine being in a sensory haven. Perhaps it's lying on the beach and listening to the ocean waves. Perhaps it's sitting on top of a hill and watching the sunset. Find that special place where you feel calm and at peace.

Try this visualization. Imagine opening up a treasure chest buried deep inside you. As you take out each jewel, you see yourself as the person you want to be, not someone driven by sensory limitations. If you are clumsy, perhaps you see a glittering blue topaz and suddenly you are gracefully swimming through water. If you are shy, perhaps you see a glittering diamond and see yourself walking down the aisle to the altar, surrounding by glittering jewels and your future spouse with arms out waiting to embrace you. Let your imagination fly.

Set aside 5-10 minutes a few times a day to envision the life you want.

Breathing Meditation

Focus on the breath is one of the easiest ways to become present and a central practice in mindfulness meditation. Here's a short breathing meditation for you to try. When your mind wanders, return to your breath. Don't try to change your breathing. Rather, be aware of the feeling of the breath rather than controlling it.

Start by bringing your attention to the area between your upper lip and your nose, where air seems cool as you breathe in and warm as you breathe out. Keep your attention there through the meditation session. When thoughts arise, acknowledge them, and continue to focus on the subtle in-breath and outbreath. Try to not let your thoughts distract you but keep refocusing your attention on the breath.

Close your eyes and settle into your body so you feel comfortable...

Relax...

Release...

Let go...

With your eyes gently closed, become aware of the space before your eye...Like a field of darkness...

Pay attention to any sounds outside the room... Just listen, curious... Let the sounds come and go... No need to judge...

Notice any sounds that may be coming from inside the room... Notice the sound of your own breathing ...Even if very soft... Just listen...

Notice the sensations as you breathe in...

Notice the sensations as you breathe out...

Feel the air touch your nostrils...feel the slight movement of your chest and tummy...

Listen to the gentle sound of your own breathing... Allow your breath to take up whatever rhythm feels natural for you at the moment...Quite effortlessly...

If your attention wanders... bring it back to the next breath...

Be aware of this breath... And this breath... Be aware of what it is to be breathing in... and breathing out...

Simply be with the breath...Aware of the breath...

Now breathe in and imagine a wave coming toward you. Breathe out and imagine the wave going away.

Breathe in... Breathe out..

Breathe in... Breathe out..

Open your eyes. Do you feel more relaxed and at peace? Good chance that you do.

Feel Spiritually Empowered

Sarah is a classic languid: hypo-responsive, fleshy, clumsy, stooped, and lacking energy. She falls easily, doesn't know right from left and is unable to cross the midline. She had great difficulty learning how to tie her shoes or cut a straight line, and never learned to dance, ride a bike, swim, or do any sports. Out of necessity, she learned how to drive but she feels fearful behind the wheel as she constantly bumps into curbs and other cars and gets lost in a flash. Fortunately, she's exceptionally bright and, though a klutz was a top student in class, albeit one with a scratchy handwriting.

All these problems made her childhood a living hell as both her parents and her sister were athletic and competent and expected the same from her. Lost, floundering, anxious, depressed, and at times suicidal, she behaved bizarrely. Her parents sent her to a psychiatrist who put her on Prozac. Though this helped take the edge off her anxiety and depression, she remained a lost soul, without direction, and tortured by obesity from an inability to control over-eating.

Having grown up the 1950's, when no one even knew of sensory processing disorder, she assumed her problems were from a chemical imbalance in her brain. That she remained depressed and suicidal despite Prozac miffed her.

For solace, she turned inward to her imagination. Highly creative, she became a sculptor and painter. Her artistry helped her cope, as did her social life: a warm, loving, charming and engaging person with a pretty face, she easily attracted people.

In her late 20's, she found Christianity. From that day on, she turned to the "Lord" for solace and guidance and her life transformed. When she gets depressed and suicidal, she prays, and that jolts her out of her dark state.

Like meditation, prayer has the same effect on calming and balancing the nervous system, and like for Sarah, can be a huge, life changing experience.

Could an association exist between being a languid and a desire to be off in the cosmos? It's possible. If you are uncoordinated and clumsy, being inside your body has been troubling. What better place to be than in the cosmos where your body disappears? In deep meditation or in deep prayer you are so unaware of your body that you are not even aware of breathing.

Science backs up this contention. The OAA or orientation association area of the brain orients you in physical space by drawing a sharp distinction between you and everything else. It is your conscious sense of self and dependent on receiving sensory input. If you can easily turn off sensation, you begin to lose self and feel a part of the larger cosmos or universe—in other words, the religious or spiritual experience. Shutting off thoughts and sense of self produces calm and well-being and is profoundly pleasant and physically beneficial. As one meditator described it: "There's a sense of timelessness and infinity. It feels like I am part of everyone and everything in existence." That kind of experience is strongly stimulating for those with low arousal who find the world often lacking with enough oomph to get them interested and involved.

Try Neurofeedback

Neurofeedback is EEG Biofeedback that helps train you to self-regulate brain activity. The clinician observes your brain in action, shows you that information and rewards your brain, specifically the part that controls stress, for changing its own activity (brain waves) to more appropriate patterns. This process trains you to be calm and stay calm over time. The process takes time, awareness, practice, and reinforcement.

Neurofeedback has shown great success in helping change the behavior of children with SPD, those with ADD and ADHD, and those on the autistic spectrum.

Another way to change your "mind," is through nature's pharmacy. Let's now explore that.

Summing Up

Present Moment: Life can be found only in the present moment. The past can't be changed and causes depression. The future creates worry and anxiety. The present moment is the only place where you can experience joy, bliss, ecstasy, serenity, peace.

Mindfulness meditation: This is the practice of purposefully paying attention to the present, neutrally and non-judgmentally.

Different Meditations:

- **Object Meditation:** In the object meditation, you can keep your eyes open and focus on an object out in the world
- **Guided Visualization:** Visualizing something in your mind lights up the same neurons in your brain as when the image is actually seen and elicits the same feelings, making it a powerhouse for controlling your thoughts.
- **Breathing Meditation:** Focus on the breath is one of the easiest ways to become present and a central practice in mindfulness meditation.

Feel Spiritually Empowered: Like meditation, prayer has the same effect on calming and balancing the nervous system and, like for Sarah, can be a huge, life changing experience.

Try Neurofeedback: Neurofeedback is EEG Biofeedback that helps train you to self-regulate brain activity. It has shown great success in helping change the behavior of children with SPD, those with ADD and ADHD, and those on the autistic spectrum.

✦

16

Nature's Pharmacy

"The art of healing comes from nature, not from the physician.
Therefore the physician must start from nature, with an open mind."

~Paracelsus

If you have SPD, at some time you have likely taken psychotropic drugs like anti-depressants and anti-anxiety medication to help balance your emotions and arousability. Many will have suffered side effects from drugs. Whether illicit, prescribed, or over-the counter, all drugs can cause side effects that upset brain chemistry and alter mood, perceiving, thinking, behavior, and sleep.

Why not try nature's pharmacy? Many alternative natural therapies exist to balance your biochemistry naturally—for instance, by boosting low serotonin that can cause anxiety, panic, and sleeplessness. Unlike Xanax and Zoloft, alternative substances within nature's pharmacy work with, not against your body's design to modify brain chemistry and they do so without side effects.

Below are options to anti-anxiety drugs and stimulants. Though you may wish to experiment at the suggested dose to see what works for you, it is best to take these supplements under the guidance of a holistic physician or naturopath.

HERBS

Generally safe, effective, and non-addictive, herbs have been used to relax body and mind for centuries.

The following herbs have been deemed safe as nature's tranquilizers:

Kava: Enhances GABA activity, the action of gamma amino butyric acid that (see below). By doing so, it relaxes both muscles and emotions and calms without sedating, as prescription tranquilizers often do. Don't use it along with benzodiazepine tranquilizers.

Valerian root: A natural relaxant that, taken together with kava, enhances GABA. It works well as a sleep aid. It is also useful for gut related problems as it seems to block the transmission of stressful nerve impulses to the bowel.

Passionflower: Has a mild relaxing effect and induces a deep, restful sleep.

Gotu kola: Mildly relaxes and revitalizes the nervous system, as well as decreasing fatigue and depression while increasing memory and intelligence.

Ginkgo biloba: Improves brain function by increasing cerebral blood flow and oxygenation, helping ease depression, anxiety, headaches, memory loss, tinnitus (ringing in the ears), vertigo, headache, and poor concentration. As it is a blood thinner, don't take it before surgery.

Sceletium: An herb from South Africa that has been used since prehistoric times to lessen anxiety, stress, and tension and raise spirits and connectedness. It has no serious side effects but should not be taken with antidepressants or with large doses of tryptophan or 5-HTP.

Holy Basil: An herb used for over 3000 years in Ayurvedic tradition to reduce anxiety. It is also helpful in regulating blood sugar and insulin metabolism.

Sensoril: A proprietary extract of Ashwaganda and a well-known Ayurvedic herbal treatment for stress and anxiety, it helps increase energy, reduce fatigue, improve sleep, decrease irritability, enhance focus and concentration, reduce stress and increase overall feeling of wellbeing.

TAKE HEED: There is a downside to herbs. Unlike drugs that attack symptoms quickly, herbs work more subtly and slowly and you may not initially feel the POW of a tranquilizer. Don't be fooled into trying a larger dose. Though generally safe if you adhere to the suggested dose on the bottle, herbs can powerfully affect the body. If the suggested dose isn't doing the trick, consult a licensed herbalist or nutritionist.

If you are pregnant or nursing always consult with a physician before taking any herb. If you are taking any medication, check with your physician to see if they interact with herbal supplements. Many herbs will interact with anti-depressants and other medication. If scheduled for surgery, always tell your physician what herbs you are taking as some are blood thinners and must be stopped before surgery. A few herbs have been shown to cause anxiety.

Unsafe Herbs

Yohimbine: An herb derived from the bark of a tree, it is a male aphrodisiac with sometimes dangerous side effects. Even standard amounts may occasionally trigger anxiety, panic attack, and mania.

Ephedra: A stimulant used for quick energy and appetite suppression, the "herbal Ecstasy" is misused for recreation, and in high doses creates rapid heart rate, dizziness, headache, anxiety and insomnia.

AMINO ACIDS

Amino Acids are a powerful natural means for balancing neurotransmitters and are commonly used to replace psychotropic drugs.

TAKE HEED: *People respond differently to amino acids so try them ideally under a physician's care.*

TO CALM DOWN:

GABA (gamma amino butyric acid): An amino acid and a neurotransmitter, GABA regulates neurotransmitters noradrenaline, dopamine, and serotonin. The brain's natural Valium, it dampens the nervous system and helps calm by naturally slowing breathing and heart rate, and relaxing muscles. Librium and Valium work by pushing GABA into the brain and blocking the re-uptake. Take it before a known stressful event to help prevent anxiety.

Taurine: An amino acid, taurine inhibits the release of adrenaline and provides similar calming as GABA. Some get pleasantly high from only a few capsules.

Tryptophan: An amino acid that is a source for both 5-HTP and serotonin, tryptophan can be taken in supplement form and has been shown to raise serotonin levels by 200%.

INTERESTING INFO: *Actress Margot Kidder manages bipolar disorder via natural means, uses 1000 mg. each of tryptophan, taurine, and GABA before bedtime to help with sleep.*

5-HTTP: A form of tryptophan, 5-HTTP helps regulate serotonin level, and induce relaxation, elevate mood, and promote healthy sleep, dreaming, and creativity. Do not take it if you are on anti-depressants.

TO REV UP:

Phenylalanine (PS): An essential amino acid that cannot be manufactured by the body, phenylalanine is used to produce tyrosine (*see below*), and directly affects mood and energy, along with treating fatigue, depression, problems with food cravings and overeating, and chronic pain.

Glutamine: When stressed, your body uses up mass amounts of glutamine that can be replaced with a supplement of L-glutamine.

Tyrosine: This amino acid is a precursor of adrenaline, dopamine and norepinephrine that are important for maintaining a sense of well-being and energy, and it also promotes a healthy metabolism and nervous system. Tyrosine and phenylalanine can be used in conjunction.

IMPORTANT INFO: In her book, **The Mood Cure,** *Julia Ross discusses the powerful role of amino acid supplementation on mood. For bipolar disorder, hyperactivity, depression, stress and anxiety, she suggests a trial dose of amino acids of 500 to 1000 mg. of L-carnitine in the morning and 3 to 5 capsules of phosphatidyl choline, a fatty acid. This will slow the spontaneous rate of neuronal firing in the brain, and, in the bipolar, does so as well as lithium without negative side effects. Proper vitamin and mineral supplementation must accompany the amino acids.*

OTHER

Many other natural calming substances exist as well, from homeopathic remedies tea to adaptogens. Here's a partial list.

Phosphatidylserine: A fatty acid, **PS** helps the hypothalamus to regulate the amount of cortisol produced by the adrenals.

Reishi: A relaxing medicinal mushroom, reishi reduces anxiety and insomnia.

Aconitum Napellus: A homeopathic remedy for panic attack, aconitum napellus has been reported to stop a panic attack within 30 seconds.

L-Theanine: Abundant in green tea, L-theanine increases brain GABA and significantly affects neurotransmitters like dopamine and serotonin, resulting in improved memory and learning ability. It is effective in treating anxiety, nervousness, sleep disturbances, premenstrual syndrome (PMS) and ADD/ADHD.

Relora: Taken from Chinese medicine, relora is an all-natural anti-anxiety and stress relief ingredient to control stress-related eating and drinking. Both non-sedating and a potential anti-depressant, it helps quiet the hypothalamic-pituitary-adrenal axis without causing drowsiness, and reduce anxiety by acting as a "precursor" to DHEA, the hormone that helps counteract the negative effects of the stress hormone cortisol.

Chinese Red Date (Red Jujube) has been used for thousands of years in traditional Chinese Medicine to treat of anxiety and insomnia.

Adaptogens: Two adaptogens shown helpful for anxiety are Rhodiola and Ashwaganda.

Calmes Forte: Homeopathic remedy for reducing stress.

This now ends our journey. As you start yours, I encourage you to do so full speed ahead, fired up to turn your life around. If the road gets bumpy and you feel off balance, use the tricks you learned in this book to get stable. If you come to a fork in the road and feel confused, ask yourself which direction will ultimately give you the most equanimity. If you need to slow down, take baby steps. If you come to a stop sign, respect what your body is telling you and take a break, regroup, recharge, and continue to forge ahead.

Think of each day as a new beginning in establishing stronger roots to the ground so you can feel centered, literally and figuratively, and wings so you can take flight to where you were meant to soar. If it rains, put up your umbrella and make a big splash!

Summing Up

HERBS

Generally safe, effective, and non-addictive, herbs have been used to relax body and mind for centuries. The following herbs have been deemed safe as nature's tranquilizers:

- Kava
- Valerian root
- Passion flower
- Gotu kola
- Ginkgo biloba
- Sceletium
- Holy basal
- Sensoril

Unsafe Herbs:

- Yohimbine
- Ephadra

AMINO ACIDS

Amino Acids are a powerful natural means for balancing neurotransmitters and very commonly used to replace psychotropic drugs.

For calming:

- GABA
- Taurine

- Tryptophan
- 5-HTTP

To rev up:

- Phenylalanine (PS):
- Glutamine
- Tyrosine

<u>OTHER</u>

Many other natural calming substances exist as well, from teas to homeopathic remedies to adaptogens. Here's a partial list.

- Phosphatidylserine
- Reishi
- Aconitum Napellus
- L-Theanine
- Relora
- Chinese Red Date
- Adaptogens: Rhodiola and Ashwaganda.
- Calmes Forte

APPENDIX A

SIGNS OF SENSORY PROCESSING DISORDER

Could you suffer sensory processing disorder and if so, what sensory or motor processes are specifically implicated? To find out, copy and the fill in the following check list. If you have checks under each category, you likely suffer it. The more checkmarks, the more severe and handicapping is the condition.

SENSORY MODULATION DISORDER

Sensory Avoiding

- ☐ **Dislike** being touched, especially unexpected light touch, and avoid crowds, lines or any situation involving close physical contact
- ☐ **Startle** to loud, sudden, piercing sounds; hard to shut out background noise
- ☐ **Wince** at bright lights like sunlight – must wear sunglasses even on rainy day – & fluorescent lights; bothered by TV, flickering lights, computer graphics
- ☐ **Bothered** by odors others don't notice, like musty sheets, or chemical odors like chlorine bleach or perfumes
- ☐ **Anxious** or panicky going down an escalator, riding in an elevator, driving through a tunnel, riding on a roller coaster or spinning rides
- ☐ **Low** pain threshold – anxious when getting injections
- ☐ **Dislike** getting hit or splashed by water – taking a shower, at the ocean, caught in rain

Sensory Seeking

- ☐ **Seem** unaware of touch unless very intense
- ☐ **Powerful** need for deep pressure from hugs, contact sports (football),

sex, sometimes abusive; may intrude on another's space
- ☐ **Drawn** to TV, flickering lights, computer graphics
- ☐ **Love** loud, pounding music; blast TV
- ☐ **Wear** strong perfumes
- ☐ **Like** intensely stimulating – malls, rock concerts, amusement parks
- ☐ **Seek** out intense sensations such as fast driving, roller coasters, parachuting, skiing, horseback riding, deep sea diving and so
- ☐ **"Thrill-seeker,"** dangerous at times
- ☐ **Enjoy** wearing, tight, flashy clothes with rough, fuzzy, or uneven texture
- ☐ **Like** excessively hot or cold water or drinks
- ☐ **Crave** excessively spicy, sweet, sour, or salty foods
- ☐ **Seek** stimulants, like caffeine, nicotine, cocaine, speed
- ☐ **Under-react** to pain
- ☐ **Self-abusive** – pinching, biting, slicing
- ☐ **Mouth** objects like pens or straws excessively
- ☐ **Fidget** constantly: with keys, change in pocket, a pen/pencil, paper clip, rubber band; twist hair; crack knuckles
- ☐ **Grind** teeth night and day
- ☐ **Crack** knuckles

Arousability (Sleep/wake cycle; ability to change, achieve appropriate states)
- ☐ **Problems** falling asleep; staying asleep; waking up
- ☐ **Hyperactive**
- ☐ **Unusually** sluggish and passive
- ☐ **Vacillate** between needing to calm down or rev up; little time in comfort zone

Rhythms
- ☐ **Irregular** heart rate
- ☐ **Fast,** shallow breathing
- ☐ **Too hot,** too cold, or vacillating between too hot and too cold

☐ **Undereat** or overeat
☐ **Problem** ingesting, digesting and eliminating
☐ **Underactive** or can't sit still
☐ **Speak** too fast or too slow

Emotional Regulation
☐ **Emotions** run away or appear hidden; in relationships, inappropriately excessive
☐ **Emotions** lack range and depths and in relationships may be deficient
☐ **Emotionally** labile
☐ **Emotionally** dead

Behavioral Organization
☐ **Messy**
☐ **Easily** disorganized
☐ **Avoid** anything new or seek novelty and thrills

Sexuality
☐ **Difficulties** in sexual relationships
☐ **Little** or no sex drive, or obsessed with sex
☐ **Sexual** touch feels aversive or overstimulating or overly sexed

SENSORY DISCRIMINATION

Poor Tactile Discrimination
☐ **Seem** out of touch with hands, as if unfamiliar appendages
☐ **Unable** to identify which body parts have been touched without looking
☐ **Fearful** in the dark
☐ **Unable** to identify objects by feel–need to see keys to perceive they are in hand
☐ **Need** visual cues to zip, button and unbutton clothes and other motor tasks
☐ **Dress** messily & look disheveled with shirt half untucked, shoes

untied, pants not pulled up

☐ **Have** difficulty with fine motor skills, such as buttoning, zipping, writing, or using silverware as may not always feel which finger is which or where each one is located

☐ **Unable** to tell if touch is friendly or threatening and may lash out aggressively to benign touch, e.g., perceiving a bump as a blow and feel as if being attacked

☐ **Misjudge** spatial relationships of objects in the environment, often bumping into furniture, mis-stepping on stairs and curbs, driving over a curb or hitting another car

Poor Body Awareness

☐ **Unsure** of where body parts are or how they interrelate

☐ **Have** poor difficulty orienting arms and hands, legs and feet to get dressed

☐ **Withdraw** from movement to avoid touch sensations, and may bump into things to figure out where you end and the world begins

☐ **May** feel separate from body – depersonalization

Poor Auditory Discrimination

☐ **Difficulty** attending to, understanding & remembering what is said or read & misinterpret requests

☐ **Fail** to understand or follow two sequential directions at a time

☐ **Trouble** articulating thoughts verbally or in writing

☐ **Problem** responding to others' questions/comments; need what is said repeated

☐ **Difficulty** discerning if a sound is near of far; may be misdiagnosed with attention deficit disorder (ADD) rather than a problem with auditory discrimination

☐ **Problems** reading (dyslexia) and especially out loud

☐ **Difficulty** identifying people's voices or instruments in the orchestra

☐ **Problem** filtering out other sounds and attending to what someone is saying

☐ **Bothered** by loud, sudden, metallic, or high-pitched sounds

☐ **Look** at others for reassurance before answering
☐ **Often** talk out of turn or "off topic"
☐ **If** not understood, have difficulty rephrasing; may get frustrated, angry, give up

Poor Visual-Spatial Discrimination

☐ **Fail** to comprehend reading or quickly lose interest
☐ **Hard** to visualize what you read
☐ **Uncomfortable** or overwhelmed by moving objects or people
☐ **Fatigue** easily when using eyes for close work
☐ **Difficulty** distinguishing foreground from background and locate items among other items—papers on a desk, socks in a drawer, items on a grocery shelf
☐ **See** double
☐ **Write** at a slant (up or down hill) on a page
☐ **Confuse** left and right
☐ **Difficulty** perceiving depth, distance, boundaries and thus judging spatial relationships; may bump into objects or people or misstep on curbs and stairs; may fear driving
☐ **Problem** scanning visual sequences and following rapid movement with eyes, as following a tennis match or video game
☐ **Difficulty** recognizing symbols or gestures and might misinterpret facial cues

Poor Smell and Taste Discrimination

☐ **Difficulty** identifying what food you are eating without looking at it
☐ **Difficulty** distinguishing particular tastes or smells, like orange from tangerine

MOVEMENT

Motor Planning Problems (Dyspraxia)

☐ **Difficulty** with organizing, and performing activities, both novel and familiar that involve a sequence of body movements, such as hitting

a tennis ball
- [ ] **Poor** self-help skills and reliance on others to get started
- [ ] **Poor** gross motor skills–jumping, catching a ball, climbing a ladder etc.
- [ ] **Poor** fine motor skills & difficulty using "tools" such as pencils, silverware, combs, scissors; gripping sandals or walking barefoot; eat messily
- [ ] **Poor** eye-hand coordination and can't catch a ball

Movement and Balance Problems
- [ ] **Appear** clumsy, awkward, and uncoordinated
- [ ] **Lose** balance easily when climbing stairs, riding a bicycle, jumping, standing on one foot, or standing on both feet with closed eyes
- [ ] **Avoid** most sports or seek intense sports with strong input into balance system (roller coasters, parachuting, bungee jumping, car racing, water or downhill skiing), or deep pressure to body (horseback riding, deep sea diving, jumping & crashing on trampoline, rock climbing)
- [ ] **Have** poor body awareness: bump into things, knock things over, trip; do things with too much force–walking, slamming doors, dressing things too hard, slamming objects down
- [ ] **Get** car or seasick

Poor Muscle Tone
- [ ] **Have** stiff muscle tone
- [ ] **Have** a limp, "floppy" body
- [ ] **Frequently** slump, lie down, and lean head on hand or arm while working at desk
- [ ] **Fatigue** easily
- [ ] **Compensate** for "looseness" by grasping objects tightly
- [ ] **Have** difficulty turning doorknobs, handles, opening and closing items; use an electric can opener or often ask someone to open can
- [ ] **Have** difficulty catching yourself if falling

Body Language Deficits
- [ ] **Facial** expression and body language hard to read

☐ **Body** language does not match communicative intent

Bilateral Coordination Problems
☐ **May** have never crawled as an baby
☐ **Have** poor body awareness
☐ **Lacked** an established hand preference by age four or five
☐ **Difficulty** learning exercise or dance steps; have two left feet
☐ **Confuse** left and right
☐ **Problem** crossing the midline, like using the right hand to cross over the left shoulder to scratch yourself or to burp a baby

SOCIAL/EMOTIONAL

Emotional Instability
☐ **Disruptive** or aggressive; at times violent
☐ **Silly**
☐ **Restless**
☐ **Tense**
☐ **Edgy**
☐ **Difficult** or willful
☐ **Easily** frustrated & frazzled
☐ **Explosive**
☐ **Moody**
☐ **Hypervigilant** even in safe environments
☐ **Attention** getting

Social Ineptitude
☐ **Poor** eye contact
☐ **Slow** responding
☐ **Inappropriate** or lack of initiating
☐ **Out** of sync
☐ **Misread** other's intent

Relationship Problems

☐ **Dependency**
☐ **False** independence
☐ **Incapacity** for intimacy
☐ **Poor Self-concept**
☐ **Low self-esteem**
☐ **Feeling "crazy," "weird"**
☐ **Negative** self-talk
☐ **Identity** confusion
☐ **Seem** lazy, bored, unmotivated, depressed, stubborn, troubled

Poor Coping Skills

☐ **Easily** frustrated, aggressive, or withdrawn when failing & give up easily
☐ **Difficulty** adjusting to a new situation
☐ **Decrease** sensory input through avoidance (flight) & by lashing out (fight) to push people away.
☐ **Control** sensory input by compulsively adhere to strict schedules & rigid routines for eating, waking, going to sleep, and so on.

COGNITION

☐ **Distracted** easily and fidgety when needing to focus and concentrate
☐ **Impulsive**
☐ **Disorganized**
☐ **Disoriented**
☐ **Lack** of use of creative skills
☐ **Poor** inner drive; feel stuck and find it hard to pursue goals
☐ **Short-term** memory problems
☐ **Poor** communication skills and often at a loss for words
☐ **Lack** good problem solving skills
☐ **Problems** academically as a child, despite normal or above normal intelligence

☐ **Lack** of strategies to modify behavior
☐ **Largely** unaware of behavior and generally not able to modify it

PSYCHIATRIC SYMPTOMS

☐ Anxiety
☐ Depression
☐ Bipolar disorder
☐ Eating disorders
☐ Obsessive-compulsive behavior
☐ Panic attack
☐ Phobias
☐ Substance Abuse
☐ Distorted hearing
☐ Depersonalization
☐ Dissociation
☐ Cutting

RESOURCES

Suggested Books:

- *Too Loud, Too Bright, Too Fast, Too Tight, What to do if you are sensory defensive in an overstimulating world,* by Sharon Heller (HarperCollins, 2002).
- *Anxiety: Hidden Causes; Why your anxiety may not be "all in your head" but from something physical,* by Sharon Heller, PhD (Symmetry, 2010).
- *The Vital Touch,* by Sharon Heller (NY: Holt, 2997).
- *Making Sense: A Guide to Sensory Issues,* by Rachel C. Schneider (Sensory World, 2016.
- *Sensory Modulation & Environment: Essential Elements of Occupation: Handbook & Reference,* by Tina Champagne (Australia: Pearson, 2011).
- *Living sensationally: Understanding your senses,* by Winnie Dunn (Jessica Kingsley Publishers, 2008).
- *The Sensory Connection Program: Activities for Mental Health Treatment,* by Karen M. Moore, (Therapro, 2005).
- *The Sensory-Sensitive Child* by Karen A. Smith & Karen R. Grouze (HarperCollins, 2004).
- *The Out-of-Sync Child. Recognizing and Coping with Sensory Integration Dysfunction,* by Carol Stock Kranowitz (Skylight/Perigee, 1998).
- *The Out-of-Sync Child Grows Up, Coping with Sensory Processing Disorder in the Adolescent and Young Adult Years.,* by Carol Stock Kranowitz (Tarcher/Perigee, 2016).
- *Sensational Kids,* by Lucy Jane Miller (Putnam Adult, 2006).
- *Self-Regulation Workbook, Learning to Use Sensory Activities to Manage Stress and Anxiety and Emotional Crisis,* by Karen M. Moore. (Sensory Connection Program, 2008).

- *Sensory Integration and Learning Disorders*, by A. Jean Ayres (Western Psychological Services, 1972).
- *Sensory Integration and the Child*, by A. Jean Ayres (Western Psychological Services, 1998).
- *Spark*, by John Ratey. (NY: Little Brown, 2008).
- *Behavioral Expressions and Biosocial Bases of Sensation Seeking*, by Martin Zuckerman, (NY: Cambridge University Press, 1994).

Articles:

- Pfeiffer B, Kinnealey M, Reed C, Herzberg G. "Sensory modulation and affective disorders in children and adolescents with Asperger's disorder." *Am J Occup Ther.* 2005 May-Jun;59(3):335-45.
- Kinnealey, Moya and Fuiek, M., "The relationship between sensory defensiveness, anxiety, depression and perception of pain in adults," *Occupational Therapy International*, 6 (3), 1999:95:206.
- Pfeiffer B, Kinnealey M., Treatment of sensory defensiveness in adults. Occup Ther Int. 2003;10(3):17584

Websites:

- sharonheller.net (adults)
- spdlife.org (adults)
- spdfoundation.net (information, research, all ages)
- sensory-processing-disorder.com (all ages)
- out-of-sync-child.com (children)
- sensoryproject.com (adults)
- sifocus.org (magazine-all ages)

Products:

- www.Southpawenterprises.com

Finding an occupational therapist:

- www.Sensory-processing-disorder.com (all ages)
- www/Spdnetwork.org (research)

Made in the USA
Middletown, DE
18 November 2023

43032079R00195